The Renaissance Imagination

Important Literary and Theatrical Texts
from the Late Middle Ages through
the Seventeenth Century

STEPHEN ORGEL, EDITOR

Davidson

A Garland Series

Reformation Biblical Drama in England

The Life and Repentaunce of Mary Magdalene

The History of Iacob and Esau

AN OLD-SPELLING CRITICAL EDITION
EDITED WITH AN INTRODUCTION BY

PAUL WHITFIELD WHITE

GARLAND PUBLISHING, INC.
New York & London
1992

Library of Congress Cataloging-in-Publication Data

Reformation biblical drama in England : an old-spelling critical edition of two plays / edited by Paul Whitfield White
p. cm. — (The Renaissance imagination)
Includes bibliographical references.
Contents: The life and repentaunce of Mary Magdalene — The history of Iacob and Esau.
ISBN 0-8153-0460-9 (alk. paper)
1. English drama—Early modern and Elizabethan, 1500-1600. 2. Jacob (Biblical patriarch)—Drama. 3. Esau (Biblical figure)—Drama. 4. Mary Magdalene, Saint—Drama. 5. Bible plays, English. I. White, Paul Whitfield. II. Wager, Lewis, fl. 1566. Life and repentance of Marie Magdalene. 1992. III. Jacob and Esau. 1992. IV. Series: Renaissance imagination (Unnumbered)
PR1263.R44 1992
822'.3080382—dc20 92-17420

Printed on acid-free, 250-year-life paper
Manufactured in the United States of America

TO

GLYNNE WICKHAM

CONTENTS

ACKNOWLEDGEMENTS

During the early stages of preparing this book for publication I was greatly aided by Barry McCann who, in addition to formatting the text for the computer and copying onto it the initial draft, offered perceptive suggestions of an editing nature. Two other graduate students in English at Baylor University to whom I am very grateful are Sara Marisol Madrazo and Pamela Susan Yoder. They each logged many hours on the computer carrying out a variety of tasks. I wish also to thank Melanie McQuere who took on the copy-editing responsibilities at short notice and then patiently put up with my delays in getting the manuscript to her. My many debts to other editors of Tudor drama, especially to F. I. Carpenter and J. S. Farmer who completed earlier modern editions of *Mary Magdalene* and *Jacob and Esau* respectively, are acknowledged in the notes.

My photographic reproduction of the fragment of the 1557/58 edition of *Iacob and Esau* (New College Mss 363/4, nos. 71-74) in Appendix A appears with the permission of the Bodleian Library, Oxford. I am indebted to its staff, as I am to the staffs of the British Library, and Moody Library, Baylor University, for assisting me with research, and to the Baylor University Research Committee, Graduate School, and English Department, for supplying financial support.

ABBREVIATIONS

All for Money	Thomas Lupton. *All for Money*. Ed. J. S. Farmer. TFT. London: Jack, 1910.
Arber, *Stationers Reg.*	Edward Arber, ed. *A Transcript of the Registers of the Company of Stationers of London; 1554-1640*, 4 vols. 1875; rpt. New York: Peter Smith, 1950.
Axton, *Classical Interludes*	Marie Axton, ed. *Three Tudor Classical Interludes: Thersites, Jack Jugeler, Horestes.* Cambridge: Brewer, 1982.
Bale, *Select Works*	John Bale. *Select Works*. Ed. Henry Christmas. PS. Cambridge: Cambridge UP, 1849.
Beer, *Rebellion & Riot*	Barrett L. Beer. *Rebellion and Riot: Popular Disorder in England during the Reign of Edward VI.* Kent, OH: Kent State UP, 1982.
Bernard, *Prosody*	J. E. Bernard. *The Prosody of the Tudor Interlude*. New Haven, CT: Yale UP, 1939.
Bevington, *Tudor Drama & Politic*	David Bevington. *Tudor Drama and Politics.* Cambridge, MA: Harvard UP, 1968
Bevington, *From Mankind to Marlowe*	David Bevington. *From Mankind to Marlowe*. Cambridge, MA: Harvard UP, 1962.
Bills, "Suppression Theory"	Bing D. Bills. "The 'Suppression Theory' and the English Corpus Christi Play: A Re-Examination." *Theatre Journal* 32 (1980): 157-68.
Blackburn, *Biblical Drama*	Ruth H. Blackburn. *Biblical Drama under the Tudors*. The Hague: Mouton, 1971.
Boas, *Univ. Drama*	Frederick Boas. *University Drama in the Tudor Age.* Oxford: Oxford UP, 1914.
Bradford, *Writings*	*The Writings of John Bradford*. Ed. E. A. Townsend. 2 vols. Cambridge: Cambridge UP, 1848.

Bradner, "Test for Udall's Authorship"	Leicester Bradner. "A Test for Udall's Authorship." *Modern Language Notes* 42 (1927): 378.
Brigden, "Youth & the English Reformation"	Susan Brigden. "Youth and the English Reformation." *Past and Present* 95 (1982): 38-67.
Calvin, *Commentary*	John Calvin. *Commentary on a Harmony of the Evangelists, Matthew, Mark, and Luke.* Trans. William Pringle. 3 vols. Edinburgh: Calvin Trans. Society, 1845.
Calvin, *Inst.*	John Calvin. *The Institution of the Christian Religion*. Trans. Thomas Norton. 1561; rpt. London: np, 1582
Carpenter, MM	Lewis Wager. *The Life and Repentaunce of Mary Magdalene*. Ed. F. I. Carpenter. Chicago: Chicago UP, 1903
Chambers, *Eliz. Stage*	E. K. Chambers. *The Elizabethan Stage*. 4 vols. Oxford: Clarendon, 1923.
Chambers, *Med. Stage*	E. K. Chambers. *The Medieval Stage*. 2 vols. Oxford: Clarendon, 1903.
Craik, *Tudor Interlude*	T. W. Craik. *The Tudor Interlude*. Leicester: Leicester UP, 1958.
Crow and Wilson, JE	John Crow and F. P. Wilson, eds. *Jacob and Esau*. MSR. Oxford: Clarendon, 1956.
Dawson, *Records of Kent*	Giles Dawson, ed. *Records of Plays and Players in Kent*. MSC VII. Oxford: Oxford UP, 1965.
Dent, *Proverbial Lang.*	R. W. Dent. *Proverbial Language in English Drama Exclusive of Shakespeare 1495-1616.* Berkeley: U of California P, 1984.
Dessen, *Elizabethan Drama*	Alan Dessen. *Elizabethan Drama and the Viewer's Eye*. Chapel Hill: U of North Carolina P, 1977.
Dictionary of Printers	*A Dictionary of the Printers and Booksellers Who Were at Work in England, Scotland, and Ireland 1557-1775*. London: Bibliographical Society, 1977.
Digby, *Mary Magdalene*	*The Digby Play of St. Mary Magdalene.* In *The Digby Plays*. Ed. F. J. Furnivall. London: EETS, 1896.
Doctor Faustus	Christopher Marlowe. *Doctor Faustus*. Ed. John D. Jump. Revels Plays. London: Methuen, 1962.

Eccles, "Brief Lives"	Mark Eccles. "Brief Lives: Tudor and Stuart Authors." *Studies in Philology* 79 (1982): 123-24.
Eccles, "William Wager"	Mark Eccles. "William Wager and His Plays." *English Language Notes* 18 (June, 1981): 258-262.
EETS	Early English Text Society
Enough	William Wager. *Enough Is as Good as a Feast*. Ed. R. Mark Benbow. Regents Renaissance Drama. Lincoln: U of Nebraska P, 1967.
Farmer, JE	J. S. Farmer, ed. *Jacob and Esau*. In *Six Anonymous Plays (Second Series)*. Early English Dramatists. London: Early English Drama Society, 1906.
Farmer, MM	Lewis Wager. *The Life and Repentaunce of Mary Magdalene*. Ed. J. S. Farmer. TFT. London: Jack, 1908.
Feuillerat, *Revels at Court*	Albert Feuillerat, ed. *Documents Relating to the Revels at Court in the Time of King Edward VI and Queen Mary*. Louvain: A. Uystpruyst, 1914.
Foxe, *Christus Triumphans*	John Foxe. *Christus Triumphans*. In *Two Latin Comedies by John Foxe*. Ed. and trans. John Hazel Smith. Ithaca: Cornell UP, 1973.
Gardiner, *Mysteries' End*	Harold Gardiner. *Mysteries' End*. New Haven: Yale UP, 1946.
Glass of Gouernment	George Gascoigne. *The Glasse of Gouerment*. TFT. London: Jack, 1914.
God's Promises	John Bale. *God's Promises*. In Happé, *Bale*, vol. II.
Greg, *Biblio. of Drama*	W. W. Greg. *A Bibliography of the English Printed Drama to the Restoration*. 4 vols. London: The Bibliographical Society, 1939-59.
Happé, *Bale*	Peter Happé, ed. *The Complete Plays of John Bale*. 2 vols. Cambridge: Brewer, 1985-86.
Happé, "Saint Play"	Peter Happé. "The Protestant Adaptation of the Saint Play." In *The Saint Play in Medieval Europe*. Ed. Clifford Davidson. Kalamazoo: Medieval Institute Publications, 1986.

Hazlitt, *Dodsley's Plays*	W. Carew Hazlitt, ed. *Dodsley's Old English Plays: Vol. II.* 4th ed. London: Reeves and Turner, 1874.
JE	*Jacob and Esau.*
Jones, "Dangerous Sport"	Robert C. Jones. "Dangerous Sport: The Audience's Engagement with Vice in the Moral Interludes." *Renaissance Drama* 6 (1973): 45-64.
Kendall, *Drama of Dissent*	Richie Kendall. *The Drama of Dissent.* Chapel Hill: U of North Carolina P, 1986.
Kendall, *Calvin*	R. T. Kendall. *Calvin and English Calvinism.* Oxford: Oxford UP, 1979.
King, *Eng. Reform. Lit.*	John N. King. *English Reformation Literature: The Tudor Origins of the Protestant Tradition.* Princeton: Princeton UP, 1982.
King Johan	John Bale. *King Johan.* In Happé, *Bale*, Vol. I.
Knowles, *Bare Ruined Choirs*	David Knowles. *Bare Ruined Choirs: The Dissolution of the English Monasteries.* Cambridge: Cambridge UP, 1976.
Lancashire, *Dramatic Texts and Records*	Ian Lancashire. *Dramatic Texts and Reccrds of Britain.* Toronto: U of Toronto P, 1984.
Le Huray, *Music & Reform. in England*	Peter Le Huray. *Music and the Reformation In England 1549-1660.* 1967; rpt. Cambridge: Cambridge UP, 1978.
Lisle Letters	*The Lisle Letters.* Ed. Muriel St Clare Byrne. 6 vols. Chicago: Chicago UP, 1981.
The Longer	William Wager. *The Longer Thou Livest the More Fool Thou Art.* Ed. R. Mark Benbow. Regents Renaissance Drama. Lincoln: U of Nebraska P, 1967.
LP: Henry 8	*Letters and Papers, Foreign and Domestic, of the Reign of Henry VIII.* Ed. J. S. Brewer, J. Gairdner, and R. H. Brodie. 21 vols. London: Longman, Green, and Roberts, 1862-1932.
Magnificence	John Skelton. *Magnificence.* Ed. Peter Happé. In *Four Morality Plays.* Harmondsworth, England: Penguin, 1979.
Melanchton & Bucer	*Melanchthon and Bucer.* Ed. Wilhelm Pauck. London: Westminster, 1969.
Miller, "The Roman Rite"	E. S. Miller. "The Roman Rite in Bale's *King Johan.*" *PMLA* 64 (1949): 802-22.

Misogonus	*Misogonus*. Ed. Lester E. Barber. New York: Garland, 1979.
Morgan, "Fragments"	Paul Morgan. "Fragments of Three Lost Plays from the Stationers Register." *Bodleian Library Record*. 7 (1962-67): 299-307.
Morgan, "Puritan Hostility"	Edmund S. Morgan. "Puritan Hostility to the Theatre." *Proceedings of the American Philosophical Society* 110 (1966): 340-47.
MM	*Mary Magdalene*
MSC	Malone Society Collections
MSR	Malone Society Reprints
Murray, *English Dramatic Companies*	John T. Murray. *English Dramatic Companies 1558-1642*. 2 vols. 1910; rpt. New York: Russell and Russell, 1963.
Nelson, *Cambridge*	Alan Nelson, ed. *Cambridge*. 2 vols. REED. Toronto: U of Toronto P, 1989.
Nice Wanton	*Nice Wanton*. TFT. London: Jack, 1909.
O'Connell, "The Idolatrous Eye"	Michael O'Connell. "The Idolatrous Eye: Iconoclasm, Anti-Theatricalism and the Image of the Elizabethan Theatre." *English Literary History* 52 (1985): 279-310.
OED	Oxford English Dictionary
Pasachoff, *Playwrights, Preachers & Politicians*	N. S. Pasachoff. *Playwrights, Preachers and Politicians: A Study of Four Tudor Old Testament Dramas*. Salzburg: U of Salzburg P, 1975.
Pattison, *Music & Poetry*	Bruce Pattison. *Music and Poetry of the English Renaissance*. New York: Da Capo, 1971.
Phelps, "Date of Lewis Wager's Death"	Wayne H. Phelps. "The Date of Lewis Wager's Death." *Notes and Queries* 223 (1978): 420-21.
Pilkington, *Works*	James Pilkington. *Works*. Ed. J. Scholefield. PS. Cambridge: Cambridge UP, 1842.
Powicke, *Reform. in Eng.*	Maurice Powicke. *The Reformation in England*. London: Oxford UP, 1941.
PS	Parker Society
Ralph Roister Doister	Nicholas Udall. *Ralph Roister Doister*. Ed. J. S. Farmer. Early English Dramatists. 1906; rpt. New York: Barnes and Nobles, 1966.
REED	Records of Early English Drama

Revels History, Vol. II	*The Revels History of Drama in English (1500-1576): Volume II.* Ed. Norman Sanders, T. W. Craik, Richard Southern, and Lois Potter. London: Methuen, 1980.
Richards, "Preachers & Players"	Douglas W. Richards. "Preachers and Players. "The Contest between Agents of Sermon and Game in the Moral Drama from *Mankind* to *Like Will to Like*." Ph.D. Diss. University of Rochester, 1986.
Roston, *Biblical Drama*	Murray Roston. *Biblical Drama in England from the Middle Ages to the Present Day.* London: Faber and Faber, 1968.
Scheurweghs, "Date of *Jacob and Esau*"	G. Scheurweghs. "The Date of 'The History of Jacob and Esau.'" *English Studies* 15 (1933): 218-19
Simon, *Education & Society*	Joan Simon. *Education and Society in Tudor England.* Cambridge: Cambridge UP, 1967.
Somerset, "Fair is Foul"	J. A. B. Somerset. "'Fair is foul and foul is fair': Vice-Comedy's Development and Theatrical Effects." *Elizabethan Theatre V.* Ed. G. R. Hibbard. Hamden, CT: Archon, 1973: 54-73.
Southern, *Staging of Plays before Shakespeare*	Richard Southern. *The Staging of Plays before Shakespeare.* New York: Theatre Arts Books, 1973.
Stevens, *Music & Poetry*	John Stevens. *Music and Poetry in the Early Tudor Court.* London: Methuen, 1961.
Stopes, *William Hunnis*	C. C. Stopes. *William Hunnis and the Revels.* Louvain: A. Uystpruyst, 1910.
Strype, *Cranmer*	John Strype. *Memorials of the most reverend father in God, Thomas Cranmer.* 2 vols. Oxford: Oxford UP, 1840.
Temptation	John Bale. *The Temptation of Our Lord.* In Happé, *Bale*, vol. II.
TFT	Tudor Facsimile Texts.
Thomas, "*Jacob & Esau*"	Helen Thomas. "Jacob and Esau - 'rigidly Calvinistic'?" *Studies in English Literature* 9 (1969): 199-213.
Three Lawes	John Bale. *Three Lawes.* In Happé, *Bale*, Vol. II.
The Tide Tarrieth	George Wapull. *The Tide Tarrieth No Man.* TFT. London: Jack, 1910.

Tilley, *Dict. of Proverbs*	Morris P. Tilley. *A Dictionary of the Proverbs in England in the Sixteenth and Seventeenth Centuries*. Anne Arbor: U of Michigan P, 1950.
The Trial	*The Trial of Treasure*. Ed. J. S. Farmer. TFT. London: Jack, 1908.
Wendel, *Calvin*	Francois Wendel. *Calvin: The Origins and Development of His Religious Thought*. Trans. Philip Mairet. Glasgow: Collins, 1965.
Westfall, *Patrons & Perform.*	Suzanne Westfall. *Patrons and Performance: Early Tudor Household Records*. Oxford: Clarendon, 1990.
Wickham, *Early Eng. Stages*	Glynne Wickham. *Early English Stages*. 3 vols. London: Routledge and Kegan Paul, 1958-80.
Wilson, *English Drama*	F. T. Wilson. *The English Drama 1485-1585*. Rev. R. K. Hunter. Oxford: Oxford UP, 1969.
Wrigley, *Pop. History of England*	E. A. Wrigley and R. S. Schofield. *The Population History of England 1541-1871*. Cambridge, MA: Harvard UP, 1981.

INTRODUCTION

We still tend to think of the Reformation as having more to do with suppressing than supporting drama in Tudor England, and as a recent article has shown, the anti-theatrical puritans of Elizabeth's reign, (who at least represented a sizeable segment of Protestant opinion) were especially hostile toward stage plays on scriptural stories.[1] According to the likes of Gosson and Stubbes, no sooner had the Roman Mass been banished from England and the preaching of God's Word restored than the new stage spectacles emerged to satisfy the idolatrous tendencies of the unregenerate majority, with players functioning as the devil's "professed Masse priests and Choristers," and the "Playhouses his Synagogues."[2]

However, this hysterical distrust of *spectacula* was not a prominent feature of English Protestantism from the beginning. While such early reformers as Thomas Cranmer, John Bale, and John Foxe were keenly aware of the potential dangers of images to corrupt the senses, mislead the intellect, and incite idolatry, they did not object to their use in principle. As Foxe would ask in defense of his own Bible-based comedy *Christus Triumphans*, "why is it less fitting for the eyes than for the ears to be trained on sacred objects?"[3] Indeed, instead of impeding the cause of Christ, such stage plays could work toward its advancement, especially among a largely illiterate populace. Backed by the Tudor Protestant administrations at least through the early decades of Elizabeth's reign, early Tudor reformers used plays as vehicles for legitimating and winning popular consent for Protestant religious policy and practice. A closer look at the first fifty years of English Protestantism (what I will call the Reformation era) will show that reform-minded leaders in all the major institutions traditionally sponsoring drama--the court, the church, noble households, civic organizations, and the schools and universities--made a concerted effort to encourage the writing and production of religious drama. To be sure, the civic-sponsored biblical cycles and parish plays,

1. O'Connell, "The Idolatrous Eye," pp. 279ff.
2. For specific references, see O'Connell, "The Idolatrous Eye," pp. 279ff, and Morgan, "Puritan Hostility," pp. 340-47.
3. Foxe even went so far as to request that his audience view the play in "sacred silence, as you are wont to do in holy churches." See Foxe, *Christus Triumphans*, pp. 229-30.

some of which retained popish elements (York, for example), were condemned by early Elizabethan ecclesiastical officials, but even these were not censored out of existence by Protestant authorities as was once thought. In towns such as Coventry, Chester, Norwich, and Chelmsford, these biblical plays were revised and brought into line with Reformation teaching, and it now appears clear that financial problems and declining public interest had as much to do with their demise.[4]

What began to supplant the old town drama on scriptural subjects during the Reformation era were biblical plays with two different types of auspices: those performed by professional playing troupes, usually of aristocratic patronage, and those arranged for performance by students in the schools and universities. Both kinds of plays are represented in this volume. *Mary Magdalene*, as its Prologue makes clear, was performed by a troupe of five professional actors on tour before provincial audiences, although originally intended to entertain and instruct adolescents (like the frivolous young heroine of the play) residing in a noble household. *Jacob and Esau*, on the other hand, is a school play composed for a large cast of amateur actors, typical of such institutions as Eton, Westminster, and the Chapel Royal. The two works represent different approaches to dramatizing biblical narrative, the troupe interlude relying on traditional medieval dramaturgy, the school play using Roman comedy (and sixteenth-century adaptations of it) as a basic model for play construction.

It is fairly obvious why Reformation stage patrons encouraged the writing of scriptural drama. For them, as for the playwrights themselves, the Bible was the infallible word of God and thus the supreme authority for all Christians on matters of doctrine and daily living, and because of the perceived timelessness and immediacy of its subject matter, the Scriptures offered answers to the most pressing personal, doctrinal, and political issues of the day. As the history of the Reformation has shown (and as *Jacob and Esau* itself illustrates) those "answers" were often based on readings of Scripture as politically motivated and self-serving as the mandates of the pope that they replaced.

In writing biblical plays, English Protestant dramatists drew inspiration and guidance from their continental counterparts, Philipp Melanchthon in Lutheran Germany, Theodore Beza in Calvin's Geneva, and John Sturm of Strasbourg, all of whom were active in the promotion, composition, and directing of sacred drama. Their experiences and opinions were disseminated among the learned in England in a book entitled *De Regno Christi* by Sturm's Strasbourg contemporary, Martin Bucer, who became Regius Professor of Divinity at Cambridge under

4. Harold Gardiner's thesis in *Mysteries' End* is challenged in Lancashire, *Dramatic Texts and Records*, p. xxxi, and Bills, "Suppression Theory," pp. 157ff.

Edward VI. In a chapter entitled "De Honestis Ludis," Bucer outlines a program in which the nation's young people could participate in plays, all of which, he suggests, should be grounded in Scripture.[5]

Bucer's commentary brings to mind one further point about English Reformation biblical drama in general before we turn our attention to *Mary Magdalene* and *Jacob and Esau* for individual analysis. With only a few exceptions, these plays (not to mention many other non-biblical Reformation plays) present adolescent or young adults in central roles, and if not dealing specifically with education issues they offer some message to wayward youths or their negligent parents. This attention devoted to youth becomes more understandable when we consider that as much as half of England's population of about three million in the mid-sixteenth century was under the age of twenty,[6] and that young adults made up a large segment of the playgoing public, so much so that legislation was proposed and passed to curb the large throngs of youths attending performances in Edwardian and early Elizabethan London.[7] The Crown did not squander the opportunity of using this popularity to its own advantage. Protestant playwrights, backed and in some instances directly patronized by the administration, used religious drama as an instrument promoting the state's religious and educational policies. They, as well as foreign and native reformers who influenced public opinion on domestic and social issues, had the foresight to realize that England's future as a Protestant nation largely depended on a sound Christian education for its young people. They recognized that Roman Catholic religion could not be effectively challenged and uprooted without it; for education, at the very least, would equip people with the ability to read the Scriptures for

5. The text is translated by Wickham, in *Early Eng. Stages, II.i,* Appendix C.
6. And an estimated 25 percent of the nation's youth were under the age of ten in 1546. See Wrigley, *Pop. History of England*, pp. 563-66. The relevance of these statistics to the Reformation is treated in Brigden, "Youth & the English Reformation," pp. 38ff.
7. On 27 May 1549, the London Court of Aldermen tried to prohibit youths and servants from attending interludes by ordering them to be kept at home between the hours of 10 p.m. and 4 a.m. until Michaelmas. Youths were not "to resort to any such unlawful assemblies and gatherings of people together at any interludes or other unlawful games upon the holy day." See Brigden, "Youth & the English Reformation," p. 61 and references cited there; Beer, *Rebellion & Riot,* p. 162. In a letter to Secretary Cecil in 1564, the Bishop of London, Edmund Grindal, called for the suppression of plays because of the "histriones, common playours; who now daylye, butt speciallye on holydayes, sett vp bylles, wherunto the youthe resorteth excessively." Interludes dramatizing Bible stories is singled out by Grindal as being especially offensive. The letter is reprinted Chambers, *Eliz. Stage*, IV, 266-67.

themselves and thereby come face to face with the true gospel without corrupt priests, idolatrous images, and superstitious ceremonies getting in the way. However, more than the nation's spiritual well-being was at stake. Many young people were needed to take leadership roles in the reformed church and the expanding state bureaucracy. With the dissolution of the monasteries and the transfer of power and property from church to state, there was a great demand for men with legal training and other skills to work within the households of prominent statesmen and provide service within the government.[8]

THE LIFE AND REPENTAUNCE OF MARY MAGDALENE

Printing, Dating, and Authorship

"An interlude of the Repentaunce of Mary Magdalen" was entered in the Stationers' Register in 1566 and printed in the same year.[9] The printer was John Charlewood, whose press at Barbican seems to have specialized in religious pamphlets, ballads, and plays during the first half of Elizabeth's reign.[10] Charlewood reissued the black-letter edition of the play in 1567, the only change being a redated title page. By sixteenth-century standards, the quality of printing is very good in both instances. The present text is based on one of the two surviving copies of the 1567 edition in the British Library (Press-mark C. 34. e. 13). The second BL copy (C. 34. e. 12) is missing the last fifteen leaves (F-I) and part of the title page. The only known copy of the 1566 edition resides in the Huntington.

The author of *Mary Magdalene*, Lewis Wager, died in 1562, indicating that the play was written at least four years before its first printing. However, the statement in the Prologue that it teaches "true obedience to the kyng" (rather than the Queen), as well as the play's extensive indebtedness to Calvin's *Institutes* which was widely circulating among university students towards the end of Edward VI's reign (more on that

8. See Simon, *Education & Society*, pp. 170, 247.
9. "Recevyd of John charlewod for his lycense for ye pryntinge of an interlude of the Repentaunce of MARY MAGDALEN &c / iiijd." See Arber, *Stationers Reg.*, I, 152.
10. See the Stationers' Register entries for Charlewood in Arber, *Stationers Reg.*, vol. I,

later), points to an Edwardian date. Just how much revision, if any, the playscript underwent between the time of its original composition and the time it fell into Charlewood's hands is impossible to say, but it is quite possible that the Prologue's passionate defense of drama as a godly pastime is designed to answer the growing chorus of puritan opposition to theatre that developed in the 1560s.

Lewis Wager, like another writer of Reformation interludes, John Bale, was a Catholic-friar-turned-Protestant-preacher. A Franciscan of the Oxford convent, Wager was ordained subdeacon by the Bishop of Sarum on 21 September 1521 and studied at Oxford sometime prior to 1540. The next we hear of him is in April 1560 when he became rector of St. James, Garlickhithe, London; he was buried in his own parish two years later in July 1562, the administration being granted to his widow Elinore.[11] In the same year in the parish church of St. James, William Wager (author of *Enough is as Good as a Feast* and other interludes) was married; his four children were subsequently christened there as well. From this and the fact that William was born about 1537, we can reasonably infer that William was Lewis' son and that Lewis Wager himself married and converted to Protestantism in the mid-1530s.[12] On the title page of *Mary Magdalene,* Lewis is described as "a learned clarke," and given the topical satire of young ladies of wealth and noble descent in the early scenes, he may have served in a major household as an almoner, chaplain, or tutor, like other playwrighting scholars of the Reformation (e.g., Thomas Becon, Ralph Radcliffe, John Foxe, and Stephen Gosson). Historians have noted that the relations between the aristocracy and the monastic orders had always been close and that the more privileged and talented among the ex-religious were awarded such positions following the dissolution.[13]

Auspices and Theatrical Background

Mary Magdalene was written for a professional troupe of "four men and a boy," the adults doubling thirteen parts among them and the child-actor portraying Mary, as the casting chart on the printed title page indicates.[14] There were many such acting companies performing in Tudor England, some of which during the Reformation era had a fairly clear-cut

11. See Eccles, "Brief Lives," pp. 123-24; Phelps, "Date of Lewis Wager's Death," pp. 420-21.
12. William was "of the age of xlj yeres and vpwards" in 1578, according to a record of his testimony in Chancery. See Eccles, "William Wager," p. 258.
13. See Knowles, *Bare Ruined Choirs*, ch. 25; Powicke, *Reform. in Eng*., p. 25; Wickham, *Early Eng. Stages,* II.i.: 109.
14. See Bevington, *From Mankind to Marlowe*, pp. 68-85.

propagandist agenda of disseminating their Protestant patrons' ideological interests not only in household revels at Christmas, Shrovetide, and on important diplomatic occasions, but on tour in regions of the country over which such lords exercised influence. Two known troupes of this type were Lord Cromwell's Men, led by John Bale in the 1530s, and the King's Men under Edward VI.[15] Like the members of these troupes, the players performing *Mary Magdalene* appear to have been experienced singers, with treble, bass, and "meane" parts assigned for the song that concludes the first phase of the action (ll. 861-64). In offering a moral lesson to youth of aristocratic descent, a performance of the play would have been appropriate for the great hall of a noble household (a reference to "without the door" [l. 1388] suggests an indoor setting), perhaps one where wards and other privileged adolescents were educated,[16] but the play's homely language and lively dialogue and action, as well as its more general evangelical theme of justification by faith through imputed grace, made it also suitable to the diverse audiences on tour.

That it was taken on tour is evident from the Prologue who tells us that he and his colleagues "haue ridden and gone many sundry waies;/Yea, we haue vsed this feate at the vniversitie" (ll. 25-26). The reference to "ridden" here suggests that the troupe travelled with a horse and perhaps a wagon. The statement also supports what we already know from records at Oxford and Cambridge of professional companies performing in those universities.[17] The Prologue, moreover, casts further light on how a professional troupe earned its keep on the road: spectators are invited to give money for the performance: "Truely, I say, whether you geue halfpence or pence. / Your gayne shalbe double, before you depart hence" (ll. 43-44). Whether or not this indicates privileged seating in addition to general admission (say, halfpence for the yard, a penny for the gallery at an inn performance), it seems likely that a hat or plate was passed around, as was evidently the case in performances of the medieval *Mankind*.

Like most contemporary troupe interludes, *Mary Magdalene*, at least in the version that survives, requires little in terms of scenery, properties, and costumes for stage presentation. The play indicates its three settings,

15. For Bale's company, see *Revels History, Vol. 2,* pp. 113-15. The anti-papal repertory of the King's Men under Edward VI is not widely recognized but clearly evident in the accounts of the Revels Office; see Feuillerat, *Revels at Court,* pp. 26-47, 245.
16. It is likely that the lost comedies of Sir Thomas Moore were written for the students of his household, which provided a model for later noblemen such as William Cecil and William Petre whose great manor houses offered facilities for teaching wards and other noblemen's children. John Skelton, Ralph Radcliffe, and Stephen Gosson are among the Tudor playwrights known to have tutored in such households.
17. See Boas, *Univ. Drama,* p. 25.

Mary's courtly household at Magdalo, a street in Jerusalem, and the home of Simon the Pharisee, imaginatively through the dialogue, with the help (in the case of Simon's house) of a table and a few stools, which are brought in and taken off with the actors at the appropriate times. As T. W. Craik observes, "Simon brings in the house by virtue of his presence, and when he departs it ceases to exist."[18] Other properties are portable, including stone (or painted wood) tablets carried in by The Law, a "horrible visage" worn by Knowledge of Sin, and perhaps a jar of the ointment Mary pours on Jesus in Simon's home. The actor playing Mary is to be attractively but not sumptuously dressed, and there is no reason to believe that at any time during the action the part required a velvet "gon grace," tight-laced stays, and a hooped skirt, which the Vices recommend Mary wear to catch prospective young lovers. Indeed, Infidelitie and his cohorts encourage her to improve her wardrobe. After her religious conversion, she is to be "sadly apparelled" (l. 1764). Other stage directions for dress apply to Infidelitie who, like Covetous in William Wager's *Enough is as Good as a Feast,* announces his plans to deceive Mary by putting on "a gowne & a cap" (l. 490). Later he dons the cap and robe of a pharisee "About the which the preceptes of the testament / Must be written in order one by one" (ll. 1079-80).

Despite the indications of sparse staging, I (unlike Craik) do not rule out Chambers' suggestion that some scenery might have been employed in *Mary Magdalene* to signify the localities of Magdalo and Jerusalem, perhaps by "houses" such as those described in the Revels accounts at Court, especially for a performance before a noble household where expenditure for staging might not pose a problem to the players. Addressing the question of how the journey taken by Mary and Infidelitie from Magdalo to Jerusalem is visualized, Chambers conjectures "that the two localities were indicated on opposite sides of the hall or stage, and that the personages travelled from one to the other over the intervening space, which was regarded as representing a considerable distance."[19] Considering the adaptability of most troupe interludes to various occasions and theatrical conditions, it seems reasonable to assume that the type of staging used for a given occasion depended on the facilities and financing available. Wager's play is no exception in this regard.

18. Craik, *Tudor Interlude*, p. 12. With the entrance of Simon and Christ (l. 1657) a table, stools, a wash basin, spoons, salt and bread are brought in. Infidelitie and Malicious Judgement seem to function as servants in the scene, with Infidelitie fetching and bringing in the food and drink.

19. Chambers' hypothesis would be consistent with what we know about the staging of plays at court and in noble households. See Chambers, *Eliz. Stage*, III, 25.

Dramatic Sources

Mary Magdalene is a Protestant adaptation of the medieval saint play.[20] Wager's choice of subject matter is readily understandable when we consider that his old order, the Franciscans, along with other monastic organizations, were believed responsible for the many dramatized saints' lives that were presumed destroyed along with the great monastic libraries.[21] Although their playbooks do not survive, we know of a Mary Magdalene play performed in the parish church at Taunton, Somerset, in 1504, an outdoor production at Chelmsford in 1561 (this may have have been the Digby version), and quite possibly another at Magdalene College, Oxford in 1506-7.[22] Whether Wager was familiar with any of these works or with the surviving East Anglian Digby *Mary Magdalene* is unknown, but his play does share some features in common with the latter play. Following the Digby author, Wager identifies the profligate woman who washes Christ's feet in Luke 7 with Mary Magdalene in Luke 8 out of whom Jesus expelled seven demons (and in both plays the exorcism is highly theatricalized), he makes references to Mary's upbringing in the castle of Magdalene, and he depicts at some length the dinner at Simon's house where Mary washes Christ's feet and listens to the parable of the two debtors. In terms of dramaturgy, both plays mingle biblical figures with characters signifying moral abstractions. Nevertheless, the similarities basically end here. As a troupe dramatist, Wager could not remotely accommodate the elaborate staging and casting requirements of the Digby spectacle. As a Protestant, he had no place for the postbiblical miracles and other legendary aspects of the saint so dear to the medieval cult of Mary Magdalene, such as her conversion of the king and queen of Marcylle, her being fed by the angels from heaven, and so on. Moreover, while he is no less committed to combining edification with entertainment in treating the saint, his play is infused with an entirely different religious outlook, one that is positively hostile to the medieval cult of saints and other Catholic dogma and iconography that underpin the Digby *Magdalene*. Wager's Protestant hagiography recalls the writings of Tyndale and Bale in which such martyrs as William Tracie, Sir John Oldcastle, Anne Askew, and King John offered models of biblical piety, evangelical zeal, and extraordinary faith in the face of Catholic persecution. This type of saint was, to quote Bale, "not canonized of the Pope but in the precious blood of his Lord Jesus

20. Happé, "Saint Play," pp. 205-40.
21. Gardiner, *Mysteries' End*, p. 56.
22. Lancashire, *Dramatic Texts and Records*, pp. 107, 244, 272.

Christ."[23] As Mary explains to the audience, "To all the worlde an example I may be, / In whom the mercy of Christ is declared" (ll. 1769-70).

As much as Wager may have been familiar with the saint-play tradition, his dramatic technique owes more to moral play dramaturgy. He has in fact interwoven a few biblical episodes into a standard psychomachia plot used to dramatize the process of religious conversion in pre-Reformation moral plays and interludes such as *Mankind* and *Youth*. As in these plays, the acting space becomes, at least on one level, a kind of spiritual landscape in which the protagonist's allegorized companions represent the motives, impulses, and thoughts that mark individual religious experience. The chief difference, of course, lies in the theological basis of that religious experience, which is explicitly Calvinist. In *Mankind*, for example, the hero begins in innocence (he is purged of original sin by Baptism), and while his fall into sin is inevitable, it is an act of his free and efficacious will. His salvation likewise is based on his voluntary acceptance of the offering of redemption. In *Mary Magdalene*, as in other Protestant interludes, unregenerate man is no longer a mutable being in the sense of being free to initiate the process leading to salvation. The action begins with Mary, the representative of universal man, depraved and already rampant in sin, and it is only when she is wrenched from sin to a state of regeneration by means of irresistible grace that salvation is awarded.

This rejection of free will in favour of predestination and irresistible grace is already evident in the plays of Bale, which Wager may have had the opportunity to see in 1537/38 when the Lord Cromwell's players, evidently led by Bale himself, visited Oxford.[24] *Mary Magdalene* does seem to have benefited from Bale's versification and stagecraft. The play follows Bale's practice (who in turn derived it from earlier moral-play convention) of employing dramatic doggerel for the Vices' speeches and heavy pentameter verse (often in rhymed couplets) for the serious characters, including the opening Prologue (whose speech is in rhyme-royal stanzas). And as in *Three Laws*, Wager introduces a Vice named Infidelitie who is associated with Catholic corruption and heads a gang of his own offspring, and he personifies the Old Law as a type of Moses who appears bearing the tables of the law. Moreover, *Mary Magdalene* inherits the Protestant typology of *King Johan* and Bale's scriptural plays in which biblical and historical narrative foreshadow the present (and universal) conflict between the forces of Christ and Antichrist. As with

23. Bale, *Select Works*, p. 59; cited in Happé, "Saint Play," p. 215.
24. See Alton, "Academic Drama at Oxford," p. 41. This reference to Cromwell's Men at Oxford is overlooked in Murray, *English Dramatic Companies*.

Bale, Christ's struggle with the pharisees is treated as the struggle of the Protestant preacher against Roman Catholic persecution and the doctrine of justification by works.

Mary Magdalene as Dramatic Homily and Topical Satire

Wager's main homiletic argument is made transparent through a sequence of interactions between Mary and her allegorical companions. Through Infidelitie, Mary is led to Pride, Cupidity, and Carnal Concupiscence. With her degeneracy complete, the process leading to salvation begins. By the declaration of the Law of God, she is brought to Knowledge of Sin, who prepares the way for Christ's preaching. Through Christ, Infidelitie is expelled along with the other sins, and Faith and Repentance are received. Mary washes Christ's feet in Simon's house to show her heartfelt love in contrast to the malice and outward sanctity of the accusing Pharisee. In the end, Justification and Love are explained as the fruits, not the causes, of Faith.

The degeneracy phase of the action, which occupies more than half the play, is worth careful consideration, for Wager overlays the familiar pattern of vice intrigue and spiritual corruption with a topical satire on the youth of the privileged classes. From the standpoint of the play's central argument, the purpose of the degeneracy phase is to dramatize the working and final dominance of sin in the heart of Mary. Mary is a willing participant in wrongdoing long before she formally meets the personifications of her sins in the play. Infidelitie, who is the "head of all iniquitie" and has replaced Pride (in the Digby play) as Mary's besetting sin, recalls cradling her in his arms when she was just a babe of three years of age, and his fellow henchmen, Pride, Cupidity, and Carnal Concupiscence, all admit to knowing and having their way with Mary from a very tender age. Together, the four vices represent the whole gamut of human sin ("In vs foure . . . be contained / As many vices as euer in this world raigned," [ll. 377-78], and have their origins in (are in fact, a condensed version of) the Seven Deadly Sins of medieval drama and art. Their homiletic function is not so much to tempt Mary as to augment the sins that she is already naturally disposed to because of her depraved condition. The scheme that they devise is a familiar one. They will appear to Mary under the assumed names and identities of virtuous counsellors. Like Bale, Wager finds the theatrical metaphor useful to convey the duplicitous and specious nature of the Vices. "In our tragedie" (l. 451), as one Vice describes the plot, Infidelitie will play Prudence, Pride will appear to her as Honour, Concupiscence as Pleasure, and Cupidity as Utility.

Following medieval practice, the degeneracy phase is depicted in lively, comic realism, and to enhance the play's appeal to youth, particularly to those of noble birth for whom it may have been originally staged, Mary is presented as a beautiful, but no less spoiled and coquettish, gentlewoman who has just come into the inheritance of a wealthy estate. Her recently deceased parents, she tells us, brought her up "In vertuous qualities and godly literature," and "nourtred [her] in noble ornature," but they also gave her much liberty and granted her every request (ll. 248-55). When she first appears before the audience, she is berating her tailors for failing to keep her fitted out in the latest fashions and chiding her maids for insubordination. Expressing her need for assistance to help her run her estate and keep her in good cheer, Infidelitie promptly offers his services, along with those of "persons of great honor and nobilitie, / Felowes that loue neither to dally nor scoffe, / But at once will tell you the veritie" (ll. 294-96). The Vices now take on a more human (and topical) dimension with Infidelitie as Mary's chamberlain and the others as her newly appointed attendants. The action that ensues gives us an engaging glimpse into sixteenth-century women's fashions and toilette, recalling the Lisle letters describing the dressing of Lady Lisle's daughters at the royal court.[25] The Vices proceed to instruct the fashion-conscious young profligate to dress provocatively in the latest style, dye her hair blonde with the help of a goldsmith and curl it with a hot needle, wearing some of it piled on her forehead, and heighten her looks with cosmetics, all in the interest of alluring rich young suitors. The scene is spiced with mimicking of courtly manners, a "song of .iv. parts," much sensuous kissing and embracing, and sexually explicit punning. Consider the following exchange between Infidelitie and Mary:

Infidelitie.
Mistresse Mary can you not play on the virginals?
Mary.
Yes swete heart that I can, and also on the regals,
There is no instrument but that handle I can,
I thynke as well as any gentlewoman.
Infidelitie.
If that you can play vpon the recorder,
I haue as fayre a one as any is in this border
Truely you haue not sene a more goodlie pipe,
It is so bigge that your hand can it not gripe.
(ll. 837-44)

25. See *Lisle Letters*, IV, 166.

The transvestism of Mary (remember, she is played by a male actor, likely a boy) must have added considerably to the humour of the scene, although this may have provoked the criticism alluded to by the play's opening Prologue.

One may ask how a contemporary audience, either noble or popular, responded to this scene and how the scurrilous behaviour of Mary and the Vices could be reconciled with Wager's homiletic intentions. There is little doubt that the burlesquing of contemporary gentlewomen's fashions and coquettish behaviour would have delighted Tudor audiences, amply supplying the "mirth" promised by the Prologue. However, before we too hastily conclude that the comedy of Mary's corruption in this scene is intended primarily to amuse the audience, we should recognize with Robert C. Jones and other critics that laughter evoked by the Vices in Tudor homiletic drama is a means of implicating and involving the audience in the very experience of temptation and corruption the protagonist undergoes. This is not to say that the comedy is always associated with evil and exclusively didactic in function (as, for example, Bernard Spivack suggests), yet it was often used to disarm audiences and seduce them along with their representative in the playing area.[26]

The audience's warm, sympathetic response to the charming Vices is brought into serious question in the conversion phase of the action that follows where their worldly counsel and behaviour are shown to have damnable consequences. Infidelitie's trio of assistants exits from the acting place (never to return), leaving Mary and Infidelitie alone before the audience. The floor is about to be occupied by a procession of godly figures who externalize the inward changes Mary is experiencing as she is transformed from abject sinner to regenerate saint. Where the Vices' inspired merriment had primarily appealed to the audience's sense of play, the serious, homiletic speeches of the Virtues now encourage critical detachment. Moreover, as Alan Dessen has observed in a perceptive analysis of the scene, their physical appearance, groupings, properties, entrances, and exits are all coordinated to objectify what is happening within Mary on the spiritual plane.[27] The acting space becomes the mirror image of the psyche, not only of Mary but of every spectator who is elected by divine grace. Entering first is the Law of God carrying tables of stone, and compelling Mary and Infidelitie to retreat to the side of the acting area ("Come asyde a little, and geue hym roume" [l. 1111]). Now holding the floor and speaking perhaps in a deep voice (for this actor doubles with Cupidity who is assigned the bass part in the song), he delivers his self-introduction in formal, dignified verse, stating that "to a

26. See Jones, "Dangerous Sport," pp. 45-64; see also Richards, "Preachers & Players," ch. 1; and Somerset, "Fair is Foul," pp. 54-73.

27. See Dessen, *Elizabethan Drama*, p. 134.

glasse compared I may be, / Wherin clerely as in the sunne lyght, / The weakenesse and sinne of him self he may se; / Yea, and his owne damnation, as it is ryght" (ll. 1137-40). Although restrained by Infidelitie, Mary's conscience is sorely afflicted as she gazes upon the Law of God. Shortly thereafter, a second figure enters who states, "By the Law commeth the knowledge of synne, / Whiche knowledge truely here I represent" (ll. 1189-90). His apparent physical ugliness (if we are to believe Infidelitie) also must have made a striking impression on the audience and accentuates his allegorical significance. Wager continually reminds the audience that the action is operating on the spiritual level, as when the Law points over to Infidelitie who is presumably still standing by Mary's side, exhorting her: "O sinner, from thy heart put that Infidelity, / Which hath drowned thee already in the pit of hell" (ll. 1245-46). And again, when Knowledge of Sin says just before he departs from the place:

Though I appere not to hir carnal syght,
  Yet by the meanes that she knoweth the lawe,
I shall trouble hir always both day and night,
  And vpon hir conscience continually gnawe.
(ll. 1305-8)

With the declaration of the Law and Knowledge of Sin showing Mary that she cannot save herself by any human means, Christ now enters to award her salvation. This is unquestionably the pivotal and most highly theatrical moment in the play. At this point, Mary seems to be flanked on one side by Infidelitie and on the other side by Christ to create a kind of "Good Angel/Bad Angel" configuration as in *The Castle of Perseverence* and later in *Doctor Faustus*, for she finds herself alternatively tempted and admonished by the two figures. Finally, Christ exclaims:

Auoide out of this woman thou infidelitie,
  With the .vii. diuels which haue hir possessed.
I banish you hence by the power of my diuinitie,
  For to saluation I haue hir dressed.
(ll. 1385-88)

The stage direction then reads: "Infidelitie runneth away. Mary falleth flat downe. Cry all thus without the doore, and roare terribly." Following this flurry of stage activity, Mary rises to her feet to signify her spiritual rebirth and is then introduced by Christ to Faith and Repentaunce, who give self-introductions similar to those of the Law and Knowledge of Sin. Faith's many references to "the Word" suggest that he may be holding a Bible like similar figures in other Reformation interludes. In typically

Calvinist fashion, they stress that they are "gifts" of God and that salvation does not result from human merit. And again to emphasize their objectifying Mary's interior experience, they inform Mary before exiting with her from the place that "Though in person we shall no more appeare, / Yet inuisibly in your heart we will remayne" (ll. 1533-34). What the spectator witnesses in this theatrically engaging and memorable sequence of actions, therefore, is a dramatization of the process of religious conversion in specifically Calvinist terms. The pageant-like figures who follow one another into the acting space symbolize the steps in that process, clarifying their significance in expository speeches; their distinctive physical appearances, properties, and movements, are all utilized to give highly memorable expression to Wager's evangelical message.

Theological Source: Calvin's Institutes of the Christian Religion

The primary theological source for *Mary Magdalene* is John Calvin's *Institutes of the Christian Religion*, the Latin version of which was circulating among Protestant reformers and university students during Edward VI's reign. The work became more generally accessible in 1561, the year Thomas Norton translated the work into English. Wager's extensive debt to Calvin is evident in what almost certainly are direct borrowings from *The Institutes*. As we have observed, three theological notions--the law, repentance, and faith--appear as personified abstractions in *Mary Magdalene*. Large portions of their speeches correspond closely with passages in *The Institutes*. These passages may be found in Appendix B. In a speech echoing *The Institutes* II.vii.6, the Law in *Mary Magdalene* states that its purpose is to declare the righteousness or "iustice" that is only acceptable unto God, to rebuke the vanity of man ("dronke and blynde in his owne loue"), and to expose his weakness and inability to obtain salvation by means of his own strength (ll. 1129-36). And following *The Institutes*, the Law is compared to a mirror in which man may see his inadequacy and sin, and his damnation, the curse of God which inevitably follows sin.[28]

Wager also repeats Calvin's definitions of repentance and faith. In addition to the view of repentance as a true turning of one's whole life unto God, Wager, like Calvin, does not confine it to a brief period preceding grace, but insists that the act of penitence must be practiced throughout the believer's life: "all the life tyme in repentyng to endure" (l. 1439; *Inst.* III.iii.2). Wager defines faith as a "sure knowledge and cognition / Of the good will of God," and that it is "grounded in the word

28. See Calvin, *Inst.* II.vii.7; *MM*, ll. 1137-40; Appendix B.

of Christes erudition" (ll. 1481-84). This is a paraphrase of Calvin's assertion that faith is a "stedfast and assured knowledge of Gods kindnesse toward vs, which being grounded vpon the trueth of the free promise in Christ" (*Inst.* III.ii.7). Moreover, Wager echoes Calvin when he says that faith is "to the mynde of man reuealed" (Calvin: "reueled to our mindes"), and sealed in his heart by the Holy Ghost. Furthermore, both writers warn that if faith is not based on the Word, it will lead to impiety and heresy (*MM*, ll. 1495-96; *Inst.* II.ii.6). The mirror image reappears, but this time it is likened to the Word, in which man may "behold" faith. Next, Wager repeats Calvin's statement that faith does not teach us to know the nature of God, but simply to know his will and goodness toward man. And finally, the playwright follows Calvin in saying that it is not enough to believe that God is true only, "which can neuer lie, nor deceaue, nor do yll"; however, in adding that it is also necessary to believe that God "has declared his will" in His Word, Wager modifies Calvin's remark that "whatsoeuer procedeth from him, is the sacred and inuiolable truthe" (*MM*, ll. 1509-16; *Inst.* III.ii.6).

It is worth noting that while others in the Reformed tradition assumed that man must repent of sin before faith is possible, Wager, like Calvin, consistently places faith before repentance in the process of conversion. On this point of doctrine the Genevan theologian was uncompromising: "As for them that thinks that repentance doth rather go before faith than flow or spring foorth of it, as a frute out of a tree, they neuer knewe the force therof, and are moued with too weake an argument to thinke so. . . . Yet when we referre the beginnings of repentance to faith, . . . we meane to shewe that a man can not earnestly apply himselfe to repentance, vnlesse he know himself to be of God" (*Inst.* III.iii.1-2). In Mary Magdalene, Wager suggests that faith leads to forgiveness of sins, which makes contrition and repentance possible:

And all that trust in hym with true beleue,
  That he is very God and man, into this world sent,
God will all their synnes for his sake forgeue,
  So that they can be contrite and repent.
(ll. 1265-68)

And in the concluding speech of the play we are told, "By the word came faith, faith brought penitence" (ll. 2129-30).

Considering his reliance on other passages in *The Institutes*, it seems probable that Wager was also familiar with Calvin's exposition of Luke 7:36-50, relating the story of Christ in the home of Simon the Pharisee (*Inst.* III.iv.37). Calvin, likewise, uses the story with its parable of the two debtors to illustrate the preeminence of faith over love in salvation. In expounding Christ's saying, "this womans sinnes are forgiuen her, because she hath loued much," Calvin writes: "In which wordes (as you see) he maketh not her loue the cause, but the proofe of the forgiuenes of her sinnes. For they are deriued vpon a similitude of that debtour, to whom fiue hundred was forgiuen, to whom he did not say that therefore it was forgiuen, because he had loued much: but therefore loued much, because it was forgiuen. . . . By what means she obtained forgiuenesse of sinnes, the Lord openly testifieth: Thy faith, saith he, hath saued thee. Therefore we obtain forgiuenesse by faith: By charitie wee giue thankes, and testifie the bountifulnesse of the Lord (*Inst.* III.iv.37). Calvin's comments upon the same verse in his *Commentary on a Harmony of the Evangelists* are also relevant, and may have been known to Wager. Here, Calvin concludes: "the cause of reciprocal love is here declared to be a free forgiveness. In a word, Christ argues from the fruits of effects that follow it, that this woman has been reconciled to God."[29] In similar terms, Wager declares: "But loue foloweth forgiuenesse of synnes euermore, / As a fruict of faith, and goth not before" (ll. 2073-74; see also ll. 2107-8).

THE HISTORIE OF JACOB AND ESAU

Printing, Dating, and Authorship

Sometime between June 1557 and June 1558 Henry Sutton was licenced "to prynte an interlude vpon the history of IACOBE and ESAWE out of the xxvij chapeter of the fyrste boke of MOYSES Called genyses and for his lycense he geveth to the howse iiij^{d}."[30] Ten years later Henry Bynneman printed what is the only complete text of *Jacob and Esau* known to survive. The six extant copies of this 1568 edition are located in the British Museum, Bodleian, Huntington, Folger, Pforzheimer, and Yale University libraries.[31] The hypothesis that Bynneman's text is actually a second edition following one printed by Sutton in 1557/58 was

29. See Calvin, *Commentary*, II, 137.
30. Arber, *Stationers Reg.*, I, 23.
31. Bynneman was one of the most respected and active printers of his day, publishing such important works as Calvin's *Sermons on Job* and Holinshed's *Chronicle* before his death in 1583. He specialized in Protestant religious works and, in addition to Sir Christopher Hatton, probably secured the patronage of the Earl of Leicester, who is the dedicatee of many books produced at his printing house at The Mermaid, Knightrider Street. See *Dictionary of Printers*, pp. 59-60.

demonstrated in 1966 by Paul Morgan who discovered a sizeable fragment of it among a collection of bound manuscripts at New College, Oxford, where it formerly lined an old deed box.[32] The fragment is sheet G4, upon which the play's last 274 lines are distributed among eight pages (G1-4). Sheets G3-4 are in good condition, but one and one-half inches of text containing the speech prefixes and the first two or three words of each line are missing from the outer edges of G1-2. Its printing composition is inferior to that of Bynneman's edition of 1568. The speakers' names are not consistently aligned with their parts, indentations are lacking to mark changes in speaking parts, and in one instance a scene heading (*Actus quinti, scena decima*) appears at the bottom of G2^{v}, with the text beginning at the top of G3^{r}.

As Morgan observes, the fact that the types and capitals of this fragment match those of a work printed by Sutton in 1559 convincingly shows that this is part of the original 1557/58 *Jacob and Esau*. It also appears that it served as the copy text for Bynneman's 1568 edition which, like the earlier one, is a playscript full of stage directions designed for the actors themselves. Indeed the two texts closely correspond, with G4v in both works matching each other line for line. There are, however, about 130 variants in spelling and capitalization, and a few additional differences in spacing and printing errors (see Notes to Text). In two instances, the stage directions differ. The direction of the earlier text, "This is the last song, & must be song after the prayer," is shortened to "This song must be song after the prayer" in the 1568 version (l. 1724). Another change occurs at l. 1739, where the "The Po/etes part" (1557/58) becomes "The Poet en-/treth" (1568). These might be explained as minor stylistic alterations. However, the differing references to the poet are intriguing, and invite two other possible explanations. The 1568 revision makes clear that the poet is separate from the cast (who all stand before the audience at this point in the action), whereas it might have been the case ten years earlier that he participated as an actor and would therefore already be on stage when called to deliver the concluding speech. On the other hand, as controversial a play as *Jacob and Esau* might have been toward the end of Queen Mary's reign (see below), perhaps the author desired to retain his anonymity by not giving the speech in person (or at least wanted this as an option).

Despite its 1557/58 entry in the Stationers' Register, many scholars believe that the play's staunchly Protestant (specifically predestinarian) theology indicates an Edwardian rather than a Marian date, assigning its composition sometime between 1547 and 1553. This is plausible, although contemporary records show that numerous pro-Protestant and

32. See Morgan, "Fragments," pp. 300-02. A photographic reproduction of the JE fragment appears in Appendix A.

anti-Catholic plays were staged during Mary's reign despite statutes prohibiting them, so numerous, in fact, that a policy of active suppression appears to have been energetically enforced in 1557 when the Crown turned over the whole process of licensing plays and players to the Church in the form of certain "Commissioners for Religion."[33] Indeed, fear of persecution may well explain why the author of *Jacob and Esau* (and the authors of many religious and politically oriented Tudor plays) chose anonymity at the time of printing. We should keep in mind, however, that the vernacular drama was not of sufficient literary merit at this time for a writer to claim authorship; few were ever intended for publication or to be considered anything other than scripts for actors.[34]

The author's identity remains a mystery, despite much conjecture. Since *Jacob and Esau* is written for child actors with singing parts, it is generally agreed that the author must have been affiliated with a choir or grammar school, perhaps himself a schoolmaster. An enthusiastic claim proposed by Leicester Bradner has been made for Nicholas Udall, grammar master of Eton (1534-41) and Westminster (1555-56) and a producer of masques and plays at court before Queen Mary in 1553/54. The case is made chiefly on the basis of the play's linguistic and prosodic similarities with *Ralph Roister Doister*, the only extant play, by the way, that we can certainly ascribe to Udall.[35] Internal evidence alone, however, is usually inconclusive, and this is especially true in a genre and at a time when patterns of speech, meter, and rhyme were so heavily ruled by convention. An equally strong, if not stronger, case can be made for William Hunnis, appointed choirmaster of the Chapel Royal by Queen Elizabeth in 1568, the same year as *Jacob and Esau*'s second printing. Hunnis reportedly wrote many "enterludes" during his period as a gentleman of the Chapel under Edward VI and Mary I (see Chambers, *Eliz. Stage*, II, 34). In *William Hunnis and the Revels*, C. C. Stopes shows a number of significant correspondences between the play's verse and Hunnis's poetry.[36] The same year that the play was licensed (1557-58), Hunnis was imprisoned in the Tower for his involvement in a plot to dethrone Mary I, "his property, books, and papers, at the mercy of friend and foe, censor or publisher," an indication of Hunnis's strong Protestant

33. Chambers, *Eliz. Stage*, I, 275; Lancashire, *Dramatic Texts and Records*, pp. 158, 216.
34. See Axton, *Classical Interludes*, pp. 1-4.
35. See Bradner, "Test for Udall's Authorship," p. 378.
36. The case for William Hunnis as author has been forwarded by Stopes, *William Hunnis* (in 1910), and more recently by Pasachoff, *Playwrights, Preachers, & Politicians*, pp. 16-55.

convictions and a possible explanation for the play's rather radical political implications.

Auspices and Theatrical Background

My own guess is that *Jacob and Esau* was written toward the end of Edward VI's reign when two of the play's thematic concerns, the raising of youth and predestinarian theology, were popular subjects for preachers and playwrights alike, and that it was acted by the Chapel children at court (as the concluding prayer suggests) at this time and possibly revived under Mary and Elizabeth. The play's music, especially the hymns, are not unlike those performed at the Chapel Royal,[37] with the solo singing assigned to little Abra clearly written for a specially gifted boy chorister. The parts of both Abra and Mido require skillful coordination of speech, song, and movement,[38] as when, for example, Abra sweeps the floor as she sings the play's second song or when Mido mimics the gesturing and speech of his elders. This high calibre of acting was demanded at the Chapel Royal where the Master was given free license by the Crown to choose his choristers from any of the choir schools throughout the realm.[39] The play's ten listed acting parts (excluding "the Poet") seem suitable for the eight children residing at the Chapel in 1553, assuming that Isaac's neighbors Hanan and Zethar (who briefly appear in the second scene never to return) involved doubling, as Bevington suggests.[40]

The rather demanding staging requirements, too, resemble those prescribed for other performances before the court by the Chapel children. In addition to two live goats brought on to the stage late in the action, the stage directions call for three greyhounds (named Lightfoot, Takepart, and Lovell) to be led in by Esau's servant Ragau for a hunting expedition as the play begins. Similar requirements for hounds and hunting horns are listed for *Narcissus,* written by Hunnis for performance by the Chapel children before Queen Elizabeth in 1569, and for *Palamon and Arcyte,* composed by Hunnis' predecessor as chapel master, Richard Edwards (1566).[41] Moreover, as Chambers supposes, Isaac's tent may have been represented by a *domus* similar to those recorded for court productions in

37. See Le Huray, *Music & Reform. in England,* pp. 57-89, 172-226.
38. See *Revels History, Vol. 2,* p. 211.
39. See Le Huray, *Music & Reform. in England, pp. 57-89.*
40. For the children in the Edwardian Chapel, see *Revels History, Vol. 2*, p. 160; for doubling see Bevington, *From Mankind to Marlowe*, p. 30.
41. "Hunting dogs" appeared in two plays at Cambridge, the first at King's College in 1552-53 for *Hyppolytus*; the second at Peterhouse in 1572-73 for an unidentified play. See Nelson, *Cambridge*, II, 1127, 1145.

the Revels Accounts, although a curtained traverse might have sufficed in more modestly set productions.[42]

As a Protestant biblical play, *Jacob and Esau* offers an interesting contrast in dramatic style, stage presentation, and treatment of biblical subject matter to *Mary Magdalene.* Indeed, the main differences are really those between a popular troupe play following medieval English dramaturgy and an academic interlude in imitation of Roman comedy, a Humanist-inspired approach to play composition known as "the Christian Terence." We may recall that in Wager's play, a few well-known biblical scenes are interwoven into a psychomachia plot, with Mary's "character" moving freely among the worlds of biblical story, spiritual allegory, and topical satire; she and her companions, moreover, are self-presentational in that they explain their significance to the audience in direct-address speeches. In *Jacob and Esau*, on the other hand, the action focuses on biblical events throughout (although it gives fictional names to the Hebrew servants: Mido, Ragau, Abra), and the author takes further measures to give the work a sense of historical reality.[43] According to the title page, the players are "to be consydered to be Hebrews, and so should be apparailed with attire," which indicates the first known attempt in an English play at "period costume."[44] The characters are as naturalistically portrayed as any in the drama of the time, with no breaking out of their roles to summarize the action or comment upon its significance as one finds commonly in the troupe plays, and they are unaccompanied by

42. That at least one tent is represented in the acting place is evident from the numerous references in the dialogue and the stage directions to the characters going into or emerging from "the tente." Chambers (*Eliz. Stage*, III, 24-25) suggests three tents are needed, one each for Isaac, Esau, and Jacob. Craik, however, has shown that only one tent might be represented, while Southern's more recent detailed analysis proposes a simple curtained traverse in front of a hall screen, with at least two openings, the main one leading into the tent proper ("Isaacs Tente"), the other into Esau's "parte of the tent." Other entrances and exits, (e.g., when characters arrive from the hunt or from the neighbouring "Tentes"), were facilitated by the screen doors. Southern also suggests that the author might have been familiar with classical stage conventions for entrances and exits: "the one on the actor's right for characters coming from the near neighborhood, and that on the left from characters coming from a distance." See Southern, *Staging of Plays before Shakespeare*, pp. 361-74; see also Craik, *Tudor Interlude*, pp. 122-23.

43. The importance of the word "history" is indicated by its appearance in title, head title, and running title (Wilson, *English Drama*, p. 94).

44. This, of course, does not mean that it was the first play to do so. See Southern, *Staging of Plays before Shakespeare*, p. 363; Bevington, *From Mankind to Marlowe*, p. 30.

personified abstractions. And in contrast to the multiple settings of Wager's play, all the action in *Jacob and Esau* takes place in a single locale, the Hebrew settlement on front of Isaac's tent. Moreover, the school play holds up to the description in the title as a "mery and wittie Comedie," consistently comic throughout (apart from Esau's angry outburst in Act 5), and is generally free of the coarseness and profanity, on the one hand, and the long serious sermon-like speeches, on the other, that characterize the dialogue of Vices and Virtues in Wager's biblical interlude. The play's five-act structure is the most salient feature derived from classical comedy.

Jacob and Esau as Dramatic Homily

We should not be misled into thinking, however, that the play is any less homiletic in purpose. The theological argument is announced in the prologue, applied to the audience in the concluding epilogue, illustrated through the contrasting characters of Jacob and Esau, and further elaborated in the dialogue and speeches of the other characters (particularly in the prayers of Rebecca and Isaac), although these are delivered "in character." The several songs add direct moral commentary on the action. But no less important in conveying the message is the biblical narrative itself. The technique of using scriptural analogy to teach a lesson was a common practice among Protestant preachers and playwrights alike, and in this respect, the author of *Jacob and Esau* is at one with Lewis Wager and Bale before him. All three dramatists regard the Bible as a storehouse of archetypal stories and characters, which not only prefigured the temporal world but were a key to understanding and resolving its religious and political crises. And in identifying with the chosen people of the Old Testament, Protestants believed that they were in a sense reliving the experiences of the Israelites.[45] Therefore, while *Jacob and Esau* lacks the explicit personification-allegory of Wager's play, the Old Testament story would have been subject to a topical reading by its contemporary audience, with explosive political implications, as we shall see shortly.

Jacob and Esau's main concern is with the theological problem of predestination versus free will. This issue is explicitly addressed at the outset by "the Prologue, a Poet," with considerable care taken to ground

45. This is clearly illustrated in Bale's *King Johan* where the English monarch is envisaged as "a faythfull Moyses," who "withstode proude Pharao, for hys poore Israel / Myndynge to brynge it out of the la[n]de of Darkenesse." See Happé, *Bale*, I, 58.

the notion of predestination in biblical verses from the books of Malachi and Romans, as well as Genesis:

> Iacob was chosen, and Esau reprobate:
> Iacob I loue (sayde God) and Esau I hate.
> For it is not (sayth Paule) in mans renuing or will,
> But in Gods mercy who choseth whome he will.
> (ll. 11-14)

The dramatic action that follows illustrates the validity of predestination chiefly through the contrasting characters of the elect Jacob and his reprobate brother Esau. In the twin brothers we encounter two different and irreconcilable types of mankind: the one God's elect who is destined to inherit worldly prosperity as well as salvation in the next life; the other an unregenerate without conscience who is deterministically bent on a course leading to eternal damnation. Jacob, as one would expect, is a faithful, obedient son, his mother's favourite, and beloved by all in the community for his piety and quiet disposition. Above all, he is portrayed as a humble servant of God, subordinating his own will to what he believes to be God's providential will. As he reveals to Rebecca early on in the play: "what soeuer he hath pointed me vnto, / I am his owne vessell his will with me to do" (ll. 237-38). Jacob may strike the modern reader as somewhat self-righteous and a crafty opportunist, but clearly this is not the author's intention. His motives to acquire Esau's birthright and blessing are not selfish or in the interests of self-advancement, but based on his conviction that he is acting in accordance with God's will. "Forasmuche as my said mother, / Worketh upon thy worde O Lorde," he prays before going through with the plot, "It shall become me to shewe mine obedience" (ll. 1207-9).

Esau, on the other hand, is as wicked as Jacob is unswervingly righteous. Deprived of the necessary grace to seek goodness, he is portrayed as a profligate youth who shows no signs of redemption. Esau is selfish and inconsiderate by nature, and so preoccupied with his favourite pursuit, hunting, that he can devote no time or attention to his parents or his responsibilities as the heir apparent.[46] In our first glimpse of him, he awakens the neighbours by his incessant hornblowing at an unearthly hour of the night, and then proceeds to drag his servant, Ragau, off to the forest, without sufficient food or sleep. An unregenerate fool, he does not value or grasp the spiritual significance of the birthright, which he sells impetuously for a morsel of food and momentary gratification.

46. Esau exemplifies the addiction of noble youth to hunting, hawking, and idle pleasures (see Simon, *Education & Society*, pp. 366, 100).

When he discovers his undoing, he explodes like a tyrant, swearing to take vengeance on all who were involved in the plot (ll. 1522-84).

Like other Protestant youth plays of its time--*Nice Wanton*, *The Disobedient Child*, *The Longer Thou Livest the More Fool Thou Art*, *The Glass of Government*, as well as *Mary Magdalene*--*Jacob and Esau* attempts to reconcile abstract theological doctrine with practical matters of upbringing and education. In juxtaposing older and younger brothers, the play explores the question of how it is that youths, given the identical Christian upbringing and education, can turn out so differently. The play that *Jacob and Esau* most resembles in this respect is George Gascoigne's *Glass of Government*, which contrasts two sets of brothers. The play's two younger brothers grow up to be of exemplary moral character, one of them becoming a successful preacher in Geneva, the center of Christian culture in the eyes of the Elizabethan puritans. The two elder black sheep, on the other hand, defiantly reject the good counsel given to them, fall in with bad company, and live out their lives in vice and crime before being brought to justice: one of them hanged for robbery, the other whipped almost to the point of death for fornication. How, then, can one explain the wickedness of these boys who have been instructed in the godly precepts since early childhood and tutored by one of the finest schoolmasters in the city of Antwerp? The answer is given by the Fourth Chorus who declares that "the grace of God it is, wheron good gyftes must growe, / And lacke of God his grace it is, which makes them lye full lowe."[47] Even more emphatically, *Jacob and Esau* illustrates the notion that since all persons are deserving of damnation by reason of original sin and deliberate disobedience, God is not bound to save any child, even if he is born into a righteous family. Esau has been nurtured in the ideal family environment, yet he still grows up to be an inveterate sinner. A key scene in the play is the one in which Isaac's two neighbours, Hanan and Zethar, discuss whether predestination or education determines human character, a sort of sixteenth-century version of the nature versus nurture debate. Zethar claims that Esau's degenerate condition is due to a lack of parental discipline and instruction on Isaac's part. If children were trained under the rod, he argues, they would eschew lewdness and other vices and embrace virtue. Hannan replies that in the case of Esau, the quality of his upbringing has not been a decisive factor, since Isaac and Rebecca have been good, conscientious parents. Esau's reprobation is apparent in his "yll inclination," a natural taste for wrongdoing and a stubborn refusal to receive godly instruction:

> Esau hath ben nought euer since he was borne.
> And wherof commeth this, of Education?

47. *Glasse of Gouernment*, sig. K2[vr].

Nay it is of his owne yll inclination.
They were brought yp bothe under one tuition,
But they be not bothe of one disposition.
Esau is gyuen to looce and leude liuying.
(ll. 180-85)

As a reprobate, Esau is denied the necessary grace to be a righteous and obedient son. In Calvinist terms, his mind has been exposed to the Word, but his heart has not been illuminated by the Spirit. There is perhaps no better gloss to the above passage than the remarks of James Pilkington, the Edwardian and Elizabethan Bishop of Durham who established two grammar schools in his diocese: "This is the secret judgement of God, that of one good father, Isaac, came two so contrary children; the one so wicked, the other so good. . . . But this is to teach us the free grace of God, without any deserts on our part, whensoever he calls any to the true knowledge and fear of him; and that it is neither the goodness or evilness of the father that makes a good or evil child; for many good fathers have had evil children, and evil fathers good children."[48]

What is extraordinary about *Jacob and Esau*, however, is its departure from the orthodox Christian view that the deceptive plotting of Jacob and Rebecca to procure Esau's inheritance was both immoral and totally unnecessary.[49] Instead of showing that they were self-seeking and presumptuously intervening in the divine plan (the standard view of Tudor biblical commentaries), the author attempts to demonstrate that the seizure of the birthright was in fact sanctioned by God as the means of unseating corrupt authority and fulfilling his promise to Jacob. This has led several scholars to recognize a political dimension to *Jacob and Esau*. As David Bevington concludes: "*Jacob and Esau*'s chief ideological purpose is to justify seizure of power, and to insist that the seizure is reluctantly undertaken," and adds that the dramatist's "theory dangerously sanctions any rebellion when divine command may be taken to oversway established order."[50] *Jacob and Esau*, in fact, appears to anticipate the political views of such Marian exiles as Bishop John Ponet, the former high-ranking official of the Edwardian Church, who settled for a time in Strasbourg, and John Knox and Christopher Goodman, who came under Calvin's influence in Geneva. After witnessing and hearing reports of the

48. Pilkington, *Works*, pp. 219-20. For Pilkington's founding of grammar schools, see Simon, *Education & Society*, p. 307, 309.
49. See Pasachoff, *Playwrights, Preachers & Politicians*, p. 24, and references to the Church Fathers cited there.
50. Bevington, *Tudor Drama & Politics*, p. 112. See also Pasachoff, *Playwrights, Preachers & Politicians*, pp. 16-55, and Wickham, *Early Eng. Stages*, III, 232.

Protestant executions under Queen Mary, these exiles abandoned the early Protestant doctrine of non resistance, hitherto unchallenged in England since Tyndale enunciated it in *The Obedience of a Christian Man*, and adopted the view that the usurpation of corrupt authority is justified on scriptural grounds. While *Jacob and Esau* lacks the strident tone and the anti-Catholic virulence of Bale's plays, the dramatist obviously sees in the analogy of the Old Testament story a two-edged sword against contemporary Catholicism. He uses the analogy of Jacob's supremacy over the elder Esau, first of all, to demonstrate the validity of the doctrine of predestination as opposed to the Roman doctrine of free will and justification by works. And secondly, Esau may be seen as the older generation of English Catholics who have no place in England's future; Jacob, on the other hand, stands for Protestant elect who are predestined to live in prosperity as the new Israel: "The one shal be a mightier people elect: / And the elder to the yonger shall be subiect" (ll. 245-46).

Theological Sources

Like Lewis Wager, the author of *Jacob and Esau* may have read Calvin's *Institutes*. This was the view of G. Scheurweghs who in a 1939 article refers to several correspondences between the speeches of the play's Prologue and Epilogue and passages in the 1539 Latin edition of Calvin's *Institutes*.[51] Scheurweghs's comparison, however, does not provide conclusive evidence of Calvin's influence on the play. For as Helen Thomas points out, the playwright may have gone directly to the ninth chapter of Paul's Epistle to the Romans for the contents of his Epilogue and Prologue, rather than to *The Institutes*. However, Thomas' own interpretation, discussed in her article, "*Jacob and Esau*--'rigidly Calvinistic'?" is suspect. She argues, on the basis of certain lines in the Epilogue, that the author's opinions on predestination go directly against the teachings not only of Calvin but of Luther as well, and that they are more representative of Roman Catholic doctrine. "It is very likely," she concludes, that the play "is a dramatic statement of the position of Erasmus on predestination."[52] The lines she refers to are as follows:

> Yet not all fleshe did he then predestinate,
> But onely the adopted children of promise:
> For he foreknewe that many would degenerate,
> And wylfully giue cause to put from that blisse.
> (ll. 1747-50)

51. See Scheurweghs, "Date of *Jacob and Esau*," pp. 218-19; Appendix B.
52. Thomas, "*Jacob & Esau*," p. 203.

Thomas comments, "Thus God's foreknowledge of man's future actions is given as the cause of His choice of the elect and the reprobated" (p. 202). From the Poet's remark that foreknowledge of sin is the basis of excluding many from bliss (the meaning of the latter two lines), Thomas has deduced that election, as well as reprobation, is a consequence of God's foreknowledge of man's actions. This is, indeed, the position of Erasmus on predestination, and one that Thomas Aquinas made orthodox in Roman Catholic theology, but it is not the view expressed in *Jacob and Esau*. Thomas, I believe, has misread the text. The Poet is saying here that while God predestined the elect to salvation, he did not actually predetermine, but only foreknew, the fate of the many others who were not elected; their degeneracy or sin is the cause of their exclusion from eternal bliss.

This moderate Calvinist position (that reprobation was not the object of a divine foreordinance but simply the state of those not chosen by God) was adopted by Martin Bucer and Peter Martyr,[53] two of Calvin's closest colleagues and supporters in England, and by many of their English contemporaries, notably John Bradford. Bradford was embroiled in the famous Marian debate over predestination in the King's Bench prison in 1554. Fortunately, his contribution to the dispute has survived, and since his written opinions upon the subject appear to have been approved by Cranmer, Ridley, and Latimer, the three leading divines of the Edwardian Church,[54] it may be said that they generally reflect the views of most committed English Protestants during the 1550s. Bradford writes that it does not hurt to "affirm, teach, and preach" the doctrine that "'Christ elected some, and not all,' since it is set forth unto man in the Bible" (*Writings*, I, 311). According to Bradford, predestination "utterly

53. Peter Martyr, who served as Doctor of Divinity at Oxford in 1550, argued that "predestination refers to saints only while the reprobate are not predestinate, since sin is the only cause of reprobation." Cited in Kendall, *Calvin,* p. 30. For Bucer's views, see Wendel, *Calvin*, pp. 280-82.

54. John Strype, who had access to many documents related to the controversy in the late 17th century, writes the following: "Bradford was apprehensive that they [the free-willers] might now do great harm in the church, and therefore out of prison wrote a letter to Cranmer, Ridley, and Latimer, the three chief heads of the reformed (though oppressed) church in England, to take some cognizance of this matter, and to consult with them in remedying it. . . . Upon this occasion, Ridley wrote a treatise of God's Election and Predestination. And Bradford wrote another upon the same subject; and sent it to those three fathers in Oxford for their approbation; and, theirs being obtained, the rest of the eminent divines, were ready to sign it also" (Strype, *Cranmer,* I, 502-3).

overthroweth the wisdom, power, ableness, and choice of man, that all glory may be given only unto God" (*Writings*, I, 315). The Edwardian Reformer follows Calvin in declaring the "election is not to be looked upon but in Christ" (*Writings,* I, 220; *Inst.* III.xxiv.5). "Christ's death is sufficient for all," he asserts, "but effectual to none but to the elect only." He comes close to advocating limited atonement in believing that Christ "prayed not" for all men, and that "for whom he 'prayed not,' for them he died not" (*Writings*, I, 320). While reprobation, as well as election, serves to glorify God, Bradford, like Calvin, places the responsibility for damnation squarely on the reprobate's shoulders (*Writings,* I, 220). Where he significantly deviates from Calvin, however, is in his assertion that God's rejection of the reprobate is based not upon a positive eternal decree (as Calvin evidently believed), but on his foreknowledge of sin: "the damned therefore have not nor shall not have any excuse, for God, foreseeing their condemnation through their own sin, did not draw them as he doth his elect unto Christ" (*Writings*, I, 219). Thus, when the Poet declares in the Epilogue that God predestined "onely the adopted children of promise," and that "he foreknewe that many [i.e., the reprobate] would degenerate, / And wylfully giue cause to be put from that blisse" (ll. 1749-50), he was expressing this more moderate Calvinist position on predestination.

The Poet goes on to say that because of the fall, all men are subject to damnation on account of their sins, so "Where he chooseth, he sheweth his great mercy: / And where he refuseth, he doth none iniury" (ll. 1752-53). In anticipation of those who may ask why Christ did not offer his mercy to all of mankind, the Poet declares that the mysteries of predestination "farre surmounteth mans intellection, / To attaine or conceiue, and much more to discusse," and adds that such matters must be referred to "Gods election, / And to his secret iudgement" (ll. 1756-57). Here, once again, the author complies with Calvin, who often warned against indulging in speculative thought on predestination, for to seek knowledge of it outside of the Scriptures is a confusing and dangerous business, and "no less madnesse than if a man haue a will to goe by vnpassable waye, or to see in darknesse" (*Inst.* III.xxi.2).

Editorial Procedure

The purpose of this edition is to reproduce, as far as it is practically possible to do so, the plays in their original published form. Thus, the irregular spelling of the sixteenth-century texts is retained. The only exceptions are the names of characters in the speech prefixes, which are standardized, and contractions, which are expanded. I have also silently capitalized words at the beginning of lines and corrected obvious printers errors; these and other emendations are cited in the notes. Modern punctuation has been added sparingly and only in instances where the meaning would be otherwise unclear. Stage directions are italicized and centered in the text (including those in *Jacob and Esau* positioned in the margins in the Tudor editions). Stage directions not belonging to the original texts are placed in square brackets. Where the verse is divided into stanzas or indented or italicized, the original is followed.

A new Enterlude, neuer

before this tyme imprinted, entreating of the Life and Repentaunce of Marie Magdalene: not only

godlie, learned and fruitefull, but also well furnished with pleasaunt myrth and pastime, very delectable for those which shall heare or reade the same.

Made by the learned clarke
Lewis Wager.

The names of the Players.

Infidelitie the Vice.	The Lawe.
Marie Magdalene.	Knowledge of Sinne.
Pride of Life.	Christ Iesus.
Cupiditie.	Fayth.
Carnall Concupiscence.	Repentaunce.
Simon the Pharisie.	Iustification.
Malicious Iudgement.	Loue.

Foure may easely play this Enterlude.

Imprinted at London, by Iohn Charlewood,
dwelling in Barbican, at the signe of the halfe Eagle
and the Key. Anno. 1567.

The Prologue.

Nulla tam modesta felicitas est
Quæ malignantis dentes vitare possit.

No state of man, be it neuer so modest,
Neuer so vnrebukeable and blamelesse,
No person, be he neuer so good and honest,
Can escape at any season now harmelesse,
But the wicked teeth of suche as be shamelesse,
Are ready most maliciously him for to byte,
Like as Valerius in his fourth booke doth write.

We and other persons haue exercised
This comely and good facultie a long season,
Which of some haue been spitefully despised,
Wherefore I thinke they can alleage no reason,
Where affect ruleth, there good iudgement is geason.
They neuer learned the verse of Horace doubtles,
Nec tua laudabis studia, aut aliena reprehendes,

Thou shalt neither praise thyne owne industrie,
Nor yet the labour of other men reprehend,
The one procedeth of a proude arrogancie,
And the other from enuie, which doth discommend,
All thyngs that vertuous persons doe intend.
For euill will neuer said well, they do say,
And worse tungs were neuer heard before this day.

I maruell why they should detract out facultie:
We haue ridden and gone many sundry waies,
Yea, we haue vsed this feate at the vniuersitie,
Yet neither wise nor learned would it dispraise:
But it hath ben perceiued euer before our dayes,
[A2v] That foles loue nothing worse than foles to be called:
A horse will kick if you touche where he is galled.

Doth not our facultie learnedly extoll vertue?
Doth it not teache, God to be praised aboue al thing?
What facultie doth vice more earnestly subdue?
Doth it not teache true obedience to the kyng?
What godly sentences to the mynde doth it bryng?
I saie, there was neuer thyng inuented
More worth, for mans solace to be frequented.

Hipocrites that wold not haue their fautes reueled
Imagine slaunder our facultie to let,
Faine wold they haue their wickednes still concealed
Therfore maliciously against vs they be set,
O (say they) muche money they doe get.
Truely I say, whether you geue halfpence or pence,
Your gayne shalbe double, before you depart hence.

Is wisedom no more worth than a peny trow you?
Scripture calleth the price therof incomparable.
Here may you learne godly Sapience now,
Which to body and soule shal be profitable.
To no person truly we couet to be chargeable,
For we shall thinke to haue sufficient recompence,
If ye take in good worth our simple diligence.

In this matter whiche we are about to recite,
The ignorant may learne what is true beleue,
Wherof the Apostles of Christ do largely write,
Whose instuctions here to you we wil geue,
Here an example of penance the heart to grieue,
May be lerned, a loue which from Faith doth spring,
Authoritie of Scripture for the same we will bring.

Of the Gospell we shall rehearse a fruictfull story,
Written in the .vii. of Luke with wordes playne
[A3r] The storie of a woman that was right sory
For that she had spent her life in sinne vile and vain,
By Christes preachyng she was conuerted agayn,
To be truly penitent by hir fruictes she declared,
And to shew hir self a sinner she neuer spared.

Hir name was called Mary of Magdalene,
So named of the title of hir possession,
Out of hir Christ reiected .vii. spirites vncleane,
As Mark and Luke make open profession.
Doctours of high learnyng, witte, and discretion,
Of hir diuers and many sentences doe write,
Whiche in this matter we intend now to recite.

Of the place aforesaid, with the circumstance,
Onely in this matter (God willing) we will treate.
Where we will shewe that great was hir repentance,
And that hir loue towards Christ was also as great.

Hir sinne did not hir conscience so greuously freate,
But that Faith erected hir heart again to beleue,
That God for Christs sake wold all hir sins forgeue.

We desire no man in this poynt to be offénded,
In that vertues with vice we shall here introduce,
For in men and women they haue depended:
And therfore figuratiuely to speak, it is the vse.
I trust that all wise men will accept our excuse.
Of the Preface for this season here I make an ende,
In godly myrth to spend the tyme we doe intende.

The ende of the Preface.

[A3v] *Here entreth Infidelitie the vice.*

Infidelitie.

With heigh down down and downe a down a,
Saluator mundi Domine, Kyrieleyson,
Ite Missa est, with pipe vp *Alleluya.*
Sed libera nos à malo, and so let vs be at one.

Then euery man brought in his owne dishe,
Lord God we had wonderfull good fare,
I warrant you there was plentie of fleshe and fishe,
Go to, I beshrew your heart and if you spare.

A gods name I was set vp at the hye deace,
Come vp syr sayd euery body vnto me:
Like an honest man I had the fyrst meace,
Glad was he that might my proper person see.

When we had dined, euery man to horsebacke,
And so vp vnto the mount of Caluarie,
I trow you neuer heard of suche a knacke,
Muche woe had some of vs to scape the pillorie.

But when we came to hye Ierusalem,
Who then but I maister Infidelitie?
Mary I was not so called among them,
No, I haue a name more nigher the veritie.

In Iurie, Moysaicall Iustice is my name,
I would haue them iustified by the lawe,

It is playne infidelitie to beleue the same,
What then? from the faithe I doe them withdraw.

There is one come into the countrey of late,
Called Christ the sonne of God, the Iewes Messias
Of the kyngdome of God he begynneth to prate,
But he shall neuer bryng his purpose to passe,

No, I Infidelitie stick so much in the Iewes harts,
That his doctrine and wonders they wyl not beleue,
[A4r] I warant that the chiefe rulers in these partes,
Will deuise somewhat his body to mischeue.

Infidelitie, no beware of me Infidelitie,
Like as Faith is the roote of all goodnesse,
So am I the head of all iniquitie,
The well and spryng of all wickednesse.

Mary syr, yet I conuey my matters cleane,
Like as I haue a visour of vertue,
So my impes, whiche vnto my person do leane,
The visour of honestie doth endue.

As these, Pride I vse to call cleanlynesse,
Enuie I colour with the face of prudence,
Wrathe putteth on the coate of manlynesse,
Couetise is profite in euery mans sentence.

Slouth or idlenesse I paint out with quiete,
Gluttonie or excesse I name honest chere,
Lechery vsed for many mens diete,
I set on with the face of loue both farre and nere.

How saie you to Infidelitie once agayne?
Infidelitie all mens heartes doe occupie:
Infidelitie now aboue true Faith doth remayne,
And shall do to the worldes ende, I thinke verily.

Yea, that same Messias doth many things,
Yet I will so occupy the rulers myndes,
Bothe of byshops, phariseys, elders and kyngs,
That fewe or none of them shalbe his frendes.

Here entreth Mary Magdalene, triflyng with her garmentes.

Mary Magdalene.

I beshrew his heart naughtye folishe knaue,
The most bungarliest tailers in this countrie,
That be in the world I thinke, so God me saue,
Not a garment can they make for my degree.

[A4v] Haue you eyer sene an ouerbody thus sytte?
Nowe a mischief on his dronken knaues eare.
The knaues drynke till they haue lost theyr wytte,
And then they marre vtterly a bodies geare.

I had liefer than .xx. shillings by this light
That I had him here now in my fume and heate.
What, I am ashamed to come in any mans sight,
Thinke you in the waste I am so great?

Nay by gis twentie shillings I dare holde,
That there is not a gentlewoman in this land,
More propre than I in the waste I dare be bolde,
They be my garmentes that so bungarly do stand.

Beshrew his heart once agayne with all my hart.
Is this geare no better than to cast away?
Let hym trust to it, I will make him to smart.
For marryng of my geare he shall surely pay.

Infidelitie.

God forbyd mistresse Mary, and you so tender and yong
For marryng of your geare he is greatly to blame.

Mary.

What haue you to do, holde your bablyng tong,
Haue you any thyng to doe with the same?

Infidelitie.

These vnhappy tailors I trowe be acurst,
Most commonly when they make gentlewomens geare
In the myddes they set the piece that is worst.
Yea, that is the fashion of them euery where.

The worst piece is in the mydst of your garment,
And it is pieced into it so vnhappily,
That by my trouthe it is past amendement,
Meddle with it, and you spyll it vtterly.

Mary.

Speake you in ernest, or I pray you do you mock?
Trow you that my garment can not be amended?

Infidelitie.

Mock? I know that you come of a worshipful stock.
He that mocketh you ought to be reprehended.

[B1r]
Of taylers craft I tell you I haue some skill,
And if I shold medle with the pece that is in the midst,
I should make it worse or at the least as yll:
Therfore to let it alone as it is, I iudge it best,

Naught it is, and so you may weare it out,
Though it be new, it will be soone worne.

Mary.

It were almose to hang suche a foolishe loute,
All they that see me now, will laugh me to scorne,

No gentlewoman is ordred in this wyse,
My maydens on the other side are suche sluts,
That if I should not for myne owne clothed deuise,
Within a while they would not be worth a couple of nuts

Infidelitie.

Of my trouth it wer pitie in myne opinion
But that your geare should be well trimmed,
For you are well fauoured, and a pretie mynion,
Feate, cleane made, wel compact, and aptly lymmed.

In Ierusalem there is not I dare say,
A sweter countenance, nor a more louyng face,
Freshe and flourishyng as the floures in May,
I haue not sene a gentlewoman of a more goodly grace

Your parents I know, were very honorable,
Whiche haue left you worshipfully to lyue here,
And certainly I iudge it very commendable.
That with your owne you can make good chere.

Mary.

I thank you for your good worde, gentle friend,
And forasmuch as you did know my parentes,
I can no lesse doe than loue you with all my mynd,
Redy to do you pleasure at your commandementes.

Infidelitie.

Verba puellarum foliis leuiora caducis,
The promise of maidens, the Poet doth say,
Be as stable as a weake leafe in the wynde,
Like as a small blast bloweth a feather away,

[B1v] So a faire word truely chaungeth a maidens mynd.

Forsothe I thanke you, O louyng worme, good lord,
Yea, I knew your fathers state and condition,
The nobilitie of Iurie can beare me record,
That he was a man of a worshipfull disposition.

Iwis mystresse Marie, I had you in myne armes,
Before you were .iii. yeares of age without doubt,
I preserued you many tymes from sore harmes,
Which in your childhode your enimies went about.

A gentlewoman of noble byrth as I doe thinke
Should haue seruants alwais at her commaundement,
You are able to geue to many both meate and drinke,
Yea honest wages, and also necessary raiment.

Mary.

I perceiue right well that you owe me good will,
Tendryng my worshipfull state and dignitie:
You see that I am yong and can little skill
To prouide for myne owne honor and vtilitie.

Wherfore I pray you in all thyngs counsell to haue,
After what sort I may leade a pleasant life here,
And looke what it pleaseth you of me to craue,
I will geue it you gladly, as it shall appere.

Infidelitie.

Say you so mistresse Mary, wil you put me in trust
In faith I will tell you, you can not trust a wiser.
You shall liue pleasantly, euen at your hearts lust,
If you make me your counseller and deuiser.

Remember that you are yong and full of dalliance
Lusty, couragious, fayre, beautifull and wise.
I will haue you to attempt all kyndes of pastance,
Usyng all pleasure at you owne heartes deuise.

Do you thinke that it is not more than madnesse,
The lusty and pleasant life of a mans youth,
Miserably to passe away in study and sadness,
[B2r] It is extreme foly mistresse Mary for a truth.

Be ye mery, and put away all fantasies,
One thyng is this, you shal neuer be yonger in dede,

Your bodily pleasure I would haue you to exercise,
Sure you are of worldly substance neuer to nede.

Mary.

Certainly my parents brought me vp in chyldhod,
In vertuous qualities, and godly literature,
And also they bestowed vpon me muche good
To haue me nourtred in noble ornature.

But euermore they were vnto me very tender,
They would not suffer the wynde on me to blowe,
My requests they would always to me render,
Wherby I knew the good will that to me they did owe.

At their departing, their goodes they distributed
Among vs their children, whom they did well loue.
But me as their dearlyng, they most reputed,
And gaue me the greatest part, as it did behoue.

Infidelitie.

Puellæ pestis, indulgentia parentum,
Of parentes the tender and carnall sufferance,
Is to yong maidens a very pestilence.
It is a prouocation and furtherance,
Vnto all lust and fleshly concupiscence.

O mistresse Mary, your parentes dyd see,
That you were beautifull and well fauoured:
They did right well as it semeth me,
That so worshipfully they haue you furthered.

As I vnderstand, you haue in your possession
The whole castel of Magdalene, with the purtenance,
Which you may rule at your discretion,
And obtaine therby riches in abundance.

O what worldly pleasure can you want,
What commodities haue you of your owne?
[B2v] About Ierusalem is not suche a plant,
As to me and many other is well knowen,

It were decent I saye, to vse the fruition
Of suche richesse as is left you here,
You neuer heard in any erudition,
But that one with his own should make good chere.

Mary.

By my trouth so would I, if I perfectly knew

Which way I should good chere makyng begyn,
A lusty disposition from me doth ensue:
But without councell, I am not worth a pyn.

Infidelitie.

Councell? In you shall want no councell in dede,
I know where a certayne company is,
Which can geue suche councell in tyme of nede,
That you folowyng them can neuer spede amys.

Mary.

Nowe I pray you helpe me to that company,
And looke what I am able to do for your pleasure,
You shall haue it I promise you verily,
Yea, whether it be landes, golde, or treasure.

Infidelitie.

The truth is so, they whom nowe I speake of,
Are persons of great honor and nobilitie,
Felowes that loue neither to dally nor scoffe,
But at once will tell you the veritie.

Mary.

Men of honour say you? tell me I you desire,
Can you cause them trowe you shortly to be here?
I wyll goe and prouide some other attire,
That accordyng to my byrthe I may appere.

Infidelitie.

Byrth? faith of my body, you are well arayde,
I warrant you with these clothes they wil be content
They had liefer haue you naked, be not afrayde,
Then with your best holy day garment.

Mary.

You are a mery man in dede, you are a wanton,
I will go and returne agayne by and by,
[B3r] As I am, I would with all my heart be known,
So that I might be plesant to euery mans eye.

Infidelitie.

I pray you heartily that I may be so bold
To haue a kisse or two before you doe depart,

Mary.

If a kisse were worth a hundred pound of gold,
You should haue it euen with my very heart.

[They kiss.]
Exit [Mary].

Infidelitie.

I thanke you mistresse Mary by my maydenhood,

Lord what a pleasant kysse was this of you?
Take her with you, I warant you wil neuer be good
She is geuen to it, I make God auow.

And I trow I shall helpe to set her forward.
Shortly my ofspryng and I shall her so dresse,
That neither law nor prophets she shall regard,
No though the sonne of God to her them expresse.

Infidelitte is my name, you know in dede,
Proprely I am called the Serpents sede,
Loke in whose heart my father Sathan doth me sow
There must all iniquitie and vice nedes growe,
The conscience where I dwell is a receptacle,
For all the diuels in hell to haue their habitacle,
You shall see that Maries heart within short space,
For the diuell hym self shall be a dwellyng place,
I will so dresse her, that there shall not be a worse.
To her the diuell at pleasure shall haue his recourse.
I will go and prepare for her such a company,
As shall poison her with all kyndes of villanie.

Here entreth Pride of Life, Cupiditie, and Carnall Concupiscence.

Pride of Life.
Whether art thou goyng nowe Infidelitie?
Infidelitie.
Pride of Life now welcom, the spryng of iniquitie,
O pride of life, thou neuer vsest to go alone
Geue me your handes also I pray you one by one.
[B3v] Welcome pride of life with my whole heart and mynde,
And thou art welcome Cupiditie myne owne friend:
What, mynikin carnall concupiscence,
Thou art welcome heartily by my conscience.
Pride of Life.
To see thee mery Infidelitie I am right glad.
Cupiditie.
When Infidelitie is in health, I can not be sad.
Carnall Concupiscence.
Infidelitie? O Infidelitie, myne owne infidelitie,
I am glad to see thee mery now for a suretie,
A maruell what thou dost in this place alone,
I thought that out of Iurie thou hadst ben gone.

Infidelitie.
Out of Iurie? no carnall lust, to thee I may tell
That with the chief princes now I do dwell:
The bishops, priestes and pharisies do me so retayne,
That the true sense of the lawe they do disdayne.

Pride of Life.
In faith there is some knauery in mynde,
That here by thy selfe alone we doe thee fynde.
Cupiditi in our fathers cause is occupied,
As within a while it shall be verified.

Infidelitie.
Am I? you would say so if ye knew all,
I was goyng forth you to call,
Know you not a wenche called Mary Magdalene?

Pride of Life.
Do I know hir? she is a prety wenche and a cleane.
Since she had discretion hir haue I knowne,
Mary Magdalen (quod he) in dede she is myne own
It is as proude a litle gyrle truely I thinke,
As euer men sawe in this world eate or drinke.

Cupiditie.
And somwhat to do with hir now and then I haue
I allure hir for hir owne profite alway to saue.
I haue dressed hir so well truely I beleue,
That alredy for Gods sake nothyng she will geue.

Carnall Concupiscence.
For my part in hir I haue kindled such a fyre,
That she beginneth to burn in carnall desyre.

Infidelitie.
[B4r] Tushe, as yet you haue but hir mynde moued,
Whom she may forsake if she be reproued:
But I would haue hir cleaue vnto you so fast,
That she shall not forsake you while her life doth last.

Pride of Life.
If then be once rooted within the hart,
Then maist thou make an entrance by thy craft and art
So that we may come into hir at pleasure,
Fillyng hir with wickednesse beyond all measure.
In vs foure without faile be contained
As many vices as euer in this world raigned.
Now if we by thy meanes may in hir remain,
She shall be sure all kyndes of vices to contain.

Carnall Concupiscence.
Within my selfe you know that I contain a sort,

Whiche by name before you here I wil report.
My name is carnall concupiscence or desyre,
Which all the pleasures of the fleshe doth require.
First the fleshe to nourishe with drinke and meate
Without abstinence like a beast alway to eate,
To quaffe and drinke when there is no necessitie,
Ioying in excesse, bealy chere, and ebrietie.
I containe in my selfe all kynd of lecherie,
Fornication, whoredom, and wicked adulterie,
Rape, incest, sacrilege, softnesse, and bestialitie,
Blyndnesse of mynde, with euery suche qualitie,
Inconstancie, headinesse, and inconsideration,
After the heartes poyson and filthy communication,
So then to the hate of God I do them bryng,
Causyng a loue in himself inordinatly to spryng.
These and suche like I containe in my person.
Thus you see that carnall lust goeth neuer alone.

Infidelitie.

Thou hast reckned an abhominable rable,
Where thou dwellest, the deuyll may haue a stable.

Cupiditie.
[B4v]

With thee I may boldly compare I trow,
For as many vices in me as in thee do grow.
You know that my name is called Cupiditie,
Whom Scripture calleth the roote of all iniquitie,
Infidelitie in dede is the seede of all syn,
But cupiditie openeth the gate, and letteth hym in:
I conteyne theft, deceate in sellyng and bying,
Periurie, rapine, dissimulation, and lying.
Hardinesse of heart otherwise called inhumanitie,
Inquietnesse of mynde falshode and vanitie,
In me is all vengeance enuie rankor and yre.
Murder, warre, treason, and gredie desyre.
I conteyne the wicked vices of vsurie,
Dice and card playing with all kynd of iniurie.
What mischief was there euer yet or synne,
But that cupiditie dyd it first of all begynne?

Infidelitie.

There can not be a more fylthy place in hell,
Than that is, where as cupiditie doth dwell.

Cupiditie.

Yea, there is impietie, the contempt of Gods lawe,
His worde is no more regarded than a vile strawe.

Pride of Life.

You contayne vices very wicked in dede,
But how wicked is he from whom al syn doth procede?
The beginning of syn, which doth man from god deuide
Scripture calleth it nothyng els but pride.
For I my selfe not onely conteyne you three,
But all vices in you, and that in euery degree,
Pride despiseth God, and committeth idolatrie
To God and man Pride is a very aduersarie,
I am full of boastyng, arrogancie, and vainglorie,
Enuious, and of all other mens wealth right sory:
Pride causeth obstinacie, and disobedience,
Yea, it engendreth idlenesse and negligence,
[C1r] The truth of Gods prophets through tirants of pride
Hath euer vnto this day ben cast asyde:
The men of God pride hath spitefully reputed,
And with tirants alway the same persecuted.
Pride would neuer suffer any vertue to raigne,
But oppressed it with great malice and disdaine.
In a short summe and fewe wordes you shall know all,
Pride caused Lucifer from heauen to hell to fall.
Yea pride lost mankynd, and did him so infect,
That God from his fauour dyd him away reiect,
Where as pride is, a token it is euident,
That all other vices be euen there resident.

Infidelitie.

Where as you and all your ofspryng doth dwell,
There is a place for all the diuels in hell:
And playne it is, where as is suche fylthy sinne,
There euen in this world their hell doth begynne.
By such time as with vs Mary be furnished,
With the deuill him self she shall be replenished.

Pride of Life.

In our tragedie we may not vse our owne names,
For that would turne to al our rebukes and shames.

Infidelitie.

Pride with all thy abhominable store,
At this tyme must be called Nobilitie and honor.

Cupiditie.

Very well, for these women that be vicious,
Are alwais high mynded and ambicious.

Carnall Concupiscence.

Neuer woman that could play a harlots part,
Was either humble, or yet meke in hart.

Infidelitie.

Yea and the same loued alway cupiditie,
Therfore thy name shall be called Utilitie.

Pride of Life.

For hym a better name you could not expresse,
For yll disposed women are alway mercylesse.

Carnall Concupiscence.

They are alwais scraping, clawing, and gathering,
To maintaine their liues in wickednesse and synne.

Infidelitie.

[C1v] Carnall concupiscence shalbe called pleasure,
And that pretie Marie loueth beyond all measure.

Pride of Life.

Infidelitie may not be called infidelitie.

Infidelitie.

No, we will worke with a litle more austeritie,
Infidelitie for diuers respectes hath names diuers,
Of the which some of them to you I purpose to reherse
With bishops, priests, scribes, seniors and pharisies,
And with as many as be of the Iewes degrees,
I am called Legall Iustice commonly:
For why by the lawe them selues they do iustifie.
It is playne Infidelitie so to beleue:
Therfore there, suche a name to my selfe I do geue.
I haue a garment correspondent to that name,
By the which I walke among them without blame.
With publicans and sinners of a carnall pretence,
I am somtime called counsel, and somtime Prudence.
I cause them the wisedome of God to despise,
And for the fleshe and the world wittily to deuise,
Prudence before Marie my name I will call,
Which to my suggestions will cause hir to fall:
A vesture I haue here to this garment correspondent,
Lo here it is, a gowne I trowe conuenient.

Pride of Life.

For our honor I pray thee heartily doe it weare.

Infidelitie.

Mary did talke with me before in this geare,
But bicause she shall the sooner to me apply,
I will dress me in these garments euen by and by.

put on a gowne & a cap.

How thynke you by me now in this aray?

Mary loueth them I tell you, that vse to go gay.

Cupiditie.

Then hadst thou nede to mend thy folysh countenance
For thou lookest like one that hath lost his remembrance

Carnall Concupiscence.

With the one eye ouermuch thou vsest to winke,
That thou meanest som fraude therby they wyl think
[C2^{r}] He that loketh with one eie, and winketh with an other,
I would not trust (say they) if he were my brother.

Infidelitie.

Lyke obstinate Friers I temper my looke,
Which had one eie on a wench, and an other on a boke.

[Enter Mary.]

Passion of God, behold, yonder commeth Marie.
See that in your tales none from other do varie.

Pride of Life.

It is a pretie wenche that it is in dede,
Muche to intreate her, I thynke we shall not nede.

Cupiditie.

No, for I thinke she is yll inough of hir selfe,
She seemeth to be a proude little elfe.

Carnall Concupiscence.

I pray you behold how she trimmeth her geare?
She would haue all well about her euery where.

Mary.

Maidens (quod she ?) there is no gentlewoman I wene
So accumbred as I am, for such were neuer sene:
Fie on them, in good faith they are to badde,
They would make some gentlewoman stark madde.
Like as I put of my geare, so I do it fynde,
And I can not tel how oft I haue told them my mynd.
By the faith of my body if they do not amend,
To lay them on the bones surely I do intend.

Infidelitie.

Maxima quæ quæ domus, seruis est plena superbis,
Euery great house, as the Poet doth say,
Is full of naughtie seruantes both night and day.

Mary.

You say truth sir in dede. What old acquaintance?
Now forsoth you were out of my remembrance:
You haue changed your aray since I was here,
I am glad to see you mery and of a good chere.

Infidelitie.

And I of yours mistresse Mary with hart and mynd
It is a ioy to see a gentlewoman so louyng and kynd
Shall I be so bold to kisse you at our metyng?

Mary.

What else? it is an honest maner of greetyng.

[Mary and Infidelitie kiss.]

Infidelitie.

Pleaseth it you to byd these gentlemen welcome?

Mary.

[C2v] Yea forsoth, are they heartily all and some.
I will kysse you all for this gentlemans sake,
He is a friend of myne as I do hym take.

[Mary kisses Pride, Cupidity, and Concupiscence.]

Pride of Life.

He is in dede, you may be sure mistresse Mary,
There is no man lyuyng can say the contrary.

Cupiditie.

He hath ben diligent to seke vs togither,
And for your sake he hath caused vs to come hither.

Carnall Concupiscence.

I dare say thus much, that he is your friende,
For he loueth you with his whole heart and mynde.
He hath ben diligent about your cause,
As it had bene his owne, and would neuer pause,
Till he had performed his desired request.
Which I am able to say is very honest.

Mary.

A gentle friend at so little acquaintance,
Will you looke so much vnto my furtherance?
It seemeth then if by me you had ben benefited,
You would haue my kyndnesse gently requited.

Infidelitie.

Quo magis tegitur, magis æstuat ignis
The more closely that you kepe fyre, no doubt
The more feruent it is when it breaks out.

Mary.

Wel friend, I know what you meane by that verse
What I wil do for you at this tyme I wil not reherse
But in one thyng truly I am muche to blame,
That all this tym I haue not inquired your name.

Infidelitie.

Swete mistresse Mary, I am called Prudence,
Or els Counsell, full of wisedome and science,
Here vnto you, honorable Honor I haue brought,
A person alway to be in your mynde and thought,
And this person is named Vtilitie,
Very profitable for your commoditie,
Pleasure is the name of this Mynion,
Conuenient for you forsothe in myne opinion.

Mary.

[C3r] Prudence, Honor, Vtilitie, and Pleasure,
Oh who would desyre in this world more treasure,
Gramercy heart of gold for your great payne,
Truly of necessitie, I must kisse you once agayne.

[Mary and Infidelitie kiss.]

Infidelitie.

Will you so? that is the thyng that haue I wold,
Euery kisse to me is worth a crowne of golde.

Pride of Life.

Leaue kissyng, and treate we of matters more ernest.
Let us reason of things concerning your request.
Honor is my name, a qualitie for you requisite,
Or rather of honor I am an appetite:
On the which must be all your meditation,
With the hearts courage and myndes eleuation:
I tell you this desyre must be euer next your hart.

[Pride embraces Mary.]

Infidelitie.

Nay hoa there, backare, you must stand apart,

[Infidelitie separates them.]

You loue me best I trow, mystresse Mary.

Mary.

For a hundred pound I would not say the contrary
And in token Prudence that I loue you best,
Here I ioyn you next vnto my heart and breast.

[Mary embraces Infidelitie.]

Cupiditie.

If ye embrace one, you must all embrace,
For our vse is to dwell all in one place.

[Cupiditie embraces Mary.]

Carnall Concupiscence.

Tushe from our purpose alway we do digresse,
Let euery one of us his qualities expresse.

Infidelitie.

Agreed, mistresse Mary heare you my counsell.
First, all thought from your heart you must expell.
Trouble not your selfe with any fantasies.
Neuer attend you to the lawe nor prophecies.
They were inuented to make fooles afrayd,
Heare them not, for they will make you dismayd.
God? tushe, when was God to any man sene,
I had not ben now aliue, if any God had bene.

Pride of Life.

Homo homini Deus.
Man, is God to man this matter is playne,
[C3^{v}] And beleue you that none other God doth raigne.

Cupiditie.

Man is the begynnyng of his owne operation:
Ergo then of none other gods creation,
Man is his owne God therfore with vtilitie,
Let hym labour here to lyue in felicitie.

Carnall Concupiscence.

Of many ladies I am certaine you haue hard,
Which the people as goddesses dyd regard:
And why? this was the cause truly in my iudgement,
They had all pleasure here at theyr commaundment,
So that they liued in ioy wealth and prosperitie,
Vsyng all pleasures for their owne commoditie.

Infidelitie.

To be a goddesse your selfe truely you must beleue,
And that you may be so, your mind therto you must geue
All other gods beside your selfe you must despise,
And set at nought their Scripture in any wise.

Pride of Life.

How say you Mistresse Mary do we not gree all in one?

Infidelitie.

Surely Mistresse Mary we will make you a Goddesse anone.

Mary.

You please me excedingly well verily,
Persons you are of great witte and policie.

Pride of Life.

You must be proude, loftie, and of hye mynde,

Despise the poore, as wretches of an other kynde:
Your countenance is not ladylike inough yet.
I see well that we had nede to teache you more wit.
Let your eies roll in your head, declaryng your pride,
After this sort you must cast your eies aside.

Mary.

How thinke you by this maner of countenance?

[Mary poses, rolls her eyes.]

Pride of Life.

Conuenient for such as be not of your acquaintance.

Cupiditie.

I doubt not but she will do right well hir part,
By that tyme that all we be fast within hir hart.

Carnall Concupiscence.

Marke the garmentes of other in any wise,
And be you sure of one of the newest guise.
Your haire me thynke is as yelow as any gold,
[C4r] Vpon your face layd about haue it I wold,
Sometime on your forehead, the breadth of an hand,
Somtime let your attire vpon your crowne stand,
That all your haire for the most part may be in sight,
To many a man a fayre haire is a great delight.

Infidelitie.

In sommer time now and then to kepe away flies,
Let some of that faire haire hang in your eies:
With a hotte nedle you shall learne it to crispe,
That it may curle together in maner like a wispe.

Mary.

By my trouth you are a merrie gentleman.
I will follow your counsell as much as I can.

Pride of Life.

By your eares somtimes with pretie tusks and toyes
You shall folde your haire, like Tomboyes.
It becommeth a yong gentlewoman be ye sure,
And yong men vnto your loue it will allure.

Cupiditie.

If the colour of your haire beginneth for to fade,
A craft you must haue, that yellow it may be made,
With some Goldsmyth you may your selfe acquaint,
Of whom you may haue water your haire for to paint.

Carnall Concupiscence.

Besydes Goldsmythes water, there is other geare,
Very good also to colour agayne the heare,

Yea, if you were not beautifull of your vysage,
A painter could make you to apere with a lusty courage
And though you were as aged as any creature,
A Painter on your face would set such an ornature,
That you should seeme yong and very faire,
And like one whose beautie doth neuer dispaire.

Infidelitie.

Mistresse Mary, had you neuer the smal pox in your youth?

Pride of Life.

You are a mad fellow Prudence, of a truth.

Mary.

I pray you Master Prudence, wherfore ask you that?

Pride of Life.

It is like that in you he hath spied somewhat.

[Mary blushes.]

Carnall Concupiscence.

Alas good gentlewoman, she blushes like coles.

Infidelitie.

[C4v] In dede about her nose there be little prety holes,
Therfore I thynk that she hath had the pockes.
I meane good faith without any gaudes or mockes.

Mary.

If there be any fautes in my face verily,
For money I trust shortly to haue remedy.

Pride of Life.

Mistresse Mary there is not a fayrer in this town.

Infidelitie.

Yea by saint Anne she is louely in color, but brown.

Carnall Concupiscence.

If she be not content with that natiue colour,
A painter will set on one of more honour.

Infidelitie.

I haue known painters that haue made old crones
To appeare as pleasant as little prety yong Iones.

Pride of Life.

Let vs returne agayne to our ornamentes,
I would haue you pleasant alway in your garments
Vpon your forhead you must weare a bon grace,
Which like a penthouse may com farre ouer your face,
And an other from your nose vnto your throte,
Of veluet at the least, without spot or moate,
Your garments must be so worne alway,
That your white pappes may be seene if you may.

Cupiditie.

If yong gentlemen may see your white skin,
It will allure them to loue, and soone bryng them in.

Carnall Concupiscence.

Both damsels and wiues vse many such feates,
I know them that will lay out their faire teates,
Purposely men to allure vnto their loue,
For it is a thyng that doth the heart greatly moue.
At such sights of women I haue known men in dede
That with talking and beholding their noses wil blede.
Through great corage moued by such goodly sights,
Labouring the matter further with al their myghts.

Mary.

Your wordes do not onely prouoke my desire,
But in pleasure they set my heart on fyre.

Infidelitie.

Sometime for your pleasure you may weare a past,
[D1r] But aboue all thyngs gyrd your self in the waste,
Vpon your ouerbody you may nothyng els weare,
But an vnlined garment without any other geare.
Let your body be pent, and togither strained,
As hard as may be, though therby you be pained.

Pride of Life.

Vse will make the thyng easy there is no doubt.

Cupiditie.

Yea pardie, gentlewomen vse it now all about.

Infidelitie.

Your nether garments must go by gymmes and ioynts
Aboue your buttocks thei must be tied on with points.
Some women a doublet of fyne lynnen vse to weare,
Vnto the which they tye theyr other nether gear,
With wiers and houpes your garments must be made,
Pleasure your mynion shall shew you in what trade.

Carnall Concupiscence.

In the wast I wil haue ye as small as a wand.
Yea so smal, that a man may span you with his hand.

Infideliti.

It skilleth not though in the buttocks you be great.

Carnall Concupiscence.

No for there she is like many tymes to be beate.

Mary.

Well wantons well, are ye not ashamed?

Pride of Life.

In dede mistresse, they are worthy to be blamed.

You must reioyce in your richesse and good,
And set muche by your kynrede and noble blood:
Boast of them, and when of them you do talke,
Of their commendations let your tong euermore walk.
Daily thus, my lord my father, or mi lady my mother
My lorde my vncle, and my maister my brother.

Mary.

I promise you I come of a stocke right honorable,
Therfore my talk of them can not be to commendable.

Infidelitie.

It is a stock (they say) right honorable and good,
That hath neither thefe nor whore in their blood.
No more words: how say you Mistresse here by pleasure?

Mary.

Forsoth swete heart, I loue him beyond al measure.

Infidelitie.

Body of god, for this al this while haue I wrought?
[D1v] By your smirking loke ofttimes on him so I thought
What do you loue hym better than you loue me?

Mary.

Which of you I should loue best truly I can not se.

Infidelitie.

This is a true prouerbe, and no fained fable,
Few womens words, be honest, constant, and stable.

Carnall Concupiscence.

Truly Mistresse Mary if ye loue me, ther is nothing lost,
Loue they say, ieopardeth all, and spareth for no cost.
Voluptas autem est sola quæ nos vocet ad se,
Et aliciat suapte natura,
Pleasure sayth one man, of his owne nature,
Allecteth to hym euery humayn creature:
Now what person soeuer doth pleasure hate,
As a beast is to be abiected both early and late.
Let me haue a worde or two in your eare.

[Infidelitie whispers in Mary's ear.]

How say you by that, like you not that pretie geare?

Mary.

Ha, ha, ha, you are a fond body, pleasure, verily.

Infidelitie.

Doth he not moue you to matrimonie?
Take hede that he bryng you not to suche dotage,

For many incommodities truely be in mariage.

Cupiditie.

Semper habent lites, alterque iurgia lectus,
In quo nupta iacet minimum dormitur in illo,
The bedde wherin lieth any maried wife,
Is neuer without chidyng, braulyng, and strife,
That woman shall neuer sleape in quiete,
Which is maried contrary to hir diete.

Pride of Life.

Of all bondage truely this is the ground,
A gentlewoman to one husband to be bound.

Carnall Concupiscence.

Tushe mistresse Mary, be ye not in subiection,
Better it is to be at your owne election.
What thyng in this world excelleth libertie?
Neither gold nor treasure for a suretie.
Take you now one, and then an other hardely,
[D2r] Such as for the tyme will to you louyngly apply.

Mary.

That will be a meane truly to lese my good name.
And so among the people I shal suffer blame.

Infidelitie.

Ye shal not kepe my counsel, if ye can not kepe your owne
Can you not make good chere, but it must be known?

Carnall Concupiscence.

As touching that, I will be to you suche a meane,
As shal teache you alwais to conuey the matter clene

Pride of Life.

Take you none but gentlemen with veluet coates,
It is to be thought, that they ar not without groates

Cupiditie.

In any wise see that your louers be yong and gay,
And suche fellowes as be well able to pay.

Mary.

Nay truely if I should attempt any such geare,
I would take where I loued alway here and there.

Carnall Concupiscence.

Spoken like a worthy swete gyrle by the masse,
I warant all this geare will well come to passe.

Infidelitie.

You must euer haue a tongue well fyled to flatter
Let your garmentes be sprinkled with rose water.
Vse your ciuet, pommander, muske, which be to sell,
That the odor of you a myle of, a man may smell,

With swete oyntments such as you can appoynt,
Vse you euermore your propre body to anoynt.

Carnall Concupiscence.

With fine meats and pure wines do your body norish
That will cause you in all pleasure to florishe:
And when one for your mynde you can espye,
Vse a smylyng countenance and a wanton eye.

Pride of Life.

Vpon all suche as ye mynd not, looke you aloft,
To them that be not of your diet be you not soft.

Mary.

Ha, ha, ha, laugh? now I pray God I dye if euer I did se,
Such pleasant companions as you all be.
You speake of many thynges here of pleasure,
Which to vse truely requireth muche treasure.

Carnall Concupiscence.

If you can wisely occupie this pretie geare,
[D2v] I will warant you to get an hundred pound a yeare.

Infidelitie.

Hold vp the market, and let them pay for the ware,
Be euer catchyng and takyng, doe you not spare.

Mary.

I may vse daliance and pastyme a while,
But the courage of youth will soone be in exile.
I remember yet since I was a little foole,
That I learned verses when I went to schoole,
Which be these:
Forma bona fragilis est, quantum accedit ad annos,
Fit minor, & spacio carpitur illa suo,
Nec semper viola, nec semper lilia florent,
Et riget amissa spina relicta rosa.
The pleasure of youth is a thyng right frayle,
And is yearely lesse, so that at length it doth faile,
The swete violets and lylies flourishe not alway:
The rose soone drieth, and lasteth not a day.
I see in other women by very experience,
That the tyme of youth hath no long permanence.

Infidelitie.

In good faith when ye ar come to be an old maude,
Then it will be best for you to play the baude.
In our countrey there be suche olde mother bees,
Which are glad to cloke baudry for their fees.
This is the order, such as wer harlots in their youth
May vse to be baudes euermore for a truth.

Pride of Life.

When the courage of them is altogither past,
In age they vse to get their liuyng with such a cast.

Cupiditie.

Tushe, your frends haue left you honest possessions,
Which you may imploy after suche discretions,
That a worshipfull state you may maintayne,
Besides that, with the other feate you may gayne.
Oppresse you tenantes, take fines, and raise rentes,
Hold vp your houses and lands with their contents.
[D3r] Bye by great measure, and sell by small measure,
This is a way to amplifie your treasure:
Sell your ware for double more than it is worth,
Though it be starke nought, yet put it forth.
A thousand castes to enriche you I can tell,
If you be content to vse alway my counsell.

Mary.

Yes by the faith of my body, els I were not wise,
For my profite is your counsell and deuise.

Infidelitie.

How say you mistresse Mary, tell vs your mynde,
To embrace vs and loue vs can you in your heart fynd?

Mary.

Truly hart rote I loue you all .iiii. with al my hart,
Trusting that none of vs from other shall depart.
In token wherof, I embrace you in myne armes,
Trusting that you will defend me from all harmes.

[Mary embraces the Vices.]

Pride of Life.

Will we? yea we will see so for your prosperitie,
That you shall lyue in ioy and felicitie.

Cupiditie.

I will see that you shall haue good in abundance,
To maintaine you in all pleasure and daliance.

Carnall Concupiscence.

And new kyndes of pastyme I will inuent,
With the which I trust ye shal be content.

Infidelitie.

Mistresse Mary can you not play on the virginals?

Mary.

Yes swete heart that I can, and also on the regals,
There is no instrument but that handle I can,

I thynke as well as any gentlewoman.

Infidelitie.

If that you can play vpon the recorder,
I haue as fayre a one as any is in this border,
Truely you haue not sene a more goodlie pipe,
It is so bigge that your hand can it not gripe.

Pride of Life.

Will you be so good as to play vs a daunce?
And we wil do you as great pleasure it may chaunce.

Mary.

Alas we haue no suche instrument here.

Carnall Concupiscence.

I knowe where you may haue all suche geare.
[D3v] No instrumentes nor pastime that you can require,
But I can bryng you vnto it at your desire.

Cupiditie.

Will you take the payne to go before thither?
And mistresse Mary and we will come togither.

Infidelitie.

How say you mistresse Mary, are you content?

Mary.

Looke what you will do, I will therto assent.

Pride of Life.

I thinke it best that we .iii. depart hence,
And let mistresse Mary com thither with Prudence.

Infidelitie.

Be it so, then you and I will come alone,
I trust that by the way we will make one,
Nay Mistresse Mary we must haue a song of .iiii. partes
At your departyng to reioyce our mery hartes.

Cupiditie.

The treble you shall maister Pleasure syng
So freshly that for ioy your heart shall spryng.
Vtilitie can syng the base full cleane,
And Noble Honor shall syng the meane.

Infidelitie.

Mistresse Mary will you helpe to syng a part?

Mary.

Yea swete heart with you with all my hart.

Infidelitie.

In faith we will haue a song of your name.
Come syrs, helpe I pray you, to syng the same.

[They sing.]

The song

Hey dery, dery, with a lusty dery,
Hoigh mistresse Mary, I pray you be mery.
Your pretie person we may compare to *Lais,*
A morsell for princes and noble kynges,
In beautie you excell the fayre lady *Thais,*
You excede the beautifull Helene in all thyngs,
To beholde your face who can be wearie?
Hoigh mystresse Mary, I pray you be merie.
The haire of your head shyneth as the pure gold,
Your eyes as gray as glasse and right amiable,
Your smylyng countenance, so louely to behold,
To vs all is moste pleasant and delectable,
[D4^r] Of your commendations who can be wearie?
Huffa mystresse Mary, I pray you be mery.
Your lyps as ruddy as the redde Rose,
Your teeth as white as euer was the whales bone,
So cleane, so swete, so fayre, so good, so freshe, so gay,
In all Iurie truely at this day there is none.
With a lusty voyce syng we Hey dery dery.
Huffa mistresse Mary, I pray you be mery.

Mary.
Suche pleasant companions I haue not sene before,
Now I pray you let vs dwell togither euermore.

Pride of Life.
To your heart we are so fast conglutinate,
That from thence we shall neuer be separate.

Cupiditie.
Yet from your syght at this tyme we will depart,
Assuryng you to remayn styll in our hart.

Carnall Concupiscence.
We thre will go before some thyng to prepare,
That shalbe to your commoditie and welfare.

Mary.
Fare you well my heartes ioy, pleasure, and blisse.

All thre.
It is good maner at our departing to kisse.

[Mary kisses Pride, Cupidity, and CarnallConcupiscence.]
Exeunt [Pride, Cupidity, and Carnall Concupiscence].

Infidelitie.
I must kisse to, if I tary styll.

Mary.

You shall haue kisses inough, euen when you will.

[Mary embraces and kisses Infidelitie.]

Infidelitie.

Gramercy in dede myne owne good louyng Iugge
It doth me good in myne armes you to hugge,
How say you now by these mynions?

Mary.

I say as you say in dede they are mynions,
And suche persons as long tyme I haue desired,
I thanke you, that for me you haue them inquired.

Infidelitie.

You must thinke on the counsell that they did geue,
They will performe their sayinges, you shall beleue.

Mary.

I am not obliuious I warant you my freinde,
For I haue printed all their wordes in my mynde,
I haue determined by them to direct my life,
So that no man shalbe able to set vs at strife.

Infidelitie.

[D4v] Will you resort with me vnto Ierusalem?
There we shall be sure in a place to fynde them.
A banket they haue prepared for you I dare say,
Suche a one as hath not ben sene before this day.

Mary.

Alas why do they suche great cost on me bestow?

Infidelitie.

Truly bicause you their good hearts should know.
There is nothyng lost that is done for such a friende,
Iwis mistresse Mary, I wold you knew al my mind

Mary.

Gentle Prudence if you haue any thyng to say,
Breake your mynd boldly to me as you go by the way.

Infidelitie.

Will you come? you had nede to go but softly,
Take hede, for the way is foule and slipperie:
If neuer so litle backward you chaunce to slippe,
Vp into your saddle forsoth I am redy to skippe.

Mary.

Go wanton, get you forth with sorow,
We shal be at Ierusalem I think to morow.

Exeunt [Mary and Infidelitie].

Here entreth Simon the Pharisie, and Malicious Iudgement.

Simon the Pharisie.

I thought surely that here we shold haue found him,
It was shewed me that he was here about in dede.

Malicious Iudgement.

The last weke he was at the Citie of Naim,
And from thens I wote not whether he did procede.

Simon.

He did a maruellous act there, as we heard say,
For the which the people do him greatly praise:
Maruels he worketh almost euery day.
At Naim a dead chylde agayne he did rayse.

Malicious Iudgement.

All things he doth by the power of the great deuill,
And that you may see by his conuersation,
He kepeth company with suche as be euyll,
And with them he hath his habitation:

A frende of sinners, and a drynker of wyne,
Neuer conuersant with suche as be honest,
[E1r] Against the law he teacheth a doctrine,
All holy Religion he doth detest,

The reuerend bishops and you the pharisies,
He calleth hipocrites, and doth you reuile,
So he doth the doctours and scribes of all degrees,
Beside that, the Saboth also he doth defile.

He vseth as great blasphemie as euer was,
The sonne of the lyuyng God he doth hymself call,
He saith that he is the very same Messias,
Prophecied before of the Prophets all.

I promise you right worshipfull Simon,
Your temple, lawe, and people shal be made captiue,
If in this sort he be suffred alone,
And you shall lose all your prerogatiue.

Simon.

We the fathers of the clergie diuers seasons,
About hym haue consulted together,
To destroy hym we haue alleaged reasons,
But many thyngs therin we do consider.

His doctrine is maruellous this is true,
And his workes are more maruellous doubtlesse,
If as yet we should chaunce hym to pursue,
Muche inconuenience might chaunce and distresse,

The people do hym for a great Prophete take,
He doth so muche good among them that be sicke,
That they wote not what on hym to make,
For he healeth bothe the madde and the lunatike.

Malicious Iudgement.

Me thinke verily, that it doth you behoue,
Which are men of learnyng and intelligence,
His doctrine and miracles wisely to proue,
And whence he had them to haue experience.

Simon.

By my faith I wil tell you what was my pretence,
To haue bidden him to dyner this day I thought,
[E1v] Where we would haue examined his science,
And by what power suche wonders he wrought.

But if I can not haue hym in my house this day,
I will appoynt an other day for the same cause.
Then will we appoint for hym some other way
If we fynd hym contrary to our lawes.

Malicious Iudgement.

Ne credas tempori, trust not the tyme he doth say,
I feare that you will permitte hym to long:
There is euer peryll in muche delay,
Neuer suffre you to raigne ought that is wrong.

Simon.

Well, seyng that at this tyme he doth not appere,
I will returne hence as fast as I may,
Take you the payne a whyle to tary here
To see if he chance at any tyme to come this way,

Or if you here where he is resident,
Let vs haue worde as fast as euer you can.

Malicious Iudgement.

As concernyng your request I will be diligent,
To doe you pleasure euermore I am your man.

[Exit Simon.]

It shall cost me a fall I promise hym truely,

Except I bryng hym shortly to an ende.
Watche for hym will I, in all places duely,
I will know what the marchant doth intende.

A beggerly wretch, that hath not of his owne,
One house or cabyn wherin he may rest his heade:
His parents for poore laboring folks ar wel known,
And haue not the things which shold stand them in stede

No man knoweth where he lerned and went to schoole,
And yet he taketh vpon hym to teache men doctrine.
But within a while he will proue him selfe a foole,
And come to vtter destruction and ruine.

Is he able, thynke you, to withstande,
So many bishops, priestes, and pharisies,
[E2^{r}] Great learned men, and seniors of the lande,
With other people that be of their affinites?

His foly by his presumption he doth declare,
A while we are content that he doth raigne.
But I trust to make him wearie of his welfare,
If I may see hym in this countrey agayne.

[Enter Infidelitie.]

Infidelitie.
Ha, ha, ha, laugh quod he? laugh I must in dede,
I neuer sawe a bolder harlot in my life,
To prompt hir forward we shall not nede,
No poynt of synne but that in hir is rife.

Malicious Iudgement.
Infidelitie? what a diuell doest thou here?
I had not knowen thee but by thy voyce.

Infidelitie.
Malicious Iudgement I pray thee what chere,
To see thee mery at my heart I doe reioyce.

Malicious Iudgement.
What a diuell meanest thou by this geare?
This garment is not of the wonted fashion.

Infidelitie.
For euery day I haue a garment to weare,
Accordyng to my worke and operation,

Among the Pharisies, I haue a Pharisies gown,
Among publicans and synners an other I vse,
I am best I tell thee now, both in citie and towne,
And chiefly among the people of the Iewes.

This is the cause: their Messias, whom Christ they cal
Is come into the world, sinners to forgeue.
Now my labour is both with great and small,
That none of them do hym nor his wordes beleue.

The bishops and pharisies I make the more hard harted
The synnes of them that are disposed to synne,
I augment, so that they can not be conuerted,
So that hard it will be any grace to wynne.

Malicious Iudgement.

Among them Malicious Iudgement is not my name
The true intellection of the law they doe me call,
[E2v] Carnally I cause them to vnderstand the same,
And accordyng to their owne malice to iudge all.

Infidelitie.

Thou knowest that among them I am Iustice legal
For by the dedes of the law they will be iustified,
So that the doctrine of the Messias euangelicall,
Shalbe despised, and he therfore crucified.

Malicious Iudgement.

The reuerend father Simon the Pharisie,
To haue spoken with him, euen now was here:
Vnder the pretence of frendship and amitie,
He would bid him to diner, and make him good chere,

Not for any good will that to hym he doth owe,
But to proue his fashion, learnyng, and power.

Infidelitie.

Good will quod he? No, no that I do know.
For yf they durst, he should die within this houre.

But let this passe, I will tell thee what I haue done,
Knowest thou not a wench called Mary Magdalen?

Malicious Iudgement.

Yes mary, I dyd see her yesterday at noone,
A pretie wenche she is in deede and a cleane.

Infidelitie.

I haue brought her now into suche a case,
That she is past the feare of God and shame of man,

She worketh priuily in euery place,
Yea and prouoketh other therto now and than,

I would thou dydst see hir disposition,
Thou hast not sene hir like I think in thy dayes.

Malicious Iudgement.

If she haue tasted of thy erudition,
I doubt not but she knoweth all wicked ways,

To se her fashion I would bestowe my forty pence,
But at this tyme I can no longer tary here,
About my busynesse I must depart hence,
Seekyng for the same Christ both farre and nere.

Infidelitie.

Very little I hope for his commoditie.
To doe hym any good doest thou intende?

Malicious Iudgement.

[E3^r] Thou knowest my mynde right well Infidelitie,
What nede we any more tyme to spende?
Farewell, thou wilt come to diner to day,
Maister Simon will haue him if it be possible.

Exit [Malicious Iudgement].

Infidelitie.

Thou knowest that I dwell with such men alway,
For in his heart I am euen now inuisible.
Well remembred, yet I must prouide a garment
Agaynst that I come to my master Simon,
About the which the preceptes of the testament
Must be written in order one by one.

Nowe will I returne to my minion againe
I may not from hir be away absent.
If hir companie I should a litle refraine,
I knowe well that she would not be content.

[Enter Mary].

Mary.

Horeson, I beshrowe your heart, are you here?
I may doe what I will for you.

Infidelitie.

Huffa, mistresse Mary, are you so neare?
I thought otherwise I make God auowe.

I pray you let me haue a worde in your eare,

[Infidelitie whispers in Mary's ear.]

I promise you he is a mynion felowe.
By my faith I thought that you had ben there,
For I sawe when you dyd hym folow.

Mary.

By my faith Prudence you haue a false eye,
A body can neuer so secretely worke,
But that theyr daliance you will espie,
I trowe for the nones you lye in corners and lurke.

But sirra, how say you to hym in the flaxen beard?
That is a knaue that horeson, wote you what he did?
In my life was I neuer worse afrayde,
When I came to bed, I found him there hid.

Out alas, quod I, here is some yll spirite,
A swete sauour of muske and ciuet I smelt,
[E3v] Come and lye with me Mary quod he, this night,
Then I knew who it was, when his beard I felt.

Infidelitie.

I beshrew your hearts, whore and thefe wer agreed
You knew the spirit wel inough before you cam there
I am sure, that so honestly he had you feed,
That the reward dyd put away the feare.
[Enter The Lawe holding stone tablets.]

Mary.

Good lord, who is this that yonder doth come?

What meane the tables that be in his hand?

Infidelitie.

Come asyde a little, and geue hym roume,
And what he is anone we shall vnderstand.

[Mary and Infidelitie withdraw to the side.]

The Lawe.

The Lawe of God at this tyme I do represent,
Written with the fynger of God in tables of stone,
Wherby the people might know their lord omnipotent
And how that he is the Lord God alone.

A peculiar people to him selfe he had elected,

Comming of the stocke of faithfull Abraham,
Whom by the lawe he would haue directed,
After that out of Egypt from Pharao they came.

In me as in a glasse it doth plainly appere,
What God of his people doth require,
What the peoples duetie is, they may see here,
Which they owe vnto God in paine of hell fyre.

In me is declared the same iustice,
Whiche vnto God is acceptable.
Mans synne is here shewed, and proude enterprise,
Wherby he is conuicted to paines perdurable.

It was necessary and it dyd behoue,
Considering mans pride and temeritie,
Whiche was dronke and blynde in his owne loue,
To make a lawe to shewe his imbecillitie.

Except the lawe had rebuked his vanitie,
So much he would haue trusted in his own strength
[E4r] And beleued, that through the power of his humanitie,
He might haue obteined saluation at length.

Wherfore as I sayd to a glasse compared I may be,
Wherin clerely as in the sunne lyght,
The weakenesse and sinne of him self he may se,
Yea and his owne damnation as it is ryght.

For the curse of God foloweth synne alway,
And damnation foloweth malediction:
By this it appereth as cleare as the day,
That my office is to fyll the mynde with affliction,

I am a ministration of death workyng yre,
I shewe Gods request, and mans vnabilitie,
I condemne hym for synne vnto eternall fyre,
I fynde not one iust of mans fragilitie.

Mary.

O Prudence, heare you not what the law doth say,
Excedingly it pricketh my conscience.
I may crie out alas nowe and welaway,
For I am damned by Gods owne sentence.

Infidelitie.

Prick of conscience, quod she? it pricketh you not so sore
As the yong man with the flaxen beard dyd I thinke
What a diuell about him here do you poare.
If euer I see any suche, I pray God I synke.

The more you loke on him, the worse like him you shal.
Come away, come away from him for very shame.
And in dede will you be gasyng on him styll?
If you repent not this, let me suffer blame.

[Mary gazes upward.]

Mary.

O frend Prudence, doe you see yonder glasse?
I will tell what therin I doe see:
I can not speake for sorowe, now out alasse,
All men for synne by Gods sentence damned be.

The spirite of God speaketh by kyng Salomon,
That no man on earth lyueth without synne.
[E4^{v}] Dauid saith there is none good, no not one,
No not a child that this day doth his life begynne.

Nowe synne I see requireth eternall damnation,
If a childe be damned that is but a day olde,
Alas, where then shall be my habituation?
Whiche hath done more synnes than can be tolde.

The Lawe.

Yea woman, God doth not onely prohibite the dede,
But he forbiddeth the lust and concupiscence,
Therfore thy heart hath great occasion to blede,
For many lustes and dedes hath defiled thy conscience.

Infidelitie.

Body of God, are you so madde him to beleue?
These thyngs are written to make folkes afrayde,
Will ye to him or to me credence geue?
Or to your frends, by whom you wer neuer dismaid?
And I put case that the wordes nowe were trewe,
He speaketh of men, but no women at all,
Women haue no soules, this saying is not newe,
Men shall be damned, and not women which do fall.

The Lawe.

By this term man, truely in holy Scripture,
Is vndertake both man, woman, and child in dede,

Yea as many of both kyndes as be of mans nature,
Whiche procede of Adam the first parents sede.

Enter Knowledge of Sinne.

By the Lawe commeth the knowledge of synne,
Whiche knowledge truely here I represent,
Whiche freate and byte the conscience within,
Causyng the same euermore to lament.

I am euermore before the conscience sight,
Shewyng before hym his condemnation,
So that by the dedes of the law, or by his own might
He can not attaine vnto saluation.

Infidelitie.

Lo Mary, haue ye not sponne a fayre threde?
Here is a pocky knaue, and an yll fauoured,
[F1^r] The deuill is not so euill fauoured I thinke in dede,
Corrupt, rotten, stinkyng, and yll sauoured.

Knowledge of Sinne.

It is not possible truly to declare here,
The horrible, lothsome, and stinkyng vilitie,
Which before the eyes of God doth appere,
Committed by this wretched womans iniquitie.

Mary.

Now wo be to the time that euer I was borne,
I see that I am but a damned deuill in hell,
I know that there with diuels I shall be torne,
And punished with more pains than my tong can tell

O blessed Lawe shew me some remedy,
The Prophete calleth thee immaculate and pure,
Thou of thy selfe in many places doest testifie,
That the kepers of thee are alway safe and sure.

The Lawe.

He that obserueth all thyngs written in me,
Shall liue in them, as Moyses doth expresse:
But neuer man yet in this world I dyd see,
Which dyd not the contentes in me transgresse.

It is beyond all mans possibilitie,
To obserue any commaundement in me required,
Therby appeareth his weaknesse and fragilitie,
Hapned through sinne, that against God he conspired.

Knowledge of Sinne.

The power of the law is mans synne to declare,
And to shew his damnation for the same,
But to giue saluation for the soules welfare,
The lawe doth no suche promise any tyme proclame.

Mary.

If there be no more comfort in the lawe than this,
I wishe that the lawe had neuer ben made:
In God I see is small mercy and Iustice,
To entangle men, and snarle them in such a trade.

Infidelitie.

I can you thanke for that Mary in dede:
Well spoken, an vniust God do you esteme.
[F1v] Euen from the heart that sentence dyd procede,
Feare not, their vniust God do you blaspheme:

You see no remedy but vtter damnation.
Folowe my counsell, and put care away,
Take here your pleasure and consolation,
And make you mery in this worlde while you may.

Of one hell I would not haue you twayne to make:
Be sure of a heauen while you dwell here,
Refresh your self, and al pleasure doe you take,
Plucke vp a lusty heart, and be of a good chere.

Mary.

O this knowledge of synne is so in my syght,
That if I should dye truely I can not be mery.

Infidelitie.

We will ridde the knaue hence anon by this light.
Or else of his life I will soon make him wearie.

The Lawe.

O synner, from thy heart put that infidelitie,
Which hath drowned thee already in the pit of hell,
Trust thou in Gods might and possibilitie,
Wherof neither angell nor man is able to tell.

Knowledge of Sinne.

That thing in dede, whiche to man is impossible,
Is a small thyng for God to bryng to passe,
This mercy to all senses is comprehensible,
Which he will declare by his holy Messias.

The Lawe.

That thing which I can not do through my infirmity
God is able by his son to perform in tyme appointed,

All my contentes be shadowes of his maiestie,
Whom now in this tyme God hath anoynted.

Knowledge of Sinne.

That Messias alone onely shall the law fulfill,
And his fulfilling shall be in suche acceptation,
That God for his sake shall pardon mankyndes yll,
Acceptyng his offeryng for a full contentation.

The Lawe.

That Messias is the stone spoken of before,
Which of vayne builders should be refused,
[F2r] Yet he shall be the corner stone of honour,
Which in the building of gods temple shal be vsed.

Knowledge of Sinne.

And all that trust in hym with true beleue,
That he is very God and man, into this world sent,
God will all their synnes for his sake forgeue,
So that they can be contrite and repent.

Mary.

I euer beleued yet vnto this day,
That God was able of nothyng all thyngs to make,
And as well I beleue also that he may,
Forgeue, and mercy vpon synners take,

But seyng that he hath made a determination,
By a law that none shall be saued good or badde,
Then he that would looke for any saluation,
Truly I take hym ten tymes for worse than madde.

Infidelitie.

He that will not the kepers of the law saue,
Which obserue diligently his commaundementes,
Much lesse truly on them mercy he will haue,
Which haue contemned all his words and iudgements.

The Lawe.

Wel Mary, I haue condemned thee vnto hell fyre,
Yet not so condemned thee, but if thou canst beleue
In that Messias, which for thee doth enquire,
There is no doubt but thy sinnes he will forgeue.

Thy sore is knowen, receiue thy salue and medicine,
I haue the sicke to the leache, geue good eare,
Hearken diligently vnto his good discipline,
And he will heale thee, doe nothyng feare.

Exit [The Lawe].

Infidelitie.

Let me fele your poulses mistresse Mary be you sick
By my trouth in as good tempre as any woman can be
Your vaines are full of bloud, lusty and quicke,
In better taking truly I did you neuer see.

Knowledge of Sinne.

The body is whole, but sick is the conscience,
Which neither the law nor man is able to heale,
[F2v] It is the word of God, receyued with penitence,
Like as the boke of wisedome doth plainly reueale.

Infidelitie.

Conscience? how doth thy conscience, litle Mall?
Was thy conscience sicked, alas little foole?
Hooreson fooles, set not a pynne by them all,
Wise inough, in dede, to folowe their foolishe schoole.

You bottell nosed knaue, get you out of place,
Auoyde stinkyng horeson, a poyson take thee,
Hence, or by God I will lay thee on the face,
Take hede that hereafter I doo you not see.

Knowledge of Sinne.

Though I appere not to hir carnall syght,
Yet by the meanes that she knoweth the lawe,
I shall trouble hir always both day and night,
And vpon hir conscience continually gnawe.

[Exit Knowledge of Sinne.]

Infidelitie.

What chere? nowe is here but we twaine alone,
Be mery, mistresse Mary, and away the mare,
A murreyn go with them, now they be gone,
Plucke vp your stomacke, and put away all care.

Mary.

O maister Prudence, my heart is sore vexed,
The knowledge of synne is before me alway:
In my conscience I am so greuously perplexed,
That I wote not what to doe truly nor say.

Here entereth Christ Iesus.

Infidelitie.

Benedicite, art thou come with a vengeance?
What wilt thou do? Mary, doe you loue me?
My wordes print well in your remembrance,
To yonder felowes saying doe you neuer gree.

Christ Iesus.

Into this worlde God hath sent his owne,
Not to iudge the world, or to take vengeance,
But to preache forgeuenesse and pardon,
Through true faith in hym, and perfect repentance.

The sonne of man is come to seke and saue,
[F3r] Suche persons as perishe and go astraye,
God hath promised them lyfe eternally to haue,
If they repent, and turne from theyr euill way,

The kyngdom of heauen is at hand, therfore repent,
Amende your lyues, and the Gospell beleue,
The sonne of God into this world is sent,
To haue mercy on men, and theyr synnes to forgeue.

Mary.

O here is the Messias, of whom we haue harde,
What say you Prudence is not this same he?

Infidelitie.

A Mary, do you my wordes no more regard,
You haue a waueryng witte now well I doe see,

Is not this a lyke person, the sonne of God to be,
And the Messias whiche the worlde should saue?
He is a false harlot you may beleue me,
Whome you shall see one day handled like a knaue.

If the lawe of God published by Moyses,
Be not able to bryng men to saluation,
Muche lesse suche a wretched man doubtlesse,
Can do ought for your soules consolation.

Tushe take one heauen in this present world here,
You remember what before to you I haue sayd:
Pluck vp your heart wenche, and be of good chere,
Neuer regard his words, tushe, be not afrayd.

Mary.

The lawe hath set my synnes before my syght,
That I can not be mery, but am in despaire:
I know that God is a Iudge, equall and right,
And that his lawe is true, pure, cleane and fayre.

By this law am I condemned alredy to hell.
The wordes he hath spoken must be fulfilled:

Of myrth and ioy it is but foly to tell,
For I perceiue that both body and soule be spilled.

Christ Iesus.

Like as the father raiseth the dead agayne,
[F3^{v}] And vnto life doth them mercifully restore:
So the sonne quickeneth the dead it is playne,
And geueth them a life to liue euermore,

Verily verily I say, he that heareth my voyce,
And beleueth on him that hath me sent,
Shall haue euerlastyng life therin to reioyce,
And shall not come into damnable torment.

But the same passe from death vnto lyfe,
Repent, and trust in Gods mercy for my sake.
With the sinnes of the world be at debate and strife,
And vnto grace my heauenly father will you take.

All they whom the law condemneth for synne,
By faith in me, I saue and iustifie,
I am come sinners by repentance to winne,
Like as the Prophet before did prophecie.

Christe Iesus speaketh to Mary.

[*Christe Iesus.*]

Thou woman, with mercy I do thee preuent,
If thou canst in the Sonne of God beleue,
And for thy former lyfe be sory and repent,
All thy sinnes and offences I doe forgeue.

Infidelitie.

Who is the sonne of God sir, of whom do ye talke?
Which hath this power wherof you do boast,
It is best for you out of this countrey to walke,
And neuer more be sene after in this coast.

The sonne of God quod he? This is a pride in dede.
Trowest thou that the father can suffer this?
They come of Abrahams stocke and holy sede,
And thou saiest that they beleue all amisse.

Christ Iesus.

Auoide out of this woman thou Infidelitie,
With the .vii. diuels which haue hir possessed,
I banish you hence by the power of my diuinitie,
For to saluation I haue hir dressed.

Infidelitie runneth away. Mary falleth flat downe.
[F4r] *Cry all thus without the doore, and roare terribly.*

Diuels.

O Iesus the Sonne of God euer liuing,
Why comest thou before the tyme vs to torment?
In no person for thee we can haue any abidyng,
Out vpon thee the sonne of God omnipotent.

Christ Iesus.

Arise woman, and thanke the father of heauen,
Which with his mercy hath thee preuented,
By his power I haue reiected from the spirits seuen,
Which with vnbelief haue thy soule tormented.

[Mary rises.]

Mary.

Blessed be thy name O father celestiall,
Honor and glory be giuen to thee world without end,
O Lord, doest thou regard thus a woman terrestriall?
To thee what tong is able worthy thanks to repend?

O what synfull wretche Lord haue I bene?
Haue mercy on me Lord, for thy names sake,
So greuous a sinner before this day was neuer sene,
Vouchsafe therfore compassion on me to take.

Christ Iesus.

Canst thou beleue in God, the maker of all thing,
And in his onely sonne, whom he hath sent?

Mary.

I beleue in one God, Lord and heauenly kyng,
And in thee his onely sonne with hearty intent.

Good Lord I confesse that thou art omnipotent,
Helpe my slender beliefe and infirmitie:
My faith Lord is waueryng and insufficient,
Strength it I pray the with the power of thy maiesty.

Christ Iesus.

No man can come to me, that is, in me beleue,
Except my father draw hym by his spirite.

Faith and Repentaunce entreth.

Behold Faith and Repentance to thee here I geue,
With all other vertues to thy health requisite.

Faith.

Note well the power of Gods omnipotencie:

That soule which of late was a place of deuils,
He hath made a place for him self by his clemencie,
Purgyng from thence the multitude of euils.

Repentaunce.

[F4v]

The mercy of Christ thought it not sufficient,
To forgeue hir synnes, and deuils to pourge,
But geueth hir grace to be penitent,
That is, hir soule euer after this day to scourge.

The vertue of Repentance I do represent,
Which is a true turnyng of the whole lyfe and state,
Vnto the will of the lord God omnipotent,
Sorowing for the sinnes past with displesure and hate.

That is to say, all the inward thoughts of the hart
And all the imaginations of the mynde,
Which were occupied euill by Sathans arte,
Must hence forth be turned after an other kynd.

Dauid my father on his synnes did alway thinke,
Howe horrible they were in God almighties sight,
Teares were his sustenance, yea both meat and drinke,
His hole meditation was in heauen both day and night

So that Repentance is described in Scripture,
To be a returnyng from syn with all the soule and hart,
And all the life tyme in repentyng to endure,
Declaring the same with the sen[s]es in euery part.

As thus, like as the eyes haue ben vaynly spent
Vpon worldly and carnall delectations,
So henceforth to wepyng and teares must be bent,
And wholly giuen to godly contemplations.

Likewise as the eares haue ben open alway
To here the blasphemyng of Gods holy name,
And fylthy talkyng euermore night and day,
Nowe they must be turned away from the same.

And glad to heare the Gospell of saluation,
How God hath mercy on them that doe call,
And how he is full of pitie and miseration:
Raisyng vp suche agayne as by synne dyd fall.

[G1r]

The tong which blasphemie hath spoken,
Yea and filthily, to the hurt of soule and body:
Wherby the precepts of God haue ben broken,
Must hence forth praise God for his mercy daily.

Thus like as all the members in tymes past,
Haue ben seruantes of vnrighteousnesse and synne,
Now Repentance doth that seruice away cast,
And to mortifie all his lustes doth begynne.

True repentance neuer turneth backe agayn:
For he that laieth his hand on the plough, and loketh away,
Is not apt in the kingdom of heauen to raigne,
Nor to be saued with my sainctes at the last day.

Mary.

O Lorde without thy grace I do here confesse,
That I am able to do nothyng at all,
Where it pleaseth thee my miserie to redresse,
Strength me now that hence forth I do not fall.

Graunt me Lord suche a perfect repentance,
And that I looke no more back, but go forward still,
Put my miserie euermore into my remembrance,
That I may forthinke my life that hath ben so yll.

Faith.

The holy vertue of Faith I do represent,
Ioyned continually with repentance:
For where as the person for synne is penitent,
There I ascertain him of helth and deliuerance.

Wherfore I am a certaine and sure confidence,
That God is mercifull for Christ Iesus sake:
And where as is a turnyng or penitence,
To mercy he will the penitent take:

Faith therfore is the gyft of God most excellent,
For it is a sure knowledge and cognition
Of the good will of God omnipotent,
Grounded in the word of Christes erudition,

[G1v]

This faith is founded on Gods promission,
And most clerely to the mynde of man reuealed,
So that of Gods will he hath an intuition,
Which by the holy ghost to his heart is sealed.

Repentaunce.

This Faith with the word hath such propinquitie,
    That proprely the one is not without the other,
Faith must be tried with the word of veritie,
    And the chyld is by the father and mother.

Christ Iesus.

Yea truly, if this faith do from Gods word decline,
    It is no faith, but a certayn incredulitie,
Which causeth the mynd to wander in strange doctrine
    And so to fall at length into impietie.

Faith.

The word to a glasse compare we may,
    For as it were therin, Faith God doth behold,
Whom as in a cloude we loke vpon alway,
    As hereafter more plainly it shal be told.

Mary.

My heart doth beleue, and my mouth doth publish.
    That my lord Iesus is the sonne of God eternall.
I beleue that my soule shall neuer perysh,
    But raigne with him in his kyngdom supernall.

Repentaunce.

The operation of Faith is not to enquire
    What God is as touchyng his propre nature,
But how good he is to vs to know faith doth desyre,
    Which thyng appereth in his holy Scripture.

Faith.

It is not inough to beleue that God is true only,
    Which can neuer lie, nor deceaue, nor do yll:
But true faith is persuaded firmly and truely,
    That in his word he hath declared his will.

And also what soeuer in that word is spoken,
    Faith beleueth it as the most certaine veritie,
Which by his spirit he doth vouchsafe to open
    To all such as seke hym with all humilitie.

Repentaunce.

[G2r] Christ the sonne of God here hath promised,
    Forgiuenesse of synnes to you syster Mary,
Of his owne mercie this to do he hath deuised,
    And not of your merites, thus you see plainly.

If in this promise you be certain and without doubt.
    Beleuing that the word of his mouth spoken
He is able, and also will do and bryng about,

Then that you haue Faith it is a token.

Mary.

O Iesu, graunt me this true faith and beleue,
Lord I see in my self as yet imperfection:
Vouchsafe to me thy heauenly grace to geue,
That it may be my gouernance and direction.

Christ Iesus.

Mary my grace shall be for thee sufficient,
Goe thy way forth with faith and repentance,
To heare the Gospell of health be thou diligent,
And the wordes therof beare in thy remembrance.

Faith.

Though in person we shall no more appeare,
Yet inuisibly in your heart we will remayne.

Repentaunce.

The grace of God shal be with you both far and nere,
Wherby from all wickednesse I shall you detaine.

Mary.

Honor, praise, and glory to the father eternall,
Thankes to the sonne, very god and very man
Blessed be the holy gost, with them both coequall,
One god, which hath saued me this day from Sathan.

Exeunt [Mary with Faith and Repentaunce].

Christ Iusus.

I thank thee O father, O lord of heuen, earth and of al
That thou hast hidden these things from the sapient,
And hast reuealed them to the litle ones and small,
Yea so it pleased thee O father omnipotent.

All things of my father are committed vnto me,
And who the sonne is, none but the father doth know
No man but the sonne knoweth who the father shold be,
And he to whom the sonne wil reueale and showe.

[G2v] Come vnto me all you that with labor are oppressed,
And are heauy laden, and I will you comfort,
Dispaire not for that you haue transgressed,
But for mercy do you boldly to me resort.

My yoake vpon your neckes do you gladly take,
And learn of me, for I am lowe and meke in hart,
And you shal fynd rest for your soules neuer to slake,
My yoake and burden is light in euery part.

I came not into the world, the righteous to call,
But the synfull persons vnto repentance:
The whoale haue no nede of the physition at all,
But the sicke haue nede of deliuerance.

Verily I say vnto you, that the angels,
Haue more ioy in one synner that doth repent,
Than in many righteous persons else,
Which are no sinners in their iudgement.

Here entreth Simon the Pharisie, and Malicious Iudgement, Simon biddeth Christ to dynner.

Simon.

God spede you syr heartily, and well to fare,
I reioyce much that I chaunce you here to fynde,
In good soth I was sory, and toke muche care
That I had no tyme to declare to you my mynde.

We know that you do much good in the countrey here
Wherfore the liuyng God is glorified:
You heale the sicke persons both farre and nere,
Like as it hath ben credibly testified.

Christ Iesus.

My father euen vnto this tyme worketh truely,
And I work according to his commandement and wil,
The sonne can do nothyng of hym selfe duely,
But that he seeth the father doyng alway still.

Whatsoeuer the Father doth, the sonne doth the same,
For the father doth the sonne entierly loue,
[G3r] And sheweth him al things to the praise of his name,
And shal shew him greter works than these as you shal proue

Malicious Iudgement.

Lo sir, what nede you haue more testimonie
You heare that he doth him self the sonne of God call,
Doth not the law condemne that blasphemie:
Commaunding such to be slaine great and small?

Simon.

For a season it behoueth vs to haue pacience,
I shewed you the reason wherfore of late:
At this season I pray you do your diligence,
And semble rather to loue hym than to hate.

Shall it please you syr, this day to take payne
With me at my house to take some repast,
You shal be welcome doubtlesse I tell you playne,
No great puruiance for you I entend to make.

Christ Iesus.

My meate is to doe his will that hath me sent.
But syr I thanke you of your great curtesy,
To come to you I shall be very well content,
So that you will appoynt the houre stedily.

Simon.

All things be in maner ready I thinke verily,
In the meane season in my gardein we will walke.
Take the paines to go with me, I pray you heartily,
Till dinner be ready, of matters we will talke.

Christ Iesus.

With a good will I will waite vpon you,
Pleaseth it you to go before, you know the way.

Simon.

Sirra, you see how that we are appointed now,
Make all thyngs ready without delay.

Malicious Iudgement.

Sir I will go about as fast as I may,

[Exit Simon and Christ Iesus.]

In good fayth I would that I might haue my will:
I would prepare for hym a galowes this day,
Vpon the whiche I desyre his bloud to spill.

[Enter Infidelitie.]

Infidelitie.

A vengeance take hym thefe, is he gone?
From Mary Magdalene he did me chace:
[G3v] From Simon the Pharisie he will driue me anon,
So that no where I shal be able to shew my face.

Malicious Iudgement.

Nay, we are so surely fixed in the Pharisies mynde,
That his blasphemous words can not driue vs thence
Womens heartes turne oft as doth the wynde,
And agayne of the law they know not the sence.

In malice I haue made them all so blynde,
That they iudge nothyng in Christ aryght:
To the letter of the law so fast I do them bynde,
That of the spirite they haue no maner of light.

Infidelitie.

I will tell thee Malicious Iudgement,
His wordes be of suche strength and great power,
That the diuell hym self and all his rablement,
He is able to expell, and vtterly to deuoure.

Malicious Iudgement.

Tushe hyde thy selfe in a Pharisies gowne,
Suche a one as is bordered with the commaundements
And then thou maist dwel both in citie and in towne,
Beyng well accepted in all mens iudgements.

Infidelitie.

As for a gowne, I haue one conuenient,
And lo here is a cappe agreing to the same.

[Infidelitie puts on the cap and gown.]

Malicious Iudgement.

As thou saiest, that geare is very ancient,
I warant thee now to escape all blame.

Mary of one thyng thou must take good hede,
As nere as thou canst let him not behold thy face,
Doubt thou not, but he shall haue his mede,
If I remayne with the Iewes any space.

Infidelitie.

And as for the reuerend byshop Cayphas,
With all the Aldermen of Ierusalem,
Will helpe to bryng that matter to passe,
For I am like for euer to dwell with them.

Malicious Iudgement.

The same Christ dineth with Simon to day,
Who commanded to prepare the table in all hast.
[G4r] Helpe to make all ready, and the cloth to lay,
For surely here he purposeth to take his repast.

Infidelitie.

By God he shall haue soure sause, it may hap,
Do thy parte, and surely I purpose to watche,
It shal be hard, but we will take hym in a trap.
He shall fynde hym here that will hym matche.

Malicious Iudgement.

Go and fetche trenchers, spoones, salt and bread,
See whether the cookes be ready also I pray thee.
They will come to dynner I dare lay my head,
Before that all things prepared well shall be.

Infidelitie.

A straw, all this geare wyll quickly be doone,
The cookes be ready also I am sure.
Let me see, byr lady it is almost noone,
I maruell that they can so long fastyng endure.

[Enter Simon and Christ Iesus.]

Malicious Iudgement.

Yonder they come, turne thy face out of sight,
Thou must make curtesy downe to the ground.

[Infidelitie bows to Simon and Christ Iesus as they approach.]

Infidelitie.

I would he were hanged by God and by this light.
For neuer before this day was I thus bound.

Simon.

Sir now are you welcome, I pray you come nere,
Fetche in meate syrs, I pray you quickly.

[Infidelitie and Malicious Iudgement exit and return with a table, tablecloth, stools, cushions, a water basin, spoons, and food.]

I promise you I byd you for no good chere,
But such as it is, you ar welcome hartily.

Infidelitie [to Simon].

Pleaseth it you to washe syr, here is water,
Let not yonder beggerly felow wash with you.

Simon [to Infidelitie].

Can you not a while dissemble the matter?
It is no tyme to talke of suche geare now.
[to Christ Iesus.]
Will you sit sir, *[to Infidelitie]* bryng hither a cushion and a stoole.
Set it down I say there, there at the tables ende.

[Infidelitie places the cushion and stoole at the end of the table.]

Infidelitie [aside].

Here is a businesse with a beggerly foole.
It greueth me the tyme about him to spende.
[to Christ Iesus.]
Go to, you are welcome hither to my maister Simon
Thinke your self at home in your owne place.

Christ Iesus.

[G4v] I thanke you sir, I will syt downe euen anone,

But first we will prayse God, and say our grace.

Blessed art thou heauenly father, which of thy mercy
Hast made man to thyne owne image and similitude
Which through Sathans wicked malice and enuie
Was spoiled of thy grace and of ghostly fortitude.

But at this tyme of thy mercy appointed,
Thou hast looked on man, of thy compassion,
And sent thyne owne sonne with thy spirit anoynted,
Which for his synne shall make satisfaction.

Let all creatures praise thee for their creation,
Glory to thy name for their preseruation,
Laude and honour to thee for their restauration,
All thankes to thee for eternall saluation,

Simon [to Christ Iesus].
I pray you sitte downe, I pray you heartily,
You are welcom, I pray you eate such as is here,
Go to, I would not haue you to make any curtesy,
I am sory that for you I haue no better chere.

Infidelitie [aside].
It is simple chere as you say, in dede,
It is to good for him by the Masse,
Haie is good ynough for hym theron to feede,
Or for any such foolishe asse.

Malicious Iudgement [to Infidelitie].
Marke you not what in his grace he dyd say?
Thou hast sent thy sonne anointed with the holy ghost
By these words euidently vnderstand we may,
That to be the son of God of him selfe he doth boast.

Simon [to Infidelitie and Malicious Iudgement].
Wherof doe you .ii. talk what is the matter,
Is there any thing that doth grutch your conscience?

Malicious Iudgement.
This is the truth of our talke yea I wil not flatter,
Your gest said a word wherof I wold haue intelligence.

He thanked God at this tyme nowe appointed,
That on mens synnes he had pitie and compassion,
[H1r] And hath sent his sonne with his spirite anointed,
Which for his sinne should make satisfaction.

Hath God into this world sent his owne sonne?

Or who is the sonne of God I wold be glad to know
Like as now he speaketh, so oft tymes he hath done,
The tyme and place I am able to showe.

Simon.

I pray you my guest his mynde do you satisfie,
It is said, that the sonne of God you do your self call.

Christ Iesus.

I am come into this world the truth to testifie,
Wherof the scripture and the Prophets do witnes all

If I of my self should beare testimonie,
My witnesse of you should not be taken as true,
But there is an other that witnesseth of me verily.
And I know that his testimonie is true.

Of man truely no testimonie do I take:
But I speake these wordes that saued you myght be.
The sonne of God is sent hither for your sake,
Whom in the glorie of his maiestie you shall se.

The workes which to me the father doth geue,
That I may doe them, those workes to you I say,
Beare witnesse, if you haue the grace to beleue,
That the father hath sent me into the world this day.

Besides these workes, the father that hath me sent,
Hath by many scriptures of me testified:
By the whiche the matter is euident,
That my wordes spoken before are verified.

But the father you haue neuer heard speaking,
And what he is by faith you haue neuer sene:
His word you haue not in you remayning.
Therfore to him whom he hath sent faithful you haue not ben

Serch the scriptures, for you think in your mind
That in them you shall obtaine life eternall,
[H1v] Them to beare witnesse of me you shall fynde,
How I am the sonne of the liuyng God immortall.

Simon.

Wel sir, you ar welcom, I wold not haue you to thi[n]k
That I did byd you hither to tempt or to proue,
But that I would haue you both to eate and drinke,
Euen as my entier friend, and for very loue.

Wherfore any thing that is here done or sayd,
Shalbe layd vnder foote, and go no further,
For surely if your wordes should be betrayd,
As a blasphemer the people would you murder,

Christ Iesus.

You know that there is .xi. houres in the day
And night commeth not till the .xii. houres be expired
It is not in mans power my life to take away,
Till the houre commeth of my father required.

Infidelitie.

Vnder the foote quod he? if I kepe counsell,
I would I were hanged vp by the very necke.
Fye on hym horeson traitour and very rebell,
Hear you not how god him self he beginneth to check?

Malicious Iudgement.

Though maister Simon doth but few wordes say
Yet I warrant you he beareth this geare in mynde,
Doubt thou not but he will fynde suche way,
That he shal be ryd and as many as be of his kynde.

Simon.

Go to I pray you, alacke you eate no meate:
You see that at this tyme we haue but plaine fare.

Christ Iesus.

When we haue sufficient before vs to eate,
Let vs thanke God, and put away all care.

[Enter] Mary Magdalen sadly apparelled [and carrying a jar of ointment].

Mary.

The more that I accustom my self with repentance,
The more I see myne owne synne and iniquitie,
The more knowledge therof, the more greuance,
To a soule that is conuerted from hir impietie.

To all the worlde an example I may be,
In whom the mercy of Christ is declared,
[H2r] O Lord, what goodnesse dydst thou in me see?
That thus mercifully thou hast me spared.

What goodnesse? nay, rather what a rable of euils,
Full of wickednesse, like one past all grace,
Replenished with a multitude of deuils,
Which as in hell in my soule had their place.

These were the merites and dedes that I had,

Onely thy vnspeakable mercy did me preuent:
And though that my life hath bene so bad,
Yet thou wilt no more but that I should repent.

O who shall geue me a fountayne of teares,
That I may shed abundantly for my synne?
This voice of the Lord alwais soundeth in myn eares
Repent, repent, and thou shalt be sure heauen to wyn

He saith also, do the fruictes of Repentance.
O Lord, who is able those worthy fruictes to do?
I am not able to doe sufficient penance,
Except thy grace good Lord, do helpe me therto.

But like as the parts of my body in tymes past,
I haue made seruants to all kynd of iniquitie,
The same iniquitie away for euer I do cast,
And will make my body seruant to the veritie.

This haire of my head which I haue abused,
I repute vile and vnworthie to wipe my lordes fete,
No obsequie therwith of me shalbe refused,
To do my Lord Iesus seruice, as it is most mete.

These fleshly eies which with their wanton lookes,
Many persons to synne and vice haue procured.
They haue ben the diuels volumes and bookes,
Which from the seruice of God haue other allured.

Nowe you synfull eyes shed out teares and water,
Wash the Lords fete with them whom you haue offended
[H2v] To shew such obsequie to hym it is a small matter,
Which by his grace hath my synfull life amended.

O wretched eies can you wepe for a thing temporall,
As for the losse of worldly goodes and parents,
And can you not wepe for the lorde celestiall?
Which losse incomparably passeth all detrimentes.

With this oyntment most pure and precious,
I was wont to make this carkas pleasant and swete
Wherby it was make more wicked and vicious,
And to alll vnthriftynesse very apt and mete.

Now would I gladly this oyntment bestowe,
About the innocent feete of my sauiour,
That by these penitent fruictes my lord may know
That I am right sory for my sinfull behauiour.

All my worldly substance abused before,
And through vnbelief of synne made instruments,
Now will I bestow them onely to his honor,
In helpyng hym, and for his sake other innocents.

I shall not ceasse to seeke till my lord I haue found,
He is in the house of Simon I heard say,
The house standeth on yonder same ground:
It was told me that he dyneth there to day.

I was not ashamed to synne before the Lordes sight
And shal I be ashamed before man the same to confesse?
To my Lord Iesus, now forth will I go right,
Acknowledgyng to him my penitent heart doubtlesse

Let Marie creepe vnder the table, abyding there a certayne space behynd, and doe as it is specified in the Gospell. Then Malicious Iudgement speaketh these wordes to Infidelitie.

Malicious Iudgement.
Lo syr, what a felow this is, it doth appere,
If he were suche a prophet, as of him self he doth say,
[H3r] He would know what maner of woman this same is here.
A sinner she is, he can not say nay.

Infidelitie.
A sinner quod he? yea she is a wicked sinner in dede
This is she, from whom he did me expell,
Behold, how boldly after hym she doth procede,
A harlot she is truly I may tell you in counsell.

Malicious Iudgement.
Yea and yet to touche hym he doth her permit,
Which is agaynst the law for persons defiled,
Ought not among the iust to intromit,
But from their company should be exiled.

[Infidelitie.]
I pray you see, how busy about hym she is,
She washeth his feet with teares of hir eyes,
Heigh, mary yonder is like to be nothyng amisse.
Behold, she anoynteth him to driue away flies.

Trow you that maister Simon thinketh not somwhat?
Yes I hold you a groate, though he say nothing.

Malicious Iudgement.

He is not content I warant you that,
Which thyng you may see by his lookyng.

Simon.

Syrs, take away here, we will no more now.
This fyrst: Are you in such things to be tought?
What meane you, wherabout do you looke,
I maruell wherabout you do occupy your thought.

Christ Iesus.

Simon, the truth is so, I haue a thing in my mynd
Which vnto you I must nedes expresse and say.

Simon.

Maister, say what you will, wordes are but wynde,
I will heare you truly, as paciently as I may.

Christ Iesus.

There are two detters, whom I dyd well know,
Whiche were in debt to a lender that was thriftie:
The one fiue hundred pence truely did owe,
And the other ought not aboue fiftie:
Neither of these debters had wherwith to pay,
Wherfore the lender forgaue both, as it dyd behoue.
[H3v] Nowe according to your iudgement I pray you say,
Which of these detters ought the lender most loue?

Simon.

Mary, he to whom most was forgiuen I suppose,
In few wordes truly you haue heard my sentence.

Christ Iesus.

You haue rightly iudged, and to the purpose.
Absoluyng my question like a man of science,

See you this woman? I know that in your hertes
You condemne her as a synner very vnmete
To enter among you, and to touche any partes,
Of my body, yea either head or feete:

Saying among your selues, if this were a Prophet,
He would know what maner a woman this is
Which thus commeth in while we be at meate,
A sinner she is, and hath done greatly amisse.

I say vnto you, that into this world I am come
To call suche great detters vnto repentance,

The iust, which in their co*n*ceits owe but a small summe
Haue no nede of their creditours deliuerance.

Infidelitie.

What a thief is this? he iudgeth our masters thoght,
If we destroy hym not, he will surely marre all.

Malicious Iudgement.

I euer sayd that he was worse than nought,
But among vs puruey for him we shall.

Simon.

Sir, you take vpon you very presumptuously,
I haue bydden you vnto my house here of good will,
And you reason of matters here contemptuously:
But take your pleasure, it shall not greatly skill.

Christ Iesus.

I say vnto you, that for this cause was I borne,
To beare witnesse vnto the veritie,
I see who be hypocrites full of dissemblyng scorne,
And who be persons of faith and simplicitie.

Where as you thinke you haue done me pleasure,
In bidding me to eate and drinke with you here,
[H4r] Your intent was to shew your richesse and treasure,
And that your holynesse might to me appeare.

But this woman hath shewed to me a little obsequie:
For these gestures whiche she sheweth to me,
Procede from a true meanyng heart verily,
As by her humilite plainly you may see.

When I came into your house the truth to say,
You gaue me no water to washe my feete withall,
This woman hath washed them here this day,
With the teares of her eies which on them did fall,

With the haire of hir head she hath wiped the same,
Thinking all other clothes therto ouer vile,
Horrible in hir sight is hir synne and blame,
Thinkyng hir self worthy of eternall exile.

You gaue me no kisse as the maner of the countrey is
But this woman since the tyme that I came in,
Would not presume my head or mouth to kisse,
But my feete, lamenting in hir heart for hir syn.

My head you did not anoynt with oyle so swete,
As men of this countrey do their guestes vse,
But with most precious balme she anointed my fete,
No cost about that oyntment she doth refuse.

Blessed are they, as the Prophete doth say,
Whose sinnes are forgiuen and couered by Gods mercy,
Not by the dedes of the lawe as you thinke this day,
But of Gods good will, fauour and grace freely.

At this womans synne you do greatly grutche,
As though your selues were iust, holy, and pure,
But many sinnes are forgiuen hir, bicause she loued muche
And of the mercy of God she is sure.

He to whom but a little is remitted in dede,
Loueth but a little, we se by experience:
[H4^{v}] All haue sinned, and of Gods glory haue nede.
Therfore humble your selues with penitence.

[to Mary]
I say to thee woman, thy synnes are forgeuen all,
God for my sake will not them to thee impute:
For strength to continue, to hym do thou call,
And see that thankes thou do to hym attribute.

Mary.
The mercy of God is aboue all his workes truely,
What is it that God is not able to bryng to passe?
I thanke thee Lord Iesu for thy great mercy,
Thou art the sonne of the liuyng God, our Messias.

Malicious Iudgement.
How say you by this, here is a greater matter yet,
He forgiueth synnes, as one with God equall.

Infidelitie.
And he may perceiue truely, that hath any wit,
That he is but a man wretched and mortall.

Christ Iesus.
Woman I say, thy faith hath saued thee go in peace:
Now art thou pacified in thy conscience,
Through thy faithe, I doe all thy sinnes releace,
Assuryng thee to haue mercy for thy negligence.

Mary.
O ioyfull tydynges, O message most comfortable.
Let no sinner be he neuer in so great dispaire.

Though he were synfull and abhominable,
Let him come, and he will make hym faire.

Blessed be the Lord of such compassion and pitie,
Praise we his name with glorie and honor,
I shall declare his mercy in towne and citie.
Thankes be to thee my Lord now and euermore.

[Exit Mary.]

Simon.

I see the wordes whiche I haue heard, proued true.
Men say that you are new fangled and friuolous,
Goyng about the law and our rulers to subdue,
Introducyng sectes perillous and sedicious.

Malicious Iudgement.

I can no longer containe, but must say my mynde,
In dede it is so, for by his diuelishe erudition,
[I1r] Which he soweth among the people of our kynde,
At length they will make a tumult and sedition.

Such blasphemy since the beginning was not heard,
That a man shal call him self Gods naturall sonne,
To condemne the law of God he is not afeard,
Despisyng all things that our fathers haue done.

Infidelitie.

Pleaseth it you reuerend father, to geue me licence
To say my mynde to this blasphemer and thiefe,
In fewe wordes you shall haue my sentence:
Of all heretikes I iudge hym to be the chiefe.

Perceiue you not how he doth begyn?
He commeth to none of the princes and gouerners,
But a sort of synners he goeth about to wyn:
As publicans, whores, harlots, and vniust occupiers.

Then he preferreth before such men as you be,
Saying, that they before you shall be saued.
An honest man in his company you shall not see,
But euen them, which haue them selues yll behaued.

Much good doe it you, here is sause for your meate.
Maister Simon, looke vpon this felow in season,
For in continuance he will worke such a feate,
That you shall not release with all your reason.

Christ Iesus.

O Simon, put away that Malicious Iudgement,
Which in your heart you do stubbornly contayne,
You shall not perceyue Gods commandement,
As long as he in your conscience doth remayne.

Malicious Iudgement.

Lo syr now that God he hath blasphemed,
Now his law he doth contemne and despise,
The Iustice therof of hym is nothyng estemed,
To destroy the same vtterly he doth deuise.

Simon.

Thinke you vs ignorant of gods law and will,
Which vpon your garments do them weare.
[I1v] Who but we doe the law of God fulfill,
For his precepts with vs in all places we beare.

Christ Iesus.

To fulfill the law requireth Gods spirite,
For the law is holy, iust, and spirituall,
Of loue to be obserued it is requisite,
And not of these obseruances externall.

As long as you haue this malicious iudgement,
Accompanied with Infidelitie,
I say you can not kepe Gods commaundement,
Though you shew an outward sanctitie.

Infidelitie.

Lo syr here he calleth me Infidelitie,
And you know that I am called Legal Iustification
You heare that it was spoken by Gods maiestie,
That a man shall liue by the lawes obseruation.

An honest guest come out, dogge, yea mary,
Good maners thus to taunt a man at his table:
But with fooles it is follie to vary,
His wordes be taken but as a tale or a fable.

Simon.

Away with this geare, how long shall we syt here?
At once: We haue somewhat els to do I thinke.

Christ Iesus.

Thankes be to thee, O Father, for this chere,
Thankes be to thee for our repast of meate and drinke.

Now sir, you shall licence me to depart,
And the heauenly Father might illumine your mynd

Expellyng this infidelitie from your hart,
Which with Malicious Iudgement kepeth you blynd.

Simon.

Fare ye well: for me you shall no countes render,
All shall be layd vnder the feete that is here spoken.

Infidelitie.

Though you forget it, yet we purpose to remember
You know the way, go I pray you, the doore is open.

Exit [Christ Iesus].

Malicious Iudgement.

For Gods sake syr, you and such as you be,
Looke vpon this felow by myne aduise:
[I2r] For what he goth about all you may see,
Yea you haue had warnyng of hym twise or thrise.

Infidelitie.

All the multitude beginneth after him to ronne,
You see hym and know his doctrine and opinion,
If you suffer hym till more people he hath wonne,
Strangers shall come and take our dominion.

Haue you not heard his open blasphemie?
The sonne of God he presumeth him self to name,
The Iustice of the lawe he condemneth vtterly,
To suffer him to lyue will turne to your shame.

Simon.

It shall behoue you to dog him from place to place,
Note whether openly he teache suche doctrine:
If he doe, accuse hym before his face,
For I will cause the byshops hym to examine.

Infidelitie.

And where as he willeth you vs to expell,
Callyng vs wicked nicknames at his pleasure,
He goeth about to make you to rebell
Against God and his lawes, as he doth without mesure

Malicious Iudgement.

For my part I wil watche hym so narowly,
That a word shall not scape me that doth sounde
Agaynst you the fathers, that liue so holyly,
But to accuse hym for it a way shalbe found.

Simon.

Well the tyme of our euenyng seruice is at hand,
We must depart, the sacrifice to prepare.

Infidelitie.

If you depart, we may not here ydle stande,
For to wayte vpon you at all tymes ready we are.

Exeunt [Simon, Infidelitie, and Malicious Iudgement].
Mary entreth with Iustification.

[Mary.]

At my beyng here euen now of late,
It pleased my Lord Iesus of his great mercy
To speake sentences here in my presence.
Of the which I haue no perfect intelligence,
The fyrst is: Many sinnes are forgiuen hir sayd he,
Because she hath loued much, meanyng me,
[I2v] I pray you, most holy Iustification,
Of this sentence to make a declaration.

Iustification.

A question right necessary to be moued,
For therby many errors shall be reproued,
It were a great errour for any man to beleue
That your loue dyd deserue that Christ shold forgeue
Your synnes or trespasses, or any synne at all:
For so to beleue is an errour fanaticall.
And how can your loue desyre forgiuenesse of your yl
Seing that the law it is not able to fulfill?
The law thus commaundeth as touchyng loue:
Thou shalt loue thy Lord God as it doth behoue,
With al thy hert, with al thy soule, and with al thy strength,
And thy neighbor as thy self. He saith also at length:
There was neuer man borne yet that was able,
To performe these preceptes iust, holy, and stable,
Saue onely Iesus Christ, that lambe most innocent
Which fulfilleth the law for suche as are penitent:
But loue foloweth forgiuenesse of synnes euermore,
As a fruict of faith, and goth not before,
In that parable which vnto you he recited,
Wherin he declared your sinnes to be acquited,
He called you a detter not able to pay.
Then your loue paid not your dets, perceiue you may
The forgiuenesse of your sinnes you must referre,
Only to Christes grace, then you shall not erre.
Of this thing playn knowledge you may haue
In these wordes go in peace thy fayth doth thee saue.
So by faith in Christ you haue Iustification

Frely of his grace, and beyond mans operation,
The which Iustification here I do represent,
Which remayn with all suche as be penitent.
[I3r] Here commeth loue a speciall fruicte of Faith,
As touchyng this, heare mekely what he saith.

Mary.

O, how much am I vnto Iesus Christ bound,
In whom so great mercy and goodnesse I haue found?
Not onely my synfull lyfe he hath renued.
But also with many graces he hathe me endued,

Loue entreth.

[Loue.]

I am named loue, from true faith procedyng,
Where I am, there is no vertue nedyng,
Loue commyng of a conscience immaculate,
And of a faith not fained nor simulate,
Is the end of the law as Scripture doth say,
And vnto eternall felicitie the very path way:
This loue grounded in Faith, as it is sayd,
Hath caused many euyls in men to be layd.
For where as the loue of God in any is perfite,
There in all good workes is his whole delite.
This true loue with Mary was present verily,
When to Christ she shewed that obsequie,
But this loue dyd procede from beleue,
When Christ of his mercy dyd hir sinnes forgeue,
Loue deserued not forgeuenesse of sinnes in dede,
But as a fruite therof truely it did succede.

Iustification.

Of this matter we might tary very long,
But then we should do your audience wrong,
Which gently hath heard vs here a long space,
Wherfore we will make an end nowe by Gods grace,
Praying God that all we example may take
Of Mary, our synfull lyues to forsake:
And no more to looke backe, but to go forward still
Folowyng Christ as she did and his holy will.

Loue.

Such persons we introduce into presence,
To declare the conuersion of hir offence.
[I3v] Fyrst, the lawe made a playne declaration,
That she was a chylde of eternall damnation:
By hearyng of the law came knowledge of synne,

Then for to lament truely she dyd begynne.
Nothyng but desperation dyd in hir remayne,
Lokyng for none other comfort but for hell payne.
But Christ whose nature is mercy to haue,
Came into this world synners to saue,
Which preached repentence synnes to forgeue,
To as many as in hym faithfully dyd beleue.
By the word came faith, Faith brought penitence,
But bothe the gyft of Gods magnificence.
Thus by Faith onely, Marie was iustified,
Like as before it is playnly verified,
From thens came loue, as a testification
Of Gods mercy and her iustification.

Mary.

Now God graunt that we may go the same way,
That with ioy we may ryse at the last day,
To the saluation of soule and body euermore,
Through Christ our Lord, to whom be all honor.

[Exit Mary with Iustification and Love.]

FINIS.

A newe mery and wittie
Comedie or Enterlude, newely
imprinted, treating vpon the Historie of
Iacob and Esau, taken out of the .xxvii.
Chap. of the first booke of Moses
entituled Genesis.

The partes and names of the Players
who are to be consydered to be Hebrews
and so should be apparailed with attire.

1. The Prologe, a Poete.
2. Isaac, an olde man, father to Iacob & Esau.
3. Rebecca an olde woman, wife to Isaac.
4. Esau, a yong man and a hunter.
5. Iacob, a yong man of godly conuersation.
6. Zethar a neighbour.
7. Hanan, a neighbour to Isaac also.
8. Ragau, servaunt vnto Esau.
9. Mido, a little Boy, leading Isaac.
10. Deborra, the nurse of Isaacs Tente.
11. Abra, a little wench, seruant to Rebecca.

Imprinted at London by Henrie
Bynneman, dwelling in Knightrider streate,
at the signe of the Mermayde.
Anno Domini. 1568.

The Prologue of the Play

In the Boke of Genesis it is expressed,
That when God to Abraham made sure promis
That in his seede al nations shold be blessed:
To send him a son by Sara he did not misse,
Then to Isaac (as there recorded it is)
By Rebecca his wife, who had long time be barain
When pleased him, at one birth he sent sons twaine.

But before Iacob and Esau yet borne were,
Or had eyther done good, or yll perpetrate:
As the prophet Malachie and Paule witnesse beare,
Iacob was chosen, and Esau reprobate:
Iacob I loue (sayde God) and Esau I hate.
For it is not (sayth Paule) in mans renuing or will,
But in Gods mercy who choseth whome he will.

But now for our comming we shal exhibite here
Of Iacob and Esau howe the story was,
Wherby Gods adoption may plainly appeare:
And also, that what euer Gods ordinance was,
Nothing might defeate, but that it muste come to passe.
That if this storie may your eyes or eares delite,
We pray you of pacience, while we it recite.

The Historie of Iacob and Esau.

Actus primi, Scæna Prima

Ragau the seruant. Esau a yong man his maister.

Ragau entreth with his horn at his back, and his huntyng staffe in hys hande, and leadeth. iij. greyhounds or one as may be gotten.

[Ragau.]

Now lette me see what tyme it is by the starre light?
Gods for his grace man, why it is not yet midnight,
We might haue slept there four houres yet I dare well say.
But this is our good Esau his common play:

Here he counterfaiteth how his maister calleth hym vp in the mornings, and of his answeres.

What the dyuell ayleth him? now truly I thinke plaine,
He hath either some wormes or bottes in his braine.
He scarcely sleepeth .vif. good houres in two weekes.
I wote wel his watching maketh me haue leane cheekes.
For there is none other life with hym day by day,
But vp Ragau, vp drousy hogges head I say:
Why when? Up, will it not be? Up. I come anon.
Up, or I shall reyse you in fayth ye drousy hooreson.
Why, when? shall I sette you? I come syr by and by.
Up with a wilde wenyon, how long wilt thou lie?
Up I say, vp at once. Up vp, let vs goe hence,
It is tyme we were in the forrest an houre sence.
Nowe the deuill stoppe that same yallyng throte (thynke I)
Somwhiles. For from he call, farewell all winke of eye.
Begin he once to call, I sleepe no more that stounde,
Though half an houres slepe wer worth .v. thousand pound.
Anon when I come in, and bydde him good morow:

Ah syr, vp at last, the deuyll gyue thee sorow.
Nowe the diuell breake thy necke (thinke I by and by)
That hast no witte to sleape, nor in thy bedde to lye.
Then come on at once, take my quiuer and my bowe,
Fette Louell my hounde, and my horne to blowe.
Then forth goe we fastyng an houre or two ere day,
Before we may well see either our handes or way,
[A2v] And there raunge we the wilde forest, no crumme of bread
From morning to starck night coming within our head,
Sometime Esaus selfe will faynt for drinke and meate:
So that he would be glad of a dead horse to eate.
Yet of freshe the next morow foorth he will againe,
And somtime not come home in a whole night or twaine:
Nor no delite he hath, no appetite nor minde
But to the wilde Forrest, to hunt the Harte or Hinde,
The Roebucke, the wilde bore, the fallow Deere, or Hare:
But howe poore Ragau shall dine, he hath no care,
Poore I, must eate Acornes or Bearies from the Tree.
But if I be founde slacke in the sute folowing,
Or if I do fayle in blowing or hallowing,
Or if I lacke my Staffe, or my Horne by my syde:
He will be quicke inough to fume chafe, and chide.
Am I not well at ease suche a mayster to serue,
As must haue such seruice, and yet will let me sterue?
But in faith his fashions displease moe than me,
And will haue but a madde ende one day we shall see.
He passeth nothing on Rebecca his mother,
And much lesse passeth he on Iacob hys brother.
But peace, mumme, no more: I see maister Esau.

Here Esau appereth in sight, and bloweth his Horne, ere he enter.

Esau.
Howe nowe, are we all ready seruaunt Ragau?
Art thou vp for all day man? art thou ready now?

Ragau.
I haue ben here this halfe houre syr waityng for you.

Esau.
And is all thing ready as I bad, to my mynde?

Ragau.
Ye haue no cause, that I know, any fault to fynde:
Except that we disease our tent and neighbours all
With rising ouer early eche day when ye call.

Esau.
Ah thou drousy draffesacke, wouldest thou ryse at noone?
Nay I trow the sixth houre with thee were ouersoone.
Ragau.
Nay I speake of your neighbours being men honest,
That labour all the day, and would faine be at rest:
Whom with blowing your Horne ye disease al aboutes.
Esau.
What care I for waking a forte of clubbishe loutes?
Ragau.
And I speake of Rebecca your mother, our dame.
Esau.
[A3r] Tutte I passe not whether she doe me prayse or blame.
Ragau.
And I speake of your good father, olde Isaac.
Esau.
Peace foolishe knaue: As for my father Isaac,
In case he be a sleepe, I doe him not disease,
And if he be waking, I knowe I do him please,
For he loueth me well from myne natiuitie,

Here Esau bloweth his horn agayne.

And neuer so as now, for myne actiuitie.
Therfore haue at it, once more will I blow my Horne
To giue my neighbour loutes an haile peale in a morne.

Here he speaketh to hys Dogges.

Now my maister Lightfoote, how say you to this geare,
Will you do your duetie to redde or fallow Deare?
And Swan mine owne good curre, I do think in my minde,
The game that runne apace, if thou come farre behinde:
And ha Takepart, come Takepart, here, how say you child
Wilt not thou do thy part? yes, else I am beguilde.
But I shrewe your cheekes, they haue had too much meat.
Ragau.
I blame not dogges to take it, if they may it geat:
But as for my parte, they coulde haue pardie,
A small releuauit of that that ye giue me.
They may runne light inough for ought of me they got,
I had not a good meales meate this weeke that I wot.
Esau.
If we haue lucke thys day to kill Hare, Teg, or Doe,

Thou shalt eate thy belly full, tyll thou cryest hoe.

Ragau.

I thanke you when I haue it, mayster Esau.

Esau.

Well, come on, let vs goe nowe seruant Ragau.
Is there any thing more, that I shoulde say or do?
For perhaps we come not againe this day or two.

Ragau.

I know nothing maister, to God I make a vow,
Except you woulde take your brother Iacob with you:
I neuer yet sawe hym with you an hunting goe,
Shall we proue hym once whether he will goe or no?

Esau.

No, no, that were in vaine: Alas good simple mome.
Nay, he must tarrie and sucke mothers dugge at home:
Iacob must keepe home I trow, under mothers wing,
[A3^v] To be from the Tentes he loueth not of all thing.
Iacob loueth no huntyng in the wylde forest:
And would feare if he shoulde there see any wylde beast.
Yea to see the game runne, Iacob would be in feare.

Ragau.

In good sooth I wene he would think eche Hare a Beare.

Esau.

What brother myne, what a worde call ye that?

Ragau.

Syr I am scarse waked: I spake ere I wyst what.

Esau.

Come on your ways my childe, take the law of the game.
I will wake you I trowe, and let your tongue in frame.

Ragau.

Oh what haue you done maister Esau, Gods apes.

Esau.

Why can ye not yet refraine from lettyng such scapes?
Come on, ye must haue three iertes for the nonce.
One.

[Esau beats Ragau.]

Ragau.

Oh, for Gods loue syr haue done, dispatche at once.

Esau.

Nay there is no remedy but byde it, there is twaine.

[Esau hits Ragau again.]

Ragau.

O ye rent my cheuerell, let me be past my paine.

Esau.

Take hede of huting termes fro hensforth, there is three.

[Esau hits Ragau again.]

Ragau.

Whoup. Nowe a mischief on all mopyng fooles for mee.
Iacob shall keepe the Tentes tenne yeare for Ragau,
Ere I moue agayne that he hunt wyth Esau.

Esau.

Come on, now let vs goe. God lende vs game and lucke,
And if my hande serue me well,

Ragau [aside].

Ye wyll kill a Ducke.

Exeant ambo.

Actus Primi, Scæna secunda

Hanan. Zethar. two of Isaacs neighbors.

[Enter Hanan.]

Hanan.

Ah syr, I see I am am early man thys morne,
I am once more begylde with Esau his horne.
But there is no suche stirrer as Esau is:
He is vp day by day before the Crowe pis:
Then maketh he with his Horne such tootyng and blowing
And with his wyde throate such shouting and hallowing,
That no neighbour shall in his Tent take any rest,
[A4r] From Esau addresseth hym to the forrest.
So that he maketh vs whether we will or no,
Better husbandes than we woulde be, abroade to go,
Eche of vs about our businesse and our warke.

[Enter Zethar.]

But whome doe I see yonder commyng in the darke?
It is my neighbor Zethar, I perceyue hym nowe.

Zethar.

What neighbour Hanan, well met, good morow to you.
I see well nowe I am not beguiled alone:
But what boote to lye still? for rest we can take none.

That I meruayle much of olde father Isaac,
Beyng so godly a man, why he is so slacke
To bryng hys sonne Esau to a better stay.

Hanan.

What shoulde he do in the matter I you pray?

Zethar.

Oh it is no small charge to fathers afore God,
So to traine their children in youth under the rod,
That when they come to age they may vertue ensue,
Wicked prankes abhorre, and all leudness eschue.
And me thinketh Isaac, being a man (as he is)
A chosen man of God, shoulde not be slacke in this.

Hanan.

Alack good man, what should he do more than he hath don?
I dare say no father hath better taught his sonne,
Nor no two haue giuen better example of life
Unto their children, than bothe he and his wife:
As by their yonger sonne Iacob it doth appeare.
He lyueth no looce life, he doth God loue and feare.
He keepeth here in the Tentes lyke a quiete man:
He geueth not hymselfe to wildnesse any whan.
But Esau euermore from his yong childehoode
Hath ben lyke to proue yll, and neuer to be good.
Yong it pricketh (folks do say) that wyll be a thorne,
Esau hath ben nought euer since he was borne.
And wherof commeth this, of Education?
Nay it is of his owne yll inclination.
They were brought vp bothe under one tuition,
But they be not bothe of one disposition.
[A4v] Esau is gyuen to looce and leude liuyng.

Zethar.

In fayth I warrant him haue but shreude thriuing.

Hanan.

Neither see I any hope that he will amende.

Zethar.

Then let hym euen looke to come to an yll ende.
For youth that will folow none but theyr owne bridle,
That leadeth a dissolute lyfe and an ydle,
Youth that refuseth holsome documentes,
Or to take example of theyr godly parentes,
Youth that is retchelesse, and taketh no regarde,
What become of them selfe, nor which ende goe forwarde,
It is great meruaile and a speciall grace,
If euer they come to goodnesse all theyr life space.

But why doe we consume this whole mornyng in talke,
Of one that hath no recke ne care what way he walke,
We had bene as good to haue kept our bedde still.

Hanan.

Oh it is our parte to lamente them that doe yll.
Lyke as very Nature, a godly heart dothe moue
Others good proceedings to tender and to loue:
So suche as in no wise to goodnesse will be brought:
What good ma but wil mourn, since god vs al hath wrought
But ye haue some busynesse, and so haue I.

Zethar.

And we haue ben long, farewell neighbour heartily.

[Exit Hanan and Zethar.]

Actus primi, scæna tertia.

Rebecca the Mother. Iacob the Sonne.

[Enter Rebecca and Iacob.]

Rebecca.

Come forth sonne Iacob, why tarriest thou behinde?

Iacob.

Forsoth mother, I thought ye had sayd al your minde.

Rebecca.

Nay, come I haue yet a worde or two more to say.

Iacob.

What soeuer pleaseth you, speake to me ye may.

Rebecca.

Seyng thy brother Esau is such an one,
Why rebukest thou hym not when ye are alone?
Why doest thou not gyue him some good sad wyse counsaile?

Iacob.

He lacketh not that mother, if it woulde availe.
[B1r] But when I doe him any thing of his fault tell,
He calleth me foolishe proude boy with him to mell.
He will somtime demaunde by what authoritee,
I presume to teache them which mine elders bee?
He will somtime aske if I learne of my mother,

To take on me teaching of mine elder brother?
Sometime when I tell hym of his leude behauour,
He will lende me a mocke or twaine for my labour:
And somtime for anger he will out with his purse
And call me as please hym, and sweare he will doe wurse.

Rebecca.
Oh Lorde, that to beare such a sonne it was my chaunce.

Iacob.
Mother, we must be content wyth Gods ordinaunce.

Rebecca.
Or, if I shoulde needes haue Esau to my soonne,
Would God thou Iacob haddest the Eldership woonne.

Iacob.
Mother, it is to late to wishe for that is past:
It will not be done now wish ye neuer so fast.
And I woulde not haue you to wish agaynst Gods wyll:
For both it is in vaine, and also it is yll.

Rebecca.
Why did it not please God, that thou shouldest as wele
Treade upon his crowne, as holde hym fast by the hele?

Iacob.
Whatsoeuer mysterie the Lorde therein ment,
Must be referred to his unserched iudgement.
And what soeuer he hath pointed me vnto,
I am his owne vessell his will with me to do.

Rebecca.
Well, some straunge thing therin of God intended was,

Iacob.
And what he hath decreed, must sure come to passe.

Rebecca.
I remember when I had you both conceiued,
A voyce thus saying from the Lorde I receiued:
Rebecca, in thy wombe are now two nations,
Of unlike natures and contrary fashions.
The one shal be a mightier people elect:
And the elder to the yonger shall be subiect.
I knowe this voyce came not to me of nothing:
Therfore thou shalt folow my counsell in o thing.

Iacob.
So it be not displeasing to the Lorde I must.

[B1v]

Rebecca.
I feare the lorde eke, who is mercifull and iust:
And loth would I be, his maiestie to offende,

But by me (I doubt not) to worke he doth intende,
Assay if thou canst, at some one tyme or other,
To buie the right of eldership from thy brother:
Do thou buye the birthright that to hym doth belong,
So mayst thou haue the blessing, and doe hym no wrong.
What thou hast once bought, is thyn owne of due right.

Iacob.

Mother Rebecca, if withouten fraude I might,
I would your aduise put in vse wyth all my hart,
But I may not attempt any such guilefull part:
To buie my brothers eldership and hys birthright,
I feare woulde be a great offence in Gods sight.
Which thyng if I wist, to redeeme I ne wolde,
Though I might get therby ten millions of golde.

Rebecca.

God, who by his worde and almightifull decree,
Hath appoynted thee Esau his lorde to bee,
Hath appointed some way to haue it brought about.
And that is thys way, my sprite doth not doute.

Iacob.

Upon your worde mother, I will assay ere long,
Yet it grudgeth my heart to doe my brother wrong.

Rebecca.

Thou shalt do no wrong sonne Iacob, on my perill.

Iacob.

Then by Gods leaue once assay I wil.

Rebecca.

Then farewell dere son, Gods blessing & mine with thee.

Iacob.

I will again to the Tent. Well you bee.

Exeat Iacob.

Rebecca.

Ah my sweete sonne Iacob, good fortune God thee sende.
The most gentle yong man aliue, as God me mende.
And the moste naturall to father and mother:
O that such a meke spirite were in thy brother,
Or thy syre loued thee as thou hast merited,
And then should Esau soone be disherited.

[Exit Rebecca.]

[B2r]

Actus Primi, Scæna quarta

Isaac the husbande, Rebecca, the wife.
Mido, the ladde that leadeth blinde Isaac.

[Enter Isaac and Mido; Rebecca stands apart.]

Isaac.
Where art thou my boy Mido, when I doe thee lacke?

Mido.
Who calleth Mido? here good maister Isaac.

Isaac.
Come leade me forth of doores a little I thee pray.

Mido.
Lay your hande on my shoulder, and come on this way.

Rebecca.
Now O Lorde of heauen, the fountaine of all grace,
If it be thy good will that my will shall take place:
Sende successe to Iacob, according to thy worde,
That his elder brother may serue hym as his lorde.

Mido.
Syr, whyther would ye goe, now that abroade ye be?

Isaac.
To my wife Rebecca.

Mido.
Yonder I doe hir see.

Rebecca.
Lorde, thou knowest Iacob to be thy seruant true,
And Esau all frowarde thy wayes to ensue.

Mido.
Yonder she is speaking, what euer she doth say:
By holdyng vp his handes, it seemeth she doth pray.

Isaac.
Where be ye wife Rebecca? where be ye woman?

Rebecca.
Who is that calleth? Isaac my good man?

Isaac.
Where be ye wyfe Rebecca, lette me understande?

[Rebecca approaches Isaac.]

Mido.
She commeth to you apace.

Rebecca.
Here my lorde, at hande.

Isaac.

Sauing that what so euer God doth is all right,
No small griefe it were for a man to lacke his sight.

Rebecca.

But what the Lord doth sende or worke by his high will,
Can not but be the best, no such thing can be yll.

Isaac.

All bodily punishement or infirmitie,
With all maimes of nature, what euer they be,
Yea and all other afflictions temporall:
As losse, persecution, or troubles mortall,
Are nothing but a triall or probation.
And what is he that firmely trusteth in the Lorde,
[B2v] Or stedfastly beleueth his promise and worde,
And knoweth him to be the God omnipotent,
That feedeth and gouerneth all that he hath sent:
Protecting his faithfull in euery degree,
And them to relieue in all their necessitie?
What creature (I say) that doth this understande,
Will not take all thing in good parte at Gods hande?
Shall we at Gods hand receyue prosperitie,
And not be content likewise with aduersitie?
We ought to be thankefull what euer God doth sende,
And our selues wholy to his will to commende.

Rebecca.

So should it be, and I thanke my lorde Isaac,
Suche dayly lessons at your hande I doe not lack.

Isaac.

Why then should not I thanke the Lorde, if it please him
That I shall nowe be blynde, and my sight ware all dim.
For who so to olde age will here liue and endure,
Must of force abide all suche defautes of nature.

Mido.

Why must I be blinde too, if I be an olde man?
How shall I grope the way, or who shall leade me than?

Isaac.

If the Lorde haue pointed thee such olde dayes to see,
He wil also provide that shall be meete for thee.

Mido.

I trowe if I were blinde, I coulde goe well inowe,
I coulde grope the way thus, and goe as I do nowe.

[Mido mimics Isaac's movements.]

I haue done so ere now both by day and by night,
As I see you grope the way, and haue hitte it right.

Rebecca.

Yea syr boy, will ye play any suche childishe knack?
As to counterfaite your blinde maister Isaac:

Mido.

Nay I neuer dyd it in any suche intent.

Rebecca.

Nay it is to tempt God before thou haue neede:
Wherby thou mayst prouoke hym in very deede,
With some great misfortune or plague to punish thee.
Then will I neuer more do so while I may see:
But against I be blinde, I will be so perfight,
[B3r] That though no man leade me, I will go at midnight.

Isaac.

Nowe wife, touching the purpose that I sought for you.

Rebecca.

What sayth my lorde Isaac to his handemayde now?

Isaac.

Ye haue ofte in couerte wordes ben right earnest
To haue me graunt vnto you a boune and request:
But ye neuer tolde me yet plainly what it was,
Therfore I haue euer yet lette the matter passe.
And now of late by ofte being from me absent,
I haue half suspected you to be scarce content.
But wife Rebecca, I woulde not haue you to mourne,
As though I did your honest petition wourne.
For I neuer ment to denie in all my life
Any lawfull or honest request to my wyfe.
But in case it be a thing unreasonable,
Then must I needes be to you untractable.
Now therfore say on, and tell me what is your case.

Rebecca.

I woulde, if I were sure in your heart to fynde grace:
Else syr, I woulde be lothe.

Isaac.

To speake do not refraine,
And if it be reasonable ye shall obtaine:
Otherwise, ye must pardon me gentle sweete wife.

Rebecca.

Sir, ye knowe your sonne Esau, and see his life,
Howe looce it is, and howe stiffe he is and stubberne,
Howe retchelesly he doth him selfe misgouerne:
He geueth himselfe to hunting out of reason,

And serueth the Lorde and vs at no time or season.
These conditions can not be acceptable
In the syght of God, nor to men allowable.
Nowe his brother Iacob your yonger sonne and mine,
Dothe more applie his heart to seeke the wayes diuine.
He liueth here quietly at home in the Tent,
There is no man nor childe but is with him content.

Isaac.

Oh wife, I perceive ye speake of affection,
To Iacob ye beare loue, and to his brother none.

Rebecca.

In deede syr, I can not loue Esau so well
As I doe Iacob, the plaine truth to you to tell.
[B3v] For I haue no comforte of Esau God wot:
I scarce know where I haue a sonne of hym or not.
He goeth abroade so early before day light,
And returneth home againe so late in the night,
And oneth I sette eye on hym in the whole weeke:
No sometime not in twaine, though I doe for hym seeke.
And all the neighbours see him as seldome as I.
But when they would take rest, they heare hym blow & cry.
Some see him so seldome, they aske if he be sicke:
Somtimes some demaunde whether he be dead or quicke.
But to make short tale, such his conditions be,
That I wishe of God he had nere bene borne of me.

Isaac.

Well wyfe, I loue Esau, and must for causes twaine.

Rebecca.

Surely your loue is bestowed on him in vayne.

Isaac.

Fyrst actiue he is, as any yong man can be:
And many a good morsell he bringeth home to me.
Then he is myne eldest and first begotten sonne.

Rebecca.

If God were so pleased, I woulde that were fordonne.

Isaac.

And the eldest sonne is called the fathers might.

Rebecca.

If yours rest in Esau, God giue vs good night.

Isaac.

A prerogatiue he hath in euery thing.

Rebecca.

More pitie he shoulde haue it without deseruing.

Isaac.
Of all the goodes his porcion is greater.
Rebecca.
That the worthy should haue it, I thinke much better.
Isaac.
Emong his bretherne, he hath the preeminence.
Rebecca.
Where Esau is chiefe, there is a gay presence.
Isaac.
Ouer his bretherne he is soueraigne and lorde.
Rebecca.
Such dignitie in Esau doth yll accorde.
Isaac.
He is the head of the fathers succession.
Rebecca.
I woulde Esau had loste that possession.
Isaac.
And he hath the chiefe title of inheritaunce.
Rebecca.
Wisedome woulde in Esau chaunge that ordinaunce.
Isaac.
To the eldest sonne is due the fathers blessing.
Rebecca.
That should be Iacobs, if I might haue my wishing.
Isaac.
And the chiefe endowement of the fathers substance.
[B4^{r}]
Rebecca.
Which will thriue well in Esau his gouernance.
Isaac.
By title of Eldership he hath his birthright.
Rebecca.
And that would I remoue to Iacob if I might.
Isaac.
He must haue double porcion to an other.
Rebecca.
That were more fitte for Iacob hys yonger brother.
Isaac.
In all maner of things diuided by a rate.
Rebecca.
Well gyuen goodes to him that the Lorde doth hate.
Isaac.
Why say ye so of Esau mine eldest sonne?

Rebecca.

I say true, if he proceede as he hath begonne.

Isaac.

Is he not your sonne too, as well as he is myne?
Wherfore do ye then against him thus sore repine?

Rebecca.

Bicause that in my spirite verily I know,
God will set vp Iacob, and Esau downe throwe.
I haue shewed you many a tyme ere this day,
What the Lorde of them beyng in my wombe dyd say.
I vse not for to lye: And I beleue certaine,
That the Lorde spake not these wordes to me in vaine.
And Iacob it is (I know) in whome the Lorde will
His promises to you made, and to your seede fulfyll.

Isaac.

I doubt not his promise made to me and my seede,
Leauing to his conueyaunce howe it shall proceede.
The Lorde after his way chaunge thinheritance,
But I may not wetingly breake our ordinance.

Rebecca.

Nowe woulde God, I coulde persuade my lorde Isaac,
Iacob to preferre, and Esau to put backe.

Isaac.

I may not do it wife, I pray you be content.
The title of birthright that commeth by descent,
Or the place of eldershyp comming by due course
I may not chaunge nor shift, for better nor for wourse.
Natures lawe it is, the eldest sonne to knowlage,
And in no wife to barre hym of his heritage.
And ye shall of Esau one day haue comforte.

Rebecca.

Set a good long day then, or else we shal come short.

Isaac.

I warrant you, he will doe well inough at length.

Rebecca.

You must nedes commend him being your might
[B4v] & strength.

Isaac.

Well, nowe go we hence, little Mido where art thou?

Mido.

I haue stoode here all thys while, listning howe you
And my Dame Rebecca haue bene laying the lawe,
But she hath as quicke answeres as euer I sawe.
Ye coulde not speake any thing vnto hir so thicke,

But she had hir answere as ready and as quicke.

Isaac.

Yea, womens answeres are but fewe times to seeke.

Mido.

But I did not see Esau neither all this same weeke:
Nor I do loue your sonne Esau so well,
As I do loue your sonne Iacob by a great deale.

Isaac.

No doest thou Mido, and tell me the cause why?

Mido.

Why? for I doe not: And none other cause knowe I.
But euery body as well one as other,
Doe wish that Iacob had bene the elder brother.

Isaac.

Well, come on, let vs goe.

Mido.

And who shall leade you? I?

Rebecca.

No, it is my office as long as I am by.
And I woulde all wiues, as the worlde this day is,
Woulde vnto their husbandes likewise do their office.

Mido.

Why dame Rebecca, then al wedded men shold be blind.

Rebecca.

What thou foolish ladde, no such thing was in my minde.

[Exit Isaac, Rebecca, and Mido.]

Actus secundi, scæna prima.

Ragau. the Seruant of Esau.

[Enter Ragau.]

Ragau.

I haue hearde it ofte, but nowe I feele a wonder,
In what grieuous paine they ~~die,~~ that die for hunger.
Oh my greedie stomacke howe it doth bite and gnawe?
If I were at a racke, I could eate hey or strawe.
Mine emptie gutts doe frette, my mawe doth euen teare,
Woulde God I had a piece of some horsebread here.
Yet is maister Esau in worse case than I.
If he haue not some meate the sooner he will die:

He hath sonke for faintnesse twice or thrice by the way.
[C1^{r}] And not one siely bitte we got since yesterday.
All that euer he hath, he woulde haue giuen to day
To haue had but three morsels his hunger to allay.
Or in the fielde to haue mette with some hoggs,
I coulde scarsely kepe him from eating of these doggs.
He hath sent me afore some meate for to prouide,
And commeth creeping after, scarce able to stride.
But if I knowe where to get of any man,
For to eate myne owne selfe, as hungry as I am,
I pray God I stinke: but if any come to me,
Die who die will, for sure I will first serued be.
I will see if any be ready here at home:
Or whether Iacob haue any that peakishe mome.
But first I must put all my dogges vp,
And lay vp thys geare, and then God sende vs the cup.

[Exit Ragau.]

Actus secundi, scæna secunda.

Esau the maister. Ragau the seruant.

[Esau] Commeth in so faint that he can scarce go.

Esau.

Oh what a grieuous pain is hunger to a man!
Take all that I haue for meate, helpe who that can.
O Lorde, some good body for Gods sake gyue me meate.
I force not what it were, so that I had to eate.
Meate or drinke, saue my life, or breade,
  I recke not what.
If there be nothing else, some man giue me a cat.
If any good body on me will doe so much cost,
I will teare and eate hir rawe, the shall nere be rost,
I promise of honestie I will eate hir rawe.
And what a nody was I, and a hooreson dawe,
To let Ragau goe with all my doggs at ones:
A shoulder of a dogge were nowe meate for the nones.
Oh what shall I doe? my teeth I can scarcely charme,
From gnawyng away the braune of my very arme.
I can no longer stande for faynt, I must needes lie.

[Esau lies down.]

And except meate come soone, remedilesse I die.
[C1v] And where art thou Ragau whome I sent before?
Unlesse thou come at once, I neuer see thee more.
Where art thou Ragau, I heare not of thee yet?

[Enter Ragau.]

Ragau.
Here as fast as I can, but no meate can I get.
Not one draught of drink, not one poore morsel of bread
Not one bit or crum though I shold streight way be dead.
Therfore ye may nowe see how much ye are to blame,
That wil thus sterue your self for folowing your game.

Esau.
Ah thou villain, tellest thou me this now?
If had thee, I woulde eate thee, to God I vowe,
Ah, meat thou horson, why hast thou not brought me meat?

Ragau.
Would you haue me bring you that I can nowhere geat.

Esau.
Come hither, let me tell thee a worde in thine eare.

Ragau.
Nay, speake out aloude: I will not come a foote nere.
Fall ye to snatching at folkes? adieu I am gone.

[Ragau motions to leave.]

Esau.
Nay for gods loue Ragau, leaue me not alone:
I will not eate thee Ragau, so God me helpe.

Ragau.
No, I shall desire you to choose some other whelpe.
Being in your best lust I woulde topple with ye,
And plucke a good crowe ere ye brake your fast with me.
What? are you mankene now? I recken it best I,
To bind your handes behind you euen as ye lye.

Esau.
Nay haue mercy on me, and let me not perishe.

Ragau.
In faith nought could I get wherwith you to cherishe.

Esau.
Was there nothing to be had among so many?

Ragau.
I coulde not finde one but Iacob that had any,

And no grannt would he make for ought that I could say,
Yet no man aliue with fairer wordes coulde him pray.
But the best redde pottage he hath that euer was.

Esau.

Go pray him I may speake with him once ere I passe.

Ragau.

That message by Gods grace shall not long be undone.

Esau.

Hie thee, go apace, and returne againe soone.
If Iacob haue due brotherly compassion,
He will not see me fainte after this fashion,
But I dare say, the wretche had rather see me throst,
[C2r] Than he would finde in his harte to do so muche cost:
For where is betwene one fremman and an other,
Lesse loue found than now betwene brother and brother?
Will Iacob come foorth to shewe comforte vnto me?
The horeson hypocrite will as soone hanged be.
Yet peace, me thinketh Iacob is comming in dede:
And my minde geueth me at his hande I shall spede.
For he is as gentle and louing as can be,
As full of compassion and pitie.
But let me see, doth he come? no I warrant you.
He come quod I? tushe, he come? then hang Esau.
For there is not this daye in all the worlde rounde,
Suche an other hodypeake wretche to be founde.
And Ragau my man, is not that a fine knaue?
Haue any mo maisters suche a man as I haue?
So idle, so loytring, so trifling, so toying!
So pratling, so tratling, so chiding, so boying!
So iesting, so wresting, so mocking, so mowing!
So nipping, so tripping, so cocking, so crowyng!
So knappishe, so snappishe, so eluishe, so frowarde!
So crabbed, so wrabbed, so stiffe, so untowarde!
In play or in pastime, so iocunde, so mery!
In worke or in labour so dead or so weary!
Oh that I had his eare betwene my teeth now,
I should shake him euen as a dog that lulleth a sow.
But in faith if euer I recouer my selfe,
There was neuer none trounced as I shal trounce that elf.
He and Iacob are agreed I dare say, I,
Not to come at all, but to suffre me here to die.
Whiche if they doo, they shall finde this same word true,
That after I am dead, my soule shall them pursue.
I wyll be auenged on all foes till I dye.

Yea and take vengeaunce when I am deade too I.
For I mistrust against me agreed they haue:
For thone is but a foole, and thother a starke knaue.

[Enter Iacob.]

[C2v]

Ragau [to Iacob some distance from Esau].
I assure you Iacob, the man is very weake.

Esau.
But hearke once again, me thinke I heare them speake.

Ragau.
I promise you I feare his lyfe be alreadie past.

Iacob.
Mary God forbidde.

[Iacob and Ragau approach Esau.]

Esau.
Loe nowe they come at last.

Ragau.
If ye beleue not me, see your selfe where he is.

Iacob.
Fye brother Esau, what foly is this?
About vaine pastime to wander abroade, and peake,
Til with hunger you make your selfe thus faint & weake.

Esau.
Brother Iacob, I pray you chide now no longer,
But giue me somewhat wherwith to slake mine honger.

Iacob.
Alack brother, I haue in my little cotage,
Nothing but a meale of grosse and homely pottage.

Esau.
Refreshe me therwithall, and boldly aske of me,
The best thing that I haue, what soeuer it be.
I were a very beast, when thou my life doest saue,
If I shoulde sticke with thee for the best thyng I haue.

Iacob.
Can ye be content to sell your birthright to mee?

Esau.
Holde, here is my hande, I doe sell it here to thee.
With all the profites thereof henceforth to be thine,
As free, as full, as large, as euer it was mine.

Iacob.
Then sweare thou hand in hande before the lyuing Lord,
This bargaine to fulfill, and to stande by thy worde.

Esau.
Before the Lord I sweare, to whom eche heart is known
That my birthright that was, from hensforth is thine owne.

Iacob.
Thou shalt also with me by this promise indent,
With this bargaine and sale to holde thy selfe content.

Esau.
If eche penie therof might be worth twentie pounde,
I willingly to thee surrender it this stounde.
And if eche cicle might be worth a whole talent,
I promise with this sale to holde me content.

Iacob.
Come, let vs set him of foote that he may goe sup.

Ragau.
Nay, fyrst I will knowe a thing, ere I helpe him vp.
Sirra, will ye eate folke when ye are long fasting?

Esau.
[C3^r] No, I pray thee helpe me vp, and leaue thy iestyng.

Ragau.
No trow, eate your brother Iacob nowe if you lust.
For you shall not eate me, I tell you, that is iust.

Iacob.
Come, that with my pottage thou mayst refreshed be.

[Iacob and Ragau help Esau to his feet.]

Esau.
There is no meate on earth that so wel liketh me.

Ragau.
Yet I may tell, you, it is potage dearely bought.

Esau.
No not a whitte, for my bargaine take thou no thought.
I defye that birthright that shoulde be of more price,
Than helping of ones selfe, I am not so vnwise.

Ragau.
And how then sir, shall poore Ragau haue no meate?

Esau.
Yes, and if thou canst my brother Iacob intreate.

Iacob.
God graunt I haue inough for Esau alone.

Ragau.
Why then I perceyue poore Ragau shall haue none.

*Esau entring into Iacobs tent [with Iacob]
shaketh Ragau off.*

Well, much good do it you with your potage of Rice:
I woulde fast and fare yll, ere I eate of that price.
Woulde I sell my birthright beyng an eldest sonne?
Forsoth then were it a faire threede that I had sponne.
And then to lette it goe for a mease of pottage,
What is that, but bothe unthriftinesse and dotage?
Alack, alack, good blessed father Isaac,
That euer sonne of thine, shoulde play such a leude knacke.
And yet I doe not thinke but God this thyng hath wrought,
For Iacob is as good as Esau is nought.
But foorth commeth Mido, as fast as he can trot:
For a cicle, whether to call me in or not?

Actus secundi, scæna tertia

Mido the boy. Ragau.

Mido cometh in clapping his hands, and laughing.

Mido.

Ha, ha, ha, ha, ha, ha
Nowe who sawe ere suche an other as Esau!
By my truthe I will not lie to thee Ragau,
Since I was borne, I neuer see any man
So greedily eate rice out of a potte or pan.
He woulde not haue a dishe, but take the pot and sup.
[C3v] Ye neuer sawe hungry dogge so stabbe potage vp.

Ragau.

Why howe did he suppe it? I pray thee tel me how?

Mido.

Mary euen thus, as thou shalte see me doo now.

[Mido mimics Esau eating the pottage.]

Oh I thanke you Iacob: with all my hart Iacob.
Gently done Iacob: A frendely parte Iacob.
I can suppe so Iacob.
Yea than wyll I suppe too Iacob.
Here is good meate Iacob.

Ragau.

As ere was eate Iacob.

Mido.

As ere I sawe Iacob.

Ragau.
Esau a dawe Iacob.
Mido.
Swete rice pottage Iacob.
Ragau.
By Esaus dotage Iacob.
Mido.
Joily good cheere Iacob.
Ragau.
But bought full deere Iacob.
Mido.
I was hungry Iacob.
Ragau.
I was an unthrift Iacob.
Mido.
Ye will none nowe Iacob.
Ragau.
I can not for you Iacob.
Mido.
I will eate all Iacob.
Ragau.
The deuyll go withall Iacob.
Mido.
Thou art a good sonne Iacob.
Ragau.
And would he neuer haue done Iacob?
Mido.
No, but styll cogeld in lik Jacke daw that cries ka kob.
That to be kylde I coulde not laughyng forbeare:
And therfore I came out, I durst not abide there.
Ragau.
Is there any pottage lefte for me that thou wotte?
Mido.
No. I left Esau about to licke the potte.
Ragau.
Lick quod thou? now a shame take him that can all lick.
Mido.
The potte shall nede no washing, he will it so licke.
And by this he is sitting sowne to bread and drinke.
Ragau.
And shal I haue no part with hym, doste thou thinke?
Mido.
No, for he praide Iacob ere he did begin,
To shutte the tent fast that no mo gestes come in.

Ragau.

[C4r] And made he no mention of me his seruant?

Mido.

He sayd thou were a knaue, and bad thee hence, auant.
Go shift where thou couldest, thou gottest nothing there.

Ragau.

God yelde you Esau, with all my stomachere.

Mido.

I must in againe, lest perhaps I be shent,
For I asked no body licence when I went.

Exeat [Mido].

Ragau.

Nay it is his nature, doo what ye can for him,
No thanke at his hand but choose you sinke or swim.
Then reason it with him in a mete time and place,
And he shall be ready to flee straight in your face.
This prouerbe in Esau may be vnderstande:
Clawe a churle by the tayle, and he will file your hand.
Well ywisse Esau, ye did knowe well ynouw
That I had as muche nede to be meated as you.
Haue I trotted and trudged all night and all day,
And now leaue me without dore, and so go your way!
Haue I spent so muche labour for you to prouide,
And you nothing regarde what of me may betide!
Haue I runne with you while I was able to go,
And now you purchase foode for your selfe and no mo!
Haue I taken so long paine you truly to serue,
And can ye be content that I famishe and sterue?
I must lackey and come lugging greyhound and hound
And carry the weight I dare say of twentie pound,
And to helpe his hunger purchasse grace and fauour,
And now to be shutte out fasting for my labour.
By my faith I may say, I serue a good maister,
Nay nay, I serue an ill husband and a waster.
That neither profite regardeth nor honestie,
What meruaile I then if he passe so light on me!
But Esau nowe that ye haue solde your birthright,
I commende me to you, and god geue you good night.
And let a friend tell him his faute at any time,
Ye shall heare him chafe beyonde all reason or rime.
Except it were a fiende or a verie helhounde,
Ye neuer sawe the matche of him in any grounde.
[C4v] When I shewe him of good will what others do say,

He wil fall out with me, and offer me a fray.
And what can there be a worser condition,
Than to doe yll, and refuse admonition!
Can suche a one prosper, or come to a good ende?
Then I care not howe many children God me sende.
Once Esau shall not beguile me, I can tell:
Except he shall fortune to amende, or doe well.
Therfore why doe I about hym wast thus much talke,
Whome no man can induce ordinately to walke?
But some man perchaunce doth not a little wonder,
Howe I who but right nowe did rore out for hunger,
Haue nowe so muche vacant and voyde time of leasure,
To walke and to talke, and discourse all of pleasure.
I tolde you at the fyrst, I woulde prouide for one:
My mother taught me that lesson a good whyle agone.
When I came to Iacob his friendshyp to require,
I drewe nere and nere tyl I came to the fyre.
There harde besyde me stode the potage pot,
Euen as God would haue it, neither colde not hot,
Good simple Iacob coulde not tourne his backe so thicke,
But I at the ladell got a goulpe or a licke.
So that ere I went I made a very good meale.
And dynde better cheape than Esau a good deale.
But here commeth nowe maister Esau forth.

Actus secundi, Scæna quarta.

Esau. and Ragau.

[Enter Esau.]

Esau.

Ah sir, when one is hungry, good meat is much worth.
And well fare a good brother yet in time of neede,
He commeth forth wiping his mouth.

The worlde is now merely well amended in deede.
By my truth if I had bidden from meate any longer,
I thinke my very mawe would haue frette asonder.
[D1r] Then had I bene dead and gone I make God a vowe.

Ragau [aside].

Surely then the world had had a great losse of you.
For where should we haue had your felow in your place?

Esau.
What shold I haue done with my birthright in this case.

Ragau [aside].
Kept it still, and ye had not bene a very asse.

Esau.
But the best pottage it was yet that euer was.
It were sinne not to sell ones soule for such geare.

Ragau [aside].
Ye haue done no lesse in my conscience I feare.

Esau.
Who is this that standeth clattering at my backe?

Ragau.
A poore man of yours sir, that doth his dinner lacke.

Esau.
Dinner whoreson knaue! dinner at this time a day?
Nothing with thee, but dinner and mounching alway.
Why thou whoreson villain slaue, who is hungry now?

Ragau.
In dede syr (as seemeth by your wordes) not you.

Esau.
A man were better fyll the bellies of some twelfe,
Than to fill the gutte of one such whoreson elfe,
That doth none other good but eate and drink and slepe.

Ragau [aside].
He shall do some thing els whom ye shall haue to kepe.

Esau.
And that maketh thee so slouthfull and so lyther,
I dare saie he was sire houres comming hither,
When I sent him to make prouision afore,
Not passing a myle hence or very litle more.
And yet being so farre past the houre of dining,
See and the knaue be not for his dinner whining.
Fast a while, fast with a mischiefe greedy slaue,
Must I prouide meate for euery glutton knaue?

Ragau [aside].
I may fast for any meate that of you I haue.

Esau.
Or deserue thy dinner before thou do it craue.

Ragau.
If I haue not deserued it at this season,
I shall neuer deserue it in mine owne reason.
Ye promised I should eate tyll I cried hoe.

Esau.
Yea that was if we toke either hare, tegge, or Doe.

Ragau.
But when your selfe were hungry, ye said I wot what.
Esau.
What thou villaine slaue, tellest thou me now of that?
Ragau.
[D1^{v}] Then, helpe, runne apace, Ragau my good seruant.
Esau.
Yea then was then, now is it otherwise: auaunt.
Haue I nothing to do but prouide meate for you?
Ragau.
Ye might haue geuen me som part when ye had ynough.
Esau.
What, of the red rice pottage with Iacob I had?
What, the crow would not geue it hir bird, thou art mad
Is that meate for you? nay it would make you to ranke.
Nay soft brother mine, I must kepe you more lanke.
It hath make me euen since so lusty and freshe,
As though I had eaten all delicates of fleshe.
I fele no maner faintnesse wherof to complaine.
Ragau.
Yet to morow ye must be as hungry againe,
Then must ye and will ye wishe againe for good chere:
And repent you that euer ye bought this so dere.
Esau.
Repent me? wherefore, then the Lorde geue me sorow,
If it were to do, I would do it to morow.
For thou foolish knaue, what hath Iacob of me bought?
Ragau.
But a matter of a strawe, and a thing of nought.
Esau.
My birthright and whole title of mine eldership.
Mary sir I pray God much good do it his maship,
If I die to morow, what good would it do me?
If he die to morow, what benefite hath he?
And for a thing hanging on suche casualtie:
Better a mease of pottage than nothing pardy.
If my father liue long, when should I it enioye?
If my father die soone, then is it but a toye.
For if the time were come, thinkest thou that Iacob,
Should finde Esau such a loute or such a lob,
To suffer him to enioy my birthright in rest?
Nay, I wil fyrst tosse him and trounce him of the beste,
I thinke to finde it a matter of conscience,
And Iacob first to haue a fart syr reuerence.

When my father Isaac shall the matter know:
He will not let Iacob haue my birthright I trow.
Or if he should kepe it as his owne, I pray you,
Might not I liue without it and doo wel ynow?
[D2r] Do none but mennes eldest sonnes prosper well?
How liue yonger brethren then, I beseche you tell?
Once, if any thing be by the sword to be got:
This falchion and I will haue part to our lot.
But now come on, go we abroade a while and walke,
Let my birthright go, and of other matters talke.

Ragau.

Who? I walk? nay I trow not, til I haue better dinde.
It is more time to seeke where I may some meate finde.

Esau.

What saist thou drawlatch? come forth with a mischeef.
Wilt thou not go with me? on forward whoreson theef.
Shall it be as pleaseth you, or as pleaseth me?

Ragau.

Nay as pleaseth you syr, me thinke it must be.

Esau.

And where be my dogs? and my hound? be they all wel?

Ragau.

Better than your man, for they be in their kenell.

Esau.

Then go see all be well in my parte of the tent.

Ragau.

With a right good will syr, I go incontinent.

Esau.

And I will to my fielde the which I clensed last,
To see what hope there is, that it will yelde fruite faste.

[Exit Esau and Ragau.]

Actus secundi, scæna [quinta]

Iacob. Mido. Rebecca. Abra, the handmayde.

[Enter Iacob and Mido.]

Iacob.

Thou knowest litle Mido where my mother is.

Mido.

I can go to hir as streight as a threde, and not misse.

Iacob.

Go cal hir, and come againe with her thine owne selfe.

Mido.

Yes, ye shall see me scudde like a litle elfe.

[Mido fetches Rebecca.]

Iacob.

Where I haue by the enticement of my mother,
Bargained and boughte the birthrighte of my brother:
Tourne it all to good O Lorde, if it be thy wyll:
Thou knowest my heart Lord, I did it for no ill.
And what euer shall please thee to worke or to do,
Thou shalt finde me prest and obedient therto.
But here is my mother Rebecca now in place.

[Enter Mido with Rebecca and Abra.]

Mido.

How say you master Iacob, ranne not I apace?

Iacob.

[D2v] Yes, and a good sonne to go quicke on your errand.

Rebecca.

Sonne how goeth the matter? let me understand.

Iacob.

Forsooth mother, I did so as ye me bade,
Esau to sell me all his birthright persuade.

Rebecca.

Hast thou bought it in dede, and he therwith content?

Iacob.

Yea, and haue his promise that he will neuer repent.

Rebecca.

Is the bargaine through? hast thou paid him his price?

Iacob.

Yea that I haue, a mease of red pottage of rice,
And he eate it vp euery whit well I wotte.

Mido.

When he had supte vp all, I sawe him licke the potte.

[Mido mimics Esau.]

Thus he licked, and thus he licked, and this way.
I thought to haue lickt the potte my selfe once to day.
But Esau beguilde me, I shrewe him for that,
And left not so muche as a licke for pusse our catte.

Rebecca.

Sonne Iacob, forasmuche as thou hast so well sped,
With an himne or psalme let the Lord be praised.
Sing we all together, and geue thankes to the Lord,
Whose promise and performaunce do so wel accord.

Mido.

Shal we sing the same himne that al our house
doth sing?
For Abraham and his seede to geue God praising.

Rebecca.

Yea the very same.

Mido.

Then must we all knele downe thus,
And Abra our maide here muste also sing with vs,
Knele downe Abra, what I say, will ye not knele downe?
Knele when I bid you, the slackest wench in this towne.

Here they knele doune to sing all foure, sauing that Abra is slackest, and Mido is quickest.

The firste song.

Blessed be thou, O the God of Abraham,
For thou art the Lord our God, and none but thou:
What thou workest to the glory of thy name,
Passeth mannes reason to searche what way or how.
Thy promise it was Abraham should haue seede,
More than the starres of the skie to be tolde,
He beleued and had Isaac in deeded
[D3r] *When both he and Sara seemed very olde.*
Isaac many yeres longed for a sonne,
Rebecca thy handmaid long time was barraine,
By prayer in thy sight such fauour he wonne,
That at one birth she brought him forth sons twaine,
Wherfore O Lorde, we do confesse and beleue,
That both thou canst and wilt thy promise fulfill:
But how it shall come we can no reason geue,
Saue all to be wrought according to thy will.
Blessed be thou O God of Abraham. etc.

Rebecca.

Now dout not Iacob, but God hath appointed thee
As the eldest sonne vnto Isaac to bee:
And now haue no dout, but thou art sure elected,
And that vnthrift Esau of God reiected.

And to sell thee his birthright since he was so madde,
I warrant thee the blessing that he should haue had.

Iacob.

Yea? how may that be wrought?

Rebecca.

Yes, yes, let me alone.
Ones good olde Isaac is blinde, and can not see,
So that by policie he maye beguiled bee.
I shall deuise howe, for no yll intent, ne thought,
But to bring to passe that I know god wil haue wrought
And I charge you twaine, Abra, and litle Mido.

Mido.

Nay ye should haue set Mido before Abra, trow.
For I am a man toward, and so is not she.

Abra.

No but yet I am more woman toward than ye.

Rebecca.

I charge you both that what euer hath bene spoken,
Ye do not to any liuing body open.

Abra.

For my parte it shall to no body vttered be.

Mido.

And slit my tongue, if euer it come out for me:
But if any tell, Abra here, will be pratling.
For they say, women will euer be clattering.

Abra.

There is none here that pratleth so much as you.

Rebecca.

No mo words, but hence we altogether now,

exeant omnes [Rebecca, Iacob, Mido, and Abra].

[D3v]

Actus tertij, scæna prima.

Esau. Isaac. Mido.

[Enter Esau.]

Esau.

Now since I last saw mine olde father Isaac,
Both I do thinke it long, and he will iudge me slack

Enter Isaac led by Mido.]

But he commeth forth, I will here listen and see,
Whether he shall chaunce to speake any worde of me.

Isaac.

On leade me forth Mido, to the benche on this hand,
That I may sitte me downe, for I can not long stand.

Mido.

Here syr this same way, and ye be at the benche now,
Where ye may sit doune in gods name if please you.

[Isaac sits on the bench.]

Isaac.

I maruel where Esau my sonne doth become,
That he doth now of daies visite me so seldome.
But it is oft sene whome fathers do best fauour,
Of them they haue lest loue againe for their labour.
I thinke since I saw him it is a whole weeke.
In faith litle Mido I would thou wouldest him seeke.

Mido.

Forsoth maister Isaac, and I knew it where,
It should not be very long ere I would be there.
But shall I at aduenture go seeke where he is?

[Esau approaches Isaac.]

Esau.

Seeke no farther Mido, already here he is.

Isaac.

Me thinketh I haue Esau his voice perceiued.

Esau.

Ye gesse truly father, ye are not deceiued.

Mido.

Here he is come now inuisible by my soule:
For I saw him not till he spake harde at my poule,

Isaac.

Now go thou in Mido, let vs twoo here alone.

Mido.

Sir if ye commaund me, full quickely I am gone.

Isaac.

Yet and if I call thee, see thou be not slacke.

Mido.

I come at the first call, good maister Isaac.

[Exit Mido.]

Privilegium regale super libertatibus magistrorum et scolarium parisiensium.

In nomine domini amen. Philippus dei gratia francorum rex. Noverint universi pre- 12
sentes pariter et futuri quod propter enorme illud flagicium quo per scelera simul et la-
ici quinque nostro a quibus malefactores interfecti fuit clerici iusticiam facientes quod
thomam illum tunc prepositum de quo super omnes alios scolares conquesti fuit quod fecit ne-
gat in perpetuo vinculis detinebimus in arta custodia et paupere victu quamdiu vixerit
nisi forte elegerit parisius publice aque subire iudicium in quo si ceciderit dampnatus erit.

by
Astrik L. Gabriel

The front page of the dust jacket depicts the body of the University of Paris kneeling before Phillip Augustus, King of France (1180-1223). He is shown handing over the charter of royal privileges dated July ? 1200. (Paris B.N.N. a Lat. 2060, fol. 55 recto XIV century).

The Paris Studium comprehends nine studies linked by a single theme putting emphasis on the international character of the mediaeval and the renaissance University of Paris. A.L. Gabriel, the author recalls the intellectual ties of the *Paris Studium* with other great Universities, first in German speaking territories: Vienna, Heidelberg, Cologne, Erfurt, Leipzig, Greifswald, Rostock, Basel, Freiburg im Br., Ingolstadt, Tübingen and Wittenberg, then in the Low Countries, Louvain (Leuven), finally in the Kingdom of Poland contacts with the University of Cracow were recorded.

The predilection of Paris masters to recruit and welcome students from *terra aliena* was early professed by Robert of Sorbonne, the founder of the "College of Poor Students", an institution named later on after him. In October, 1266 he accepted the donation and Arnoldus Foykini from Hague (prior 1462), Johannes de Lapide (prior 1468 and 1470-71) diocese of Speyer. The college hailed among its ranks of fellows (socii) the German Johannes Gaisser from Grönenbach and Gervasius Wain from Memmingen.

In Chapter I Gabriel outlined the spiritual portrait of *Robert of Sorbonne*, explained his country origin, and revealed his facility for using popular proverbs and analyzed his moral treatises. In Chapter II the motives of *Migration of Paris Students and Masters* to other universities is explained within the framework of their philosophical background according to their training in realism or nominalism, in the *via antiqua* or *via moderna*. The history of the *House of Poor German Students* from the XIVth to the beginning of the XVIth century is told in Chapter III. It includes a new discovery about a Czech student, who lived in the House where he copied the works of Johannes Versorius (died after 1482). *The Intellectual Contacts between the University of Louvain (Leuven) and Paris* during the XVth century is told in Chapter IV and the contacts with Cracow are related in Chapter V. A survey of German speaking *Officers at the English-German Nation at the University of Paris:* the list of elected "receptors" or treasures, "proctors" legal heads of the Nation, and "reformators" or supervisors of the discipline in Paris colleges is given in Chapter VI. The intellectual portraits of three outstanding subjects of the same Nation were depicted in the three final chapters, *Georgius Wolff*, famous German printer, studied at the Univer-

Isaac.
Sonne Esau.
Esau.
Here father.
Isaac.
Is none here but we?
Esau.
None to herken our talke father, that I doo see.

[Enter Rebecca unseen and listening.]

Isaac.
Sonne Esau, why hast thou bene from me so long?
Esau.
I cry you mercy father, if I haue done wrong.
[D4r] But I am loth to trouble you hauing nothing
To present you withall, nor veneson to bring.
Isaac.
Sonne Esau, thou knowest that I do thee loue.
Esau.
I thancke you for it father as doth me behoue.
Isaac.
And now thou seest my dayes draw towardes an ende.
Esau.
That is to me great ruth if I coulde it amende.
Isaac.
I must go the way of all mortall fleshe.
Therfore while my memory and witte is yet freshe,
I woulde thee endow mine heritage to succeede:
And blisse thee, (as I ought) to multiply my seede.
The God of my father Abraham, and of me,
Hath promised, that our seede as the sande shal be.
He is a God of truth, and in his wordes iust.
Therfore in my workyng shall be no faute I trust.
Now therfore sonne Esau, get thee forth to hunte,
With thy bowe and quiuer, as erst thou hast bene wont,
Bring me of thy venison that is good.
Esau.
Ye shall haue of the best that runneth in the wood.
Isaac.
When thou commest home, to dresse it, it shall behoue:
And to make for mine owne tooth such meate as I loue.
Thus doo mine owne dere sonne, and then I shal thee kisse
With the koosse of peace, and thee for euer blisse.

Esau.

Your will t'accomplishe moste dere father Isaac,
With all good hast and spede, I shall not be found slack.

Isaac.

Then helpe lead me home, in my tente that I were set.
And then go when thou wilt.

Esau.

I shall withouten lette.

[Exit Isaac and Esau.]

Actus tertij, scæna secunda.

Rebecca.

Rebecca.

This talke of Isaac in secrete haue I heard.
And what end it should come to my hert is afeard.
Nere had I so muche ado to forbeare to speake.
But the Lorde (I trust) will Isaacs purpose breake.

Here she kneleth doune and prayeth.

[D4v] O God of Abraham, make it of none effecte:
Let Iacob haue the blessing whom thou hast elect.
I for my part shall worke what may be wrought,
That it may to Iacob from Esau be brought,
And in will I go to see what I can deuise,
That Isaacs intent may fayle in any wise.

[Exit Rebecca.]

Actus tertij, Scæna tertia.

Ragau. Esau.

[Enter Ragau.]

Ragau.

Nay, we must on hunting go, yet once more again

Here he commeth forth with hunting staffe and others and a bag of vitailes.

And neuer com home now except we spede certain
But I trowe for hunger I haue prouided here:
That what euer befall, I Ragau shall haue chere.
I haue no time to tell what delicates here be,
But (thinke this to be true) for better men than me.
And what? shall Esau hereof haue any parte?
Nay I trust to conueigh it by such prety arte,
That till the bag be clere, he shal it neuer see.
I shall, and if he faint, feede him as he fedde me.
I shall requite his shutting me out of the dore.
That if he bidde me runne to get him meat afore,
I shall runne as fast as my feet were made of leade,
And tell him, there is none, though I may wel be spead.
I will be euen with him for my fare last day
When he was with Iacob.

[Enter Esau behind Ragau.]

Esau.

What is it that thou doest say?

Ragau.

Sir on your behalfe I earnestly wishe and pray,
That if like nede chaunce, ye may fare as last day
When ye were with Iacob.

Esau.

Well, come on, let vs go.

Ragau.

Euen when ye will, is there let in me or no!

Exeant ambo [Esau and Ragau].

[E1r]

Actus quarti, scæna prima.

Rebecca. Iacob.
[Enter Rebecca and Iacob.]

Rebecca.

Sonne Iacob euen now is come the very houre,
That if thou haue any grace or hearte or power,
To play thy parte well, and sticke vnto it throughout,
Esau his blessing will be thine without dout.

Iacob.

Mother I know your good will to be vnfained:
But I see not which waye the thing may be attained.

Rebecca.

I haue it contrived how all thing shall be done,
Do thou as I shall bid thee, and it will be wonne.

Iacob.

Mother in me shall be no faulte or negligence.

Rebecca.

Then herken very well vnto this my sentence.
I hearde olde Isaac in a long solempne talke,
Bid thy brother Esau to the fielde to walke,
And there with his bowe to kill him some venison,
Which brought and dressed, he to haue his benison.
For I am aged (sayd Isaac) truly:
And would blesse thee dere sonne before that I dye.
Now is Esau gone to do it euen so.
But while he is away, I would haue thee to go,
Abroade vnto the flocke, and set me kiddes twain.
Of which I shall with a trice make such meate certain,
As shall say come eate me, and make olde Isaac
Licke his lippes therat, so toothsom shall it smacke.
I shall make him therof such as he doth loue,
Which in thy brothers steede to blisse thee shall him moue.

Iacob.

O swete and dere mother, this deuise is but vaine,
For Esau is rough, and I am smothe certaine.
And so when I shal to my father bring this meate,
Perchaunce he will feele me, before that he will eate.
Old men be mistrustfull: he shall the matter take,
That I went about my father a foole to make.
Mother by such a pranck the matter will be wurse:
And I in stede of blissing shal purchase me his curse.

Rebecca.

On me be thy curse my sonne, let it light on me.
[E1v] Only set thou the kiddes hither, as I bid thee.
Doo thou thy true deuoire, and let God worke therein.

Iacob.

Upon your worde mother, I will the thing begin,
Send me litle Mido to helpe me beare a kidde.

Rebecca.

He shal come by and by, for so I shall him bidde.
Now lord, & if thou please, that this thing shall take place,
Further this our enterprise, helping with thy grace.

[Exit Rebecca and Iacob.]

Actus quarti, scæna secunda.

[Enter Iacob with Mido following behind.]

Mido.

Are ye here maister Iacob? I came you to looke:
And here dame Rebecca hath sent you your shepecroke
And hath commaunded me to wayte on you this day,
But wherfore or why, she woulde nothing to me say.

Iacob.

Come on then, folow me Mido a litle wayes.

Mido.

Whether ye shall leade me, I am at all assayes.

Iacob.

And art thou able to beare a kidde on thy backe?

Mido.

I am able (I trowe) to beare a quarter sacke.
How say you to this corps? is it not fat and round?
How say ye to these legges? come they not to the ground?
And be not here armes able your matter to spede?
Be not here likely shoulders to do such a deede?
Therfore come maister Iacob, if this your dout be,
For bringing home of kiddes, lay the biggest on me,
So that if we make a feast, I may haue some parte.

Iacob.

Yes that shalt thou Mido, right worthy thou art.

[Exit Mido and Iacob.]

Actus quarti, scæna tertia.

Rebecca. Abra.
[Enter Rebecca.]

Rebecca.

I come to see if Iacob be gone a fielde yet,
A litle slacking may all our purpose let.
But now that he is gone, he will be here at once.
Therfore I will call my maide Abra for the nonce,
That all thing within may be in a redinesse.

Abra, where be ye Abra?

Abra [offstage].

Here within maistresse.

Rebecca.

[E2r] Come forth: when? Abra, what Abra I say.

Abra.

Anone.

[Enter Abra.]

Rebecca.

Must I call so oft? why come ye not by and by?

Abra.

I was washing my vessell forsooth maistresse I.

Rebecca.

And in very deede, looke that all your vessell be clene.

Abra.

There is not one foule peece in all our tent I wene,

Rebecca.

Then make a great fyre, and make redy your pot
And see there be plenty of water colde and hotte.
And see the spitte be scoured as cleane as any pearle.

Abra.

If this be not quickly done cal me noughtie gyrle.

Rebecca.

Nay, soft, whither away! I haue not yet all done.

Abra.

I thought ye would haue had me as quicke to be gone,
As when ye call Abra, ye would haue me to come.

Rebecca.

Than see ye haue made redy cloaues, mace, and sinamom
Peper and saffron, then set hearbes for the potte,

Abra.

We will haue the best that by me can be got.

Rebecca.

And let no foule corner be about all the tent.

Abra.

If ye find any fault, hardly let me be shent.
Is there any thing else but that I may go now?

Rebecca.

Nought, but that when I come I finde no faut in you.

Abra.

No I warrant you, I will not let my matters slepe.

Rebecca.

Any good wenche will at hir dames bidding take kepe.
Now God of Abraham, as I trust in thy grace,

Sende Iacob the blissing in Esau his place.
As thou hast ordeyned right so must all thing be.
Performe thine own wordes lord which thou spakest to me.
Now will I go in to see that mine olde husband,
May of my secrete working nothing understand.
Or in case he smell what we haue thus farre begonne,
He may thinke it all for Esau to be done.

[Exit Rebecca.]

Actus quarti, scæna quarti.

Abra the mayde, Deborra, the nourse,
[Enter Abra.]

Abra.

He that were now within, should find all thing I wene,
As trimme as a trencher, as tricke, as swete, as cleane.
And seing that my dame prepareth suche a feast,
I will not I trow be found such a sluttishe beast,
[E2v] That there shall any filthe about our tent be kepte,
But that both within and without it shall bee swepte.

*Then let her sweepe with a brome, and while she
doth it, sing this song, and when she hath song,
let her say thus*

The second song.
It hath bene a prouerbe before I was borne,
Yong doth it pricke that wyll be a thorne.
Who will be euill, or who will be good,
Who geuen to truth or who to falshood,
Eche bodies youth sheweth a great likelihood.
For yong doth it pricke that will be a thorne.
Who so in youth will no goodnesse embrace.
But folow pleasure, and not vertues trace,
Great meruaile it is if such come to grace.
For yong doth it pricke that will be a thorne.
Suche as in youth will refuse to be tought,
Or will be slacke to worke as he ought,
When they come to age, their proofe will be nought.
For yong doth it pricke that will be a thorne.
If a childe haue bene giuen to any vice,

Except he be guided by such as be wyse,
He will therof all his lyfe haue a spice.
For yong doth it pricke that will be thorne.
It hath bene a prouerbe. etc

Abra.

Now haue I done, and as it should be for the nonce,
My sweeping and my song are ended both at once.
Now but for fetting mine herbes I might go play.
Deborra nurse Deborra, a worde I you pray.

[Enter Deborra.]

Deborra.

What is the matter? Who calleth me Deborra?

Abra.

Forsoth gentle nourse euen I litle Abra,
I pray you sweete Deborra take in this same brome,

[Abra hands Deborra the broom.]

And looke well to all thing till I returne home:
I must to the gardine as fast as I can trotte,
As I was commaunded to fet hearbes for the potte.
But in the meane time, I pray you nourse looke about
And see well to the fyre that it go not out,
I will aumble so fast, that I will soone be there,
And here again I trow, ere an horse licke his eare.

[Exit Abra.]

[E3r]
Deborra.

There is not a pretier gyrle within this mile,
Than this Abra will be within this litle while.
As true as any stele: ye may trust her with gold.
Though it were a bushell, and not a peny tolde.
As quicke about her worke that must be quickly spead
As any wenche in twenty mile about her head.
As fine a peece it is as I knowe but a few,
Yet perchaunce her husbande of her maye haue a shrewe.
Cat after kinde (saith the prouerbe) swete milke wil lap,
If the mother be a shrew, the daughter can not scape.
Once our marke she hath, I maruell if she slippe:
For hir nose is growing aboue hir ouer lippe.
But it is time that I into the tent be gone.
Lest she come and chide me, she will come now anone.

[Exit Deborra.]

Actus quarti, scæna quinta.

Abra.

[Enter Abra.]

Abra.

How say ye? haue not I dispatched me quickely?
A straw for that wenche that doth not somwhat likely,
I haue brought here good herbes, & of them plenty
To make both broth and farcing, and that full deinty,
I trust to make such broth, that when all things are in,
God almighty selfe may wet his finger therein.
Here is time and percelie, spinache, and rosemary.
Endiue, suckorie, lacteux, violette, clary,
Liuerworte, marigolde, sorell, hartes tong, and sage:
Peniryal, purselane, buglosse and borage,
With many very good herbes mo than I do name.
But to tary here thus long, I am muche to blame,
For if Iacob should come, I not in readinesse:
I must of couenaunt be shent of our maistresse.
And I would not for twenty pounde I tell ye,
That any pointe of default should be found in me.

[Exit Abra.]

Actus quarti, scæna sexta.

Rebecca. Mido. Iacob.

[E3v] *[Enter Rebecca.]*

Rebecca.

I come to see if Iacob do not returne yet,
I can not maruell enough what should be his let,
And greatly wonder he is away thus long.
I feare much of his absence, lest som thing be wrong.
As well as hearte can wishe all thing is ready here.
And now to me eche moment semeth a whole yere.
But hearke, me thinketh I here a yong kidde blee

[The kid bleets offstage.]

It is so in deede, I see Iacob, well is mee.

[Enter Mido and Iacob with the kid.]

Mido.

Hearke maister Iacob, hearde ye euer kidde blea so!
I wene she knoweth afore hande wherto she shall go.

Iacob.

I would not my father Isaac should heare:

Mido.

Nay, she will scarsly be stil, when she is dead, I do feare.

Iacob.

But loe I see my mother stande before the tent.

Rebecca.

O Lord, me thinketh long sonne Iacob since thou went.

Iacob.

And me thinketh mother, we haue hyed vs well:

Mido.

I haue made many feete to folowe, I can tell.

Rebecca.

Geue me thy kidde my sonne, and nowe leat me alone,
Bring thou in thine Mido, and see thou bee a stone.

Mido.

A stone? howe shoulde that be maistresse? I am a lad:
And a boy aliue, as good as ere ye had:

[Mido fetches and brings his kid to Rebecca.]

And nowe in bringyng home this kyd I haue I trow,
Tried my selfe a man, and a preatie fellow,

Rebecca.

I ment thou shouldest nothing saye.

Mido.

One warning is enough, ye bad vs so last day.

Rebecca.

Well let me go in, and venison hereof make:

Iacob.

And hearest thou Mido? see that good hede thou take,
In any wise to come in my fathers sight.

Mido.

Why he seeth no better at noone than at midnight.
Is he not blinde long since, and dooth his eyes lacke?
Therfore go in dame, I beare an heauy packe.

Rebecca.

I leaue you here Iacob, and hartely you pray,

That when neede shall require, you be not farre away.

Iacob.

I shall be ready mother, when so ere you call.

[Exit Rebecca with the two kids.]

Actus quarti, scæna septima.

Iacob. Mido.

[E4r]

Iacob.

O how happy is that same daughter or that sonne,
Whome the parentes loue with harty affection.
And among all others howe fortunate am I,
Whome my mother Rebecca tendreth so greatly!
If it lay in her to do any good ye see,
She would do her earnest deuoire to preferre me.
But as for this matter which she doth now intende,
Without thy aide O Lorde, howe should it come to ende.
Neuerthelesse forasmuche as my said mother,
Worketh upon thy worde O Lorde, and none other,
It shall become me to shewe mine obedience,
And to thy promise O Lorde, to giue due credence.
For what is so possible to mans iudgement,
Which thou canst not with a beck performe incontinent?
Therfore thy will O Lord, be done for euermore.

Mido.

Oh Iacob, I was neuer so afearde afore.

Iacob.

Why what newe thing is chaunced Mido, I pray thee?

Mido.

Old Isaac your father, hearde your yong kidde blea.
He asked what it was, and I said, a kidde.
Who brought it from the folde, I said you did.
For what purpose? forsoth syr saide I,
There is some matter that Iacob would remedy:
And where hast thou ben so long litle Mido, quod he,
That all this whole houre thou wert not once with me?
Forsooth (quod I) when I went from you last of all,
You bade me be no more but be ready at your call.

Iacob.

But of the kiddes bleayng he did speake no more.

Mido.

No, but and if he had called me afore,
I must haue told him al, or els I must haue made a lye,
Which woulde not haue bene a good boyes part truely.
But I will to him, and no longer here remaine,
Lest he should happen to call for Mido againe.

[Exit Mido.]

Actus quarti, scæna octaua.

Iacob. Rebecca. Deborra.
]

Iacob.

I were best also to get me into the tent,
[E4v] That if my mother neede me, I may be present.
But I see hir come forth, and nourse Deborra also,
And bring geare with them what so ere it shall do.

*[Enter Rebecca with Deborra,
carrying a collar and sleeves made of kid's hair,
and a garment belonging to Esau.]*

Rebecca.

Where is my sonne Iacob? I do him now espie.
Come apace Deborra, I pray thee let vs hye,
That all thing were dispatched somwhat to my minde.

Deborra.

It is happy that Iacob ready here ye finde.

Iacob.

Mother, what haue ye brought? & what things are those?

Rebecca.

Geare that I haue prepared to serue our purpose.
And bicause that Esau is so rough with heare:
I haue brought sleues of kid next to thy skin to weare.
They be made glouelike, and for eche finger a stall:
So that thy fathers feeling soone beguile they shall.

Then haue I brought a coller of roughe kiddes heare,
Fast vnto the skinne round about thy necke to weare.
Come, let me do it on, and if Isaac feele,
He shall therwyth be beguiled wondrous wele.

Here she doth the sleues vpon Iacobs armes.

Iacob.

And what shall this geare do, that ye haue brought?

Rebecca.

It shall serue anon I warraunt you, take no thought.
Now, throughly to rauishe thy father Isaac,
Thou shalt here incontinent put vpon thy backe,
Esau his best apparell, whose fragraunt flauour,
Shall coniure Isaac to beare thee his fauour.

Deborra.

Mary sir now is maister Iacob trimme in deede,
That is all triksie and gallaunt so God me speede,
Now I see apparell setteth out a man.
Doth it become Esau so? nay beshrewe me then.

Rebecca.

Ye may now go in nourse, and leaue lookyng on him.

Deborra.

I go, mary sir Iacob is now gay and trim.

[Exit Deborra;] Iacob standeth looking on himselfe.

Iacob.

No forsoth mother, this raiment liketh not me.
I could with mine owne geare better contented be.
And but for satisfying of your minde and will,
I would not weare it, to haue it for mine owne still.
I loue not to weare an other birdes feathers.
Mine owne poore homely geare will serue for all wethers.

Rebecaa.

Well content thy selfe, and folow my minde this day.
[F1r] Now the meate by this time is ready I dare say.
Before that with to much enough it be all spilt,
Take thy time, and assaile thy father when thou wilt.

Iacob.

Yea, but haue ye prouided mother I you pray,
That no body within may your counsaille bewray?

Rebecca.

I warrant the matter all safe from vttering,
I haue stopped all mouthes for once muttering.
Therfore whyle the tyme serueth, I thee warne,
To slacke when all thinges are ready may do harme.

Iacob.

Goe before, & I folow: but my chekes will blushe red,
To be sene among our folke thus apparailed.

[Exit Rebecca with Iacob following.]

Actus quarti, scæna nona.

Isaac. Mido. Iacob.

[Isaac enters and sits on the bench; Mido follows.]

Isaac.
Come Mido, for without thee I can nothing do.

Mido.
What is it syr, that ye would haue my helpe vnto?

Isaac.
Nothing but to sitte abrode, and take th'open aire.

Mido.
That shalbe well done, the weather is very faire,

Isaac.
Praised be the God of my father Abraham.
Who sendeth all thing nedefull for the vse of man,
And most tenderly prouideth he for me Isaac,
Better than I can feele or perceiue what I lacke.

[Enter Iacob disguised as Esau.]

Iacob.
Where is my most dere father? as I would haue it,
Taking the open ayre, here I see him sitte.
O my most deere father Isaac, well thou be.

Isaac.
Here I am my sweete sonne, and who art thou tell me?

Iacob.
Dere father, I am Esau thine eldest sonne,
According as thou baddest me, so haue I done.
Come in dere father, and eate of my venison,
That thy soule may geue vnto me thy benison.

Isaac.
But how hast thou sped so soone? let me vnderstande.

Iacob.
The Lorde thy God at the first brought it to my hande.

Isaac.
And art thou Esau mine elder sonne in deede?

Iacob.
To aske that question father, what dooth it neede?

Isaac.
Come nere that I may feele whether thou be he or not,
For Esau is rough of heare as any goate.

[Iacob approaches Isaac at the bench.]

[F1v] Let me feele thy hande, right Esau by the heare,

And yet the voice of Iacob sowneth in mine eare.
God blesse thee my sonne, and so will I do anone,
As soone as I haue tasted of thy venison.
Come on, leade me in, I will eate a pittance.
A litle thing God wotte to me is suffisance,

[Exit Iacob leading Isaac.]

Mido.

I may now go play, Iacob leadeth Isaac.
But I neuer saw such a prety knacke,
How Iacob beguiled his father, how slightly.
Now I see it true the blinde eate many a flye.
I quaked once for feare lest Iacob would be caught,
But as happe was, he had his lesson well taught.
But what will Esau say, when he commeth home?
Choose him, but for me to go in it is wisedome.

[Exit Mido.]

Actus quarti, scæna decima.

Rebecca. Abra.
[Enter Rebecca.]

Rebecca.

Now I beseche the Lorde prosper Iacob my sonne,
In our hardy enterprise which we haue begonne.
Isaac is eating such meate as he doth loue,
Which thing to blesse Iacob I dout not will him moue:
If he obteyne the blessing as I trust he shall,
Then shall my soule geue to God laude perpetuall.
But I will in to harken how the thing doth frame.

Abra [offstage].

Come in dame Rebecca,

Rebecca.

Who is it that doth me name?

Abra.

My maister Isaac is comming foorth streight way.

Rebecca.

He shall not finde me here in no wise if I may.

Actus quarti, scæna vndecima.

Isaac. Iacob.

[Enter Iacob leading Isaac to the bench.]

Isaac.

Set me down on the bench where thou didst me first find:

[Isaac sits on the bench.]

Now forsooth I haue eate meate euen to my minde.
It hath refreshed my soule wonderfully well.
Nor neuer dranke I better wine that I can tell.

Iacob.

If it were to your liking I am very glad.

[Isaac.]

[F2r] It was the best meat and wine that euer I had.
Come kysse me sonne Esau with the kysse of peace,

Iacob kisseth Isaac:
and then kneleth down to haue his blessing.

That my loue towardes thee may the more increase.
I blesse thee here for euer my sonne in this place,
The Lorde my God of might endue thee with his grace.
What swete flauour my sonnes raiment dooth yelde,
Euen the fragrant smell that commeth from a fielde.
Which the Lord hath blessed, and the same lord blesse thee:
With the dewe of heauen, the Lorde thy ground encrease
That the fatnesse of the earth may neuer cease.
The Lorde send thee abundaunce of corne and wine,
And prosper continually all thing that is thine.
The Lord make great people seruants vnto thee:
And nations to do homage and fealty.
And here to succede my place, mine heyre I thee make,
Of all things that I haue, possession to take.
Lord and ruler be thou ouer thy brethern all,
And bowe to thee as head, thy mothers children shall.
Cursed be that man that shall thee curse or missay:
And who that blesseth thee, blessed be he for aye.
Thus here haue I made my last will and testament,
Which the Lord God ratifie neuer to repent.
Serue the Lord our God, and then wel shalt thou speede,
And he shall kepe promise to multiply thy seede.
My day draweth on, for olde and feeble I am.

When I dye, put me to my father Abraham.
Now kisse me once again my sonne, and then depart,
And enter vpon all wherof now Lorde thou art.

Iacob.

The Lord God reward your fatherly tendernesse.
Which ye haue here shewed me of your mere goodnesse.

Isaac.

Go in peace my dere sonne, leauing me here alone:
And send litle Mido to leade me in anone.

Exeat Iacob.

Lord God when thou shalt see time as thou thinkest best,
Dissolue this feeble carkesse, and take me to thy reste.

[Enter Mido.]

Mido.

How do ye maister Isaac? I am here now.
[F2v] For my maister Iacob did bid me come to you,

Isaac.

Nay boye, it was not Iacob, I dare well say so.

Mido.

Forsooth it was Iacob, if my name be Mido.

Isaac.

If that be a true tale, some body is come slacke,
But lord that haue done, I will not now call backe.
But yet I will go see if I be deceiued:
For in deede me thought Iacobs voyce I perceiued.

[Exit Isaac led by Mido.]

Actus quarti, scæna duodecima

Rebecca.

[Enter Rebecca.] Then she speaketh kneeling, and holding vp her handes.

Rebecca.

O Lorde, the God of Isaac and Abraham,
I render thanks to thee though a sinfull woman.
Bicause of thy worde and promise true arte thou,
In sending Iacob the blessing of Esau.
And for thus regarding a sinner as I am,
I eftsoones thanke thee O Lorde God of Abraham,

Thy mercy and wysedome shall I sing euermore:
And magnifie thy name, for Gods there is no more.
But I will to my husbande Isaac, and see,
That for this matter he take no greefe at me.

[Exit Rebecca.]

Actus quinti, scæna prima.

Ragau.
Ragau bringeth venison at his backe.

Ragau.

Nay, now at last we haue will sped I warrant you:
Good lucke is not euermore against Esau.
He coursed and coursed again with his dogges here:
But they could at no time take either hare or dere.
At last he killed this with his bowe as God wold.
And to say that it is fatte venison be bolde.
But dressed it must be at once in all the haste,
That olde father Isaac may haue his repast.
Then without delay Esau shall blessed be,
Then faith cock on houpe, al is ours, then who but he?
But I must in that it may be drest in time likely,
And I trow ye shall see it made ready quickly.

[Exit Ragau.]

Actus quinti, scæna secunda.

[F3r] Mido.
[Enter Mido.]

Mido.

Nay now olde maister Isaac (I warrant you)
Hath blessed Iacob in the place of Esau.
At home here with vs it is iudged no small change
But a case wonderfull, and also very strange.
The yonger brother is made elder, and againe,
The elder brother must nowe serue the yonger
as his swayne.
And from hensforth we must all make curtesie and bow,

Unto maister Iacob, and not to Esau now:
And Esau him selfe must vnder Iacob bee,
At his commaundement euen as well as we.
But I care not I warrant you: for our householde
Loue Iacob better than Esau twenty folde.
None loueth Esau but for his fathers sake:
But all good folkes are glad Iacobs parte to take.
And now by Esau no man wyll sette a pinne,
But yonder he commeth nowe, I will gette me in.

[Exit Mido.]

Actus quinti, scæna tertia.

Esau.
[Enter Esau.]

Esau.

I trow I haue now wonne my spurres for euer,
For once better venison killed I neuer.
And though it wer somwhat long er I coulde it take,
Yet the goodnesse therof dooth some recompence make.
My father Isaac shall therof haue suche meate,
As in all his life he hath not the better eate.
Whervpon I doubt not, after tender kyssing,
To be streight endowed with his godly blyssing.
As his full and true heire in his place to succeede,
And t'enioye the promise that God made to his seede,
And when I am once in my place of succession,
And haue all maner thinges in full possession:
I shall wring all loutes and make them stoupe (I trowe)
I shall make the slaues couche as lowe as dog to bow.
I shall ruffle among them of an other sort,
Than Isaac hath done, and with an other port.
[F3v] But nowe will I go see what hast within they make
That part of my hunting my olde father may take.

Actus quinti, scæna quarta.

Isaac. Mido. Esau.
[Enter Isaac with Mido following.]

Isaac.

Mido, come Mido, where art thou litle Mido?

Mido.

Here redy maister Isaac, what shall I do?

Isaac.

Come leade me to mine old place, that I may sit doune

Mido.

That can I as well as any boy in this towne.

[Mido leads Isaac to the bench.]

Isaac.

O Lorde my God, how deepe and unsercheable
Are all thy iudgements, and how immutable!
Of thy iustice, whom it pleaseth thee, thou doest reiect,
Of thy mercy, whome pleaseth thee, thou doest electe.
In my two sonnes O Lord, thou hast wrought thy will,
And as thy pleasure hath wrought, so shall it stand still.
Sence thou hast set Iacob in Esau his place:
I committe him to the gouernaunce of thy grace.

[Enter Esau.]

Esau.

Now where is Isaac that he may come and eate?
Lo where he is sitting abroade vpon his seate.
Deare father Isaac, the Lord thy God thee saue.

Isaac.

Who art thou my son? & what thing woldest thou haue?

Esau.

I am your eldest sonne Esau by my name,
Newe come home from hunting, where I had ioyly game,
I haue made meate therof for your owne appetite,
Meate for your owne tooth, wherin ye will much delite.
Come eate your part, dere father, that when ye haue don,
Your soule may blesse me as your heire and eldest son.

Isaac.

Ah Esau, Esau, thou commest to late,
An other to thy blessing was predestinate.
And cleane gone it is from thee Esau.

Esau.

Alas,
Then am I the vnhappiest that euer was,
I would the saluage beastes had my body torne.

Isaac.

The blessing that thou sholdest haue had, an other hath

Esau.

Alas, what wretched villaine hath done me such scath?

Isaac.
Thy brother Iacob came to me by subtiltee.
[F4r] And brought me venison, and so preuented thee.
I eate with him ere thou camst, and with my good will,
Blessed him I haue, and blessed he shall be still.

Esau.
Ah Iacob, Iacob, well may he be called so:
For he hath vndermined me times two.
For first mine heritage he toke away me fro
And see, now hath he awaye my blessing also.
Ah father, father, though Iacob hath done this thing:
Yet let me Esau also haue thy blessing.
Shall all my good huntings for thee be in vaine?

Isaac.
That is done and past, can not be called againe.
Mine act must now stand in force of necessitie.

Esau.
And hast thou neuer a blessing then left for me?

Isaac.
Behold, I haue made thy brother Iacob thy Lord.

Esau.
A most poinant sworde vnto my heart is that word.

Isaac.
All his mothers children his seruantes haue I made.

Esau.
That worde is to me sharper than a rasers blade.

Isaac.
I haue also stablished him with wine and corne.

Esau.
Wo be the day and houre that euer I was borne.

Isaac.
What am I able to do for thee my sonne?

Esau.
Ah Iacob, Iacob, that thou hast me thus vndone.
Oh unhappy happe: oh misfortune, well away,
That euer I should liue to see this wofull day.
But hast thou one blissing and no mo my father?
Let me also haue some blessing good sweete father.

Isaac.
Well, nature pricketh me some remorse on thee to haue.
Behold, thy dwelling place the earthes fatnesse shal haue,
And the dew of heauen whiche doune from aboue shall fall:
And with dinte of sworde thy liuing get thou shall.
And to thy brother Iacob thou shalt be seruant.

Esau.

Oh, to my yonger brother must I be seruant?
Oh, that euer a man should be so oppressed.

Isaac.

Thine owne fault it is that thou art dispossessed.

Esau.

Father, chaunge that piece of thy sentence & iudgement.

Isaac.

Things done can not be vndone, therfore be content,
Let me be in quiet, and trouble me no more.
[F4v] Come Mido, in goddes name leade me in at the dore.

[Exit Isaac led by Mido.]

Esau.

Oh woulde not this chafe a man, and fret his guts out!
To liue as an vnderling vnder such a loute!
Ah hypocrite, ah hedgecreeper, ah sembling wretche:
I will be euen with thee for this subtill fetche.
O God of Abraham, what reason is herein,
That to slea ones enimy it should be made sinne?
Were not one as good his part of heauen forgoe,
As not to be reuenged on his deadly foe?
God was angry with Caim for killing Abell:
Els might I kill Iacob meruellously well.
I may fortune one day him to dispatche and ridde:
The Lord will not see all things, some thing may be hid.
But as for these misers within my fathers tent,
Which to the supplanting of me put their consent,
Not one, but I shal coyle them till they stinke for pain,
And then for their stinking, coyle them of freshe again.
I will take no daies, but while the matter is hotte,
Not one of them shall scape but they shall to the potte.

[Exit Esau.]

Actus quinti, scæna quinta.

Ragau.
[Enter Ragau.]

Ragau.

Where are we now become? marie syr here is araye,
With Esau my maister this is a blacke daye.

I told you, Esau one day woulde shite a ragge,
Haue not we well hunted, of blessing to come lagge?
Nay I thought euer it would come to suche a passe,
Since he solde his heritage like a very asse.
But in faith some of them I dare ieopard a grote,
If he may reache them, will haue on the peticote.

Actus quinti, scæna sexta.

Esau. Ragau. Abra. Mido.
[Enter Esau]

Esau.
Come out whores & theues, come out, come out I say.

Ragau [aside to the audience].
I told you, did I not? that there would be a fray?

Esau.
[G1r] Come out litle whoreson ape, come out of thy denne.

Mido.
Take my lyfe for a peny, whether shall I renne?

Esau.
Come out thou litle fende, come out thou skittish Gill.
[Enter Abra, Mido, and Deborra.]

Abra.
Out alas, alas, Esau will vs all kill.

Esau.
And come out thou mother Mab, out olde rotten witche,
As white as midnightes arsehole, or virgin pitche.
Where be ye? come together in a cluster.

Ragau.
In faith and these three wil make a noble muster.

Esau.
Ere ye escape my fingers, ye shall all be tought.
For these be they which haue all this against me wrought.

Mido.
I wrought not a stroke this day but led Isaac.
If I wrought one stroke to day, lay me on the iacke.

Esau.
Hence then, get thee in, and do against me no more.

Mido.
I care as muche for you now, as I did before.

Esau.
What sayest thou litle theefe? if I may thee catche,

Mido.
Ye shall runne apace then I wene, so God me snatche.

[Exit Mido.]

Ragau.
Now to go Mido, or thou art caught in a trippe,

Esau.
Nay for his sake, Abra, ye shall drinke of the whippe.

Abra.
Nay for Gods loue good sweete maister Esau,
Hurt not me for Mido: speake for me Ragau.

Ragau.
Sir spare litle Abra, she hath done none euill.

Esau.
A litle fiende it is, and will be a right deuill,
And she is one of them that loue not me a deale.

Abra.
If ye let me go, I will loue you very wele.

Esau.
And neuer any more ado against me make?

Abra.
Ragau shalbe surety.

Ragau.
Sir I vndertake.

Esau.
Then hence out of my sight at once, and get thee in.

Abra.
Adew, I set not a strawe by you nor a pinne.

[Exit Abra.]

Esau.
What saiest thou thou Tib! once ye shal haue a rappe.

Ragau.
The best ende of suretiship is to get a clappe,

Esau.
Now come on thou olde heg, what shal I say to thee?

Deborra.
Say what ye lust, so ye do not touche me.

Esau.
Yes, and make powder of thee, for I dare say, thou,
Hast bene the cause of all this feast to Esau.

Deborra.
[G1v] No it was Iacobs feast that I did helpe to dresse.

Esau.

Nay I thought such a witche would do such businesse.

Deborra.

But by my truth if I should dye incontinent,
I knew not of the purpose wherfore it was ment.

Esau.

But wilt thou tell me truth if I do forgeue thee?

Deborra.

Yea if I can maister Esau, beleue me.

Esau.

Is it true that when I and my brother were first borne,
And I by Gods ordinaunce came forth him beforne,
Iacob came forthwith, holding me fast by the hele?

Deborra.

It is true, I was there, and saw it very wele.

Esau.

Is it true? well Iacob I pray God I be dead,
But for my heles sake, I will haue thee by the head.
What diuel was in me, that I had not the grace
With kicking backe my hele to marre his mopishe face?
But my father Isaac will not long liue nowe,
If he were gone, Iacob I would soone meete with you.
For my soule hateth Iacob euen to the death,
And I will nere but hate him while I shall haue breath.
I may well dissemble vntill I see a day:
But trust me Iacob, I will pay thee when I may.
But if euer I heare that thou speake worde of this,
I shall cut out thy tongue, I will not mysse.

This he speaketh to Deborra.

But come on Ragau with me, so mote I thriue,
I will get a good sword, so therby must I liue.

Ragau.

Liue quod you! we are like to liue God knoweth how.

Esau.

What ye saucie merchaunt, are ye a prater now?

[Exit Esau and Ragau.]

Actus quinti, scæna septima.

Deborra. Rebecca.

Deborra.

I am glad that Esau is now gone certes.
For an euill disposed man he is doutlesse.
Yet am I no gladder of his departure hence,
Than I am that Rebecca is come in presence.

[Enter Rebecca.]

Rebecca.

Deborra, what doost thou tarying here so long?
I came full ill afeard least some thing had ben wrong
[G2r] For Mido and Abra tolde me of Esau.

Deborra.

In dede here he was, and departed hence but nowe:
And one thing I tell you dame, let Iacob beware,
For Esau to mischiefe Iacob dothe prepare,

Rebecca.

Call Iacob hyther, that I may shew him my minde.
Sende him hyther quickly, and tary ye behinde.
That he geue place awhyle, it is expedient,
And howe he may be sure, I wyll the way inuent.

Actus quinti, scæna octaua.

Iacob. Rebecca.
[Enter Iacob.]

Iacob.

Mother Rebecca, did ye sende for me hyther?

Rebecca.

Yea and the cause is this, thou must go somwhither,
To hyde thee from thy brother Esau a space.

Iacob.

In dede to mens malice we must somtime geue place.

Rebecca.

He lieth in awayte, to slea thee if he can.
Thou shalt therfore by my rede flee hence to Haran.
And lye with my brother Laban, a man aged,
Tyll Esaus wrath be somwhat asswaged.

When all thinges are forgotten, and his fury past,
I shall sende for thee again in all goodly haste.

Iacob.

Yea, but howe wyll my father herewith be content?

Rebecca.

Thou shalt see me wynne hym thereto incontinent.

[Enter Isaac led by Mido.]

And here he commeth happily, Iacob heare me,
Make a signe to Mido, that he do not name thee,
Then gette thee in priuely tyl I do thee call.

Iacob.

As ye commaunde me mother Rebecca, I shall.

[Exit Iacob.]

Actus quinti, scæna nona.

Isaac. Mido. Rebecca. Iacob.

Isaac.

Where be ye good wyfe?

Mido.

My dame Rebecca is here.

Rebecca.

I am glad sweete husband that I see you appere,
For I haue a worde or two vnto you to say.

[Isaac.]

Whatsoeuer it be, tell it me I you pray.

Rebecca.

Sir ye know, that now our life daies are but short
[G2v] And we had neuer so great neede of comfort,
Now Esau his wiues being Hethites both,
Ye know to please vs are much vnwilling and loth.
That if Iacob eke would take any Hethite to wife,
Small ioy should we both haue or comforte of our life.

Isaac.

Wife ye speake this well, and I will prouide therfore,
Call Iacob quickly, that he appeare me before.

Mido.

I can runne apace for him if ye bidde me go.

Rebecca.
Go hye thee at once then like a good sonne Mido.

[Exit Mido, returning shortly afterwards with Iacob.]

Isaac.
O Lorde saue thou my sonne from miscarying.

Mido.
Come maister Iacob, ye must make no tarying,
For I it is that shall be shent if you be slacke,
Here is your sonne Iacob now, maister Isaac.

Isaac.
Sonne Iacob, make thee ready as fast thou can,
And in all hast possible get thee vnto Laban.
He is thine owne uncle, and a right godly man,
Marry of his daughters, and not of Canan.
In Mesopotamia shalt thou leade thy life.
The lorde prosper thee there, without debate or strife.
And the God of Abraham prosper thee in peace.
He multiply thy seede, and make it to encrease,
Nowe kisse me deare sonne Iacob, and so go thy way.

[Iacob kisses Isaac.]

Rebecca.
Kisse me also sweete sonne, and hence without delay.

[Iacob kisses Rebecca.]

Iacob.
Now most tender parents, as wel with heart and word,
I bid you well to fare, and leaue you to the Lord.

Mido.
Nay maister Iacob, let me haue an hande also.

Iacob.
Euen with all my heart farewell litle Mido.

[Iacob embraces Mido, then exits.]

Isaac.
Now will I departe hence into the tent againe.

Rebecca.
As pleaseth God and you, but I will here remaine.

[Exit Isaac with Mido.]

Actus quinti, scæna decima.

Esau. Ragau. Rebecca. Isaac. Mido.
[Enter Esau and Ragau; enter Rebecca some distance apart.]

[*Esau.*] And is he gone in deede to mine vncle Laban,
In Mesopotamia at the toune of Haran?
And is Iacob gone to the house of Bethuel?
[G3r] The whirlewynd with him, and flyngyng fende of hel.
But I shall mete with him yet one daye well enough.
And who is this? my mother, whom I see here now?

Ragau.
She stoode here al this while sir, did ye not her see?

Esau.
Didst thou see her stand here, and wouldest not warne me?

Rebecca.
Sonne Esau, afore God thou art much to blame,
And to do as I heare of thee, is a foule shame.

Esau.
Mother what is it ye heard of me of late?

Rebecca.
That thou doest thy brother Iacob deadly hate.

Esau.
Hate Iacob? I hate him and will do till I dye.
For he hath done me both great wrong and vilanny.
And that shal he well know if the Lord geue me lyfe.

Rebecca.
Fye vpon thee to speake so like a lewde caytife.

Ragau.
My maister Esau is of nature much hote,
But he will be better than he saith, feare not.

Esau.
My birthright to sell did he not make me consent?

Rebecca.
But the same to do were not thy selfe content?
There is no man to blame for it but thine owne selfe.

Esau.
Yea mother, see that ye holde with that mopishe elfe.
It is your deinty dearlyng, your princkore, your golpoll,
He can neuer be praised enough of your soule,
He must euer be extolled aboue the Moone,
It is neuer amisse that he hath said or done.
I would he were rocked or dandled in your lappe:
Or I would with this fauchon I might geue him pap.

I meruail why ye should so loue him, and me not!
Ye groned as well for the one as thother I wotte.
But Iacob must be aduaunced in any wyse:
But I shall one day handle him of the new guise.

Rebecca.

Both on thy fathers blessyng and mine I charge thee,
That thy soule entend neuer such iniquitie,
Beware by the example of Caym I thee rede,
That thou bring not the Lordes curse upon thy head.

Esau.

And what should I take all this wrong at Iacobs hande?

Rebecca.

Forgeue, and the Lorde shall prosper thee on the lande.
[G3^{v}] My sonne Esau heare me, I am thy mother:
For my sake let passe this grudge against thy brother.

Ragau.

Syr, your mothers request is but reasonable,
Which for you to graunt shal be muche commendable.

Esau.

Mother, though it be a great thing that ye require:
Yet must all malice passe at your desire.
And for your cause mother, this mine angre shall slake.

Rebecca.

I thanke thee my sonne, that thou doost it for my sake

Esau.

For your sake with Iacob I will be at accorde.

Rebecca.

And shall I call thy father to be as recorde?

Esau.

As pleaseth you mother, I can be well content.

Rebecca.

Then wyll I go call hym hyther incontinent.
And where he dooth already loue thee very well,
This wyll make hym to loue thee better a greate deale.

[Rebecca exits and shortly after returns with Isaac.]

Ragau.

Truely syr, this is of you a right gentill part:
At least yf it come from the bottome of your harte.

Esau.

It must nowe be thus, but when I shall Iacob fynde,
I shall then do, as God shall put into my minde.

Rebecca.

He hath at my woorde remitted all his quarele.

Isaac.

Forsooth I loue him the better a great deale.
And if he be here, I would commende his doing.

[Esau.]

All prest here father to tary on your comming.

Isaac.

Sonne Esau, thou haste thy selfe well acquited.
That all quarell to Iacob thou haste remitted.
It was the Lordes pleasure that it should thus be,
Against whose ordinance to stande is not for thee:
But nowe to the entent it may please the Lorde,
To knitte your hartes one day in a perfect concorde,
We shall first in a song geue laude vnto his name,
And than with all gladnesse, within confirme the same.

Rebecca.

As ye thinke best dere husbande I agree therto.

Esau.

Mee ye may commaunde to what ye will haue me to do:
And so maye ye do also Ragau my man.

Isaac.

I see none, but praise we the Lorde the best we can.
Cal foorth all our household that with one accord,
[G4r] We may all with one voyce syng vnto the Lorde.

Ragau calleth al to syng.

This song must be song after the prayer.

O Lorde the God of our father Abraham,
Howe deepe and unsearcheable are thy iudgementes?
Thy almightifull hande did create and frame,
Both heauen and earth and all the elementes.
Man of the earth thou haste formed and create,
Some do thee worship, and some stray awrye,
Whome pleaseth thee, thou doste choose or reprobate,
And no fleshe can aske thee wherfore or why!
Of thine owne will thou didst Abraham electe,
Promising him seede as sterres of the skie,
And them as thy chosen people to protecte,
That they might thy mercies praise and magnifie.
Performe thou O Lorde, thine eternall decree,
To me and my seede the sonnes of Abraham,
And whom thou haste chosen thine owne people to bee,
Guide and defende to the glorie of thy name. FINIS.

Then entreth the Poete, and the rest stand still, til he haue done.

The Poet entreth

Whan Adam for breakyng Gods commaundement
Had sentence of death, and all his posteritie:
Yet the lorde our God who is omnipotent,
Had in his owne selfe by his eternall decree,
Appointed to restore man, and to make him free,
He purposed to saue mankynde by his mercie,
Whome he once had created vnto his glorie.
  Yet not all fleshe did he then predestinate,
But onely the adopted children of promise:
For he forknewe that many would degenerate,
And wylfully giue cause to be put from that blisse:
So on Gods behalfe no maner default there is,
[G4v] But where he chooseth, he sheweth his great mercy:
And where he refuseth, he doth none iniury,
  But thus farre surmounteth mans intellection,
To attaine or conceiue, and much more to discusse:
All must be referred to Gods election,
And to his secret iudgement, it is meete for vs,
With Paule the Apostle to confesse and say thus:
Oh the deepnesse of the riches of Gods wisedome,
How unsearcheable are his wayes to mans reason!
Our parte therfore is first to beleue Gods worde,
Not doubtyng but that he wil his elected saue:
Then to put full trust in the goodnesse of the Lorde,
That we be of the number which shall mercy haue:
Thirdly so to liue as we may his promise craue.
Thus if we do, we shall Abrahams chyldren be:
And come with Iacob to endlesse felicitie.

All the rest of the actours aunswer Amen.
Then foloweth the prayer.

Isaac.

Now vnto God let vs pray for all the whole clergy,
To geue them grace to auance gods honor and glory.

Rebecca.

Then for the Quenes maiesty let vs pray,
Unto God to kepe her in helth and welth night and day,
And that of his mere mercy and great benignitie,
He will defend and maintaine hir estate and dignitie,

That she beeing greeued with any outward hostilitie,
May against her enimies, alwaye haue victorie.

Iacob.

God saue the Quenes counsailours most noble and true,
And with all godlinesse their noble heartes endue.

Esau.

Lord saue the nobilitie and preserue them all:
And prosper the Quenes subiects vniuersall.
Amen.

Thus endeth this Comedie or Enterlude
of Iacob and Esau.

APPENDIX A

Fragment of the 1557/58 Edition of *Iacob and Esau*

The following pages offer for the first time in publication the entire surviving fragment of the original edition of *Jacob and Esau*, probably published by Henry Sutton shortly after he entered the title in the Stationers Register sometime between June 1557 and June 1558. The fragment consists of eight pages covering the last 274 lines of the play's text. The document is housed in the Bodleian Library, Oxford, marked as New College Manuscript 363/4, nos. 71-74.

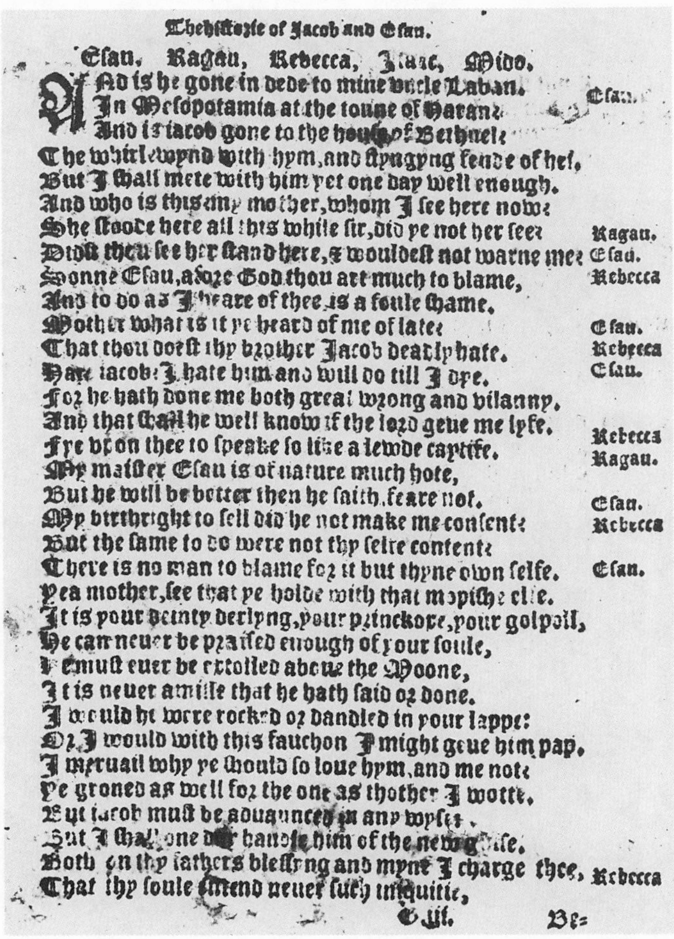

The historie of Jacob and Esau.

Esau, Ragau, Rebecca, Isaac, Mido.

And is he gone in dede to mine uncle Laban. Esau.
In Mesopotamia at the towne of Haran?
And is iacob gone to the house of Bethuel?
The whirlewynd with hym, and styngyng feude of hel,
But I shall mete with him yet one day well enough.
And who is this, my mother, whom I see here now?
She stoode here all this while sir, did ye not her see? Ragau.
Didst thou see her stand here, & wouldest not warne me? Esau.
Sonne Esau, afore God thou art much to blame, Rebecca
And to do as I heare of thee is a foule shame.
Mother what is it ye heard of me of late? Esau.
That thou doest thy brother Jacob deadly hate. Rebecca
Hate iacob? I hate him and will do till I dye. Esau.
For he hath done me both great wrong and vilanny.
And that shall he well know if the lord geue me lyfe.
Fye vpon thee to speake so like a lewde captife. Rebecca
My maister Esau is of nature much hote, Ragau.
But he will be better then he saith, feare not.
My birthright to sell did he not make me consent? Esau.
But the same to do were not thy selfe content? Rebecca
There is no man to blame for it but thyne own selfe. Esau.
Yea mother, see that ye holde with that mopishe elfe.
It is your deinty derlyng, your princkoxe, your golpoll,
He can neuer be praised enough of your soule,
He must euer be extolled aboue the Moone,
It is neuer amisse that he hath said or done.
I would he were rocked or dandled in your lappe:
Or I would with this fauchon I might geue him pap.
I meruail why ye should so loue hym, and me not?
Ye groned as well for the one as thother I wotte.
But iacob must be aduaunced in any wyse.
But I shall one day hanse him of the new guise.
Both on thy fathers blessyng and myne I charge thee, Rebecca
That thy soule attend neuer such iniquitie,

G iii. Be-

The historie of Jacob and Esau.

Esau, Ragau, Abra, M

Come out whores & theues, come out
I told you, did I not: that there would b
Come out little whoreson ape, come out
Take my lyfe for a peny, whether shall I
Come out thou little fende, come out tho
Out alas, alas, Esau will us all kill.
And come out thou mother Mab, out ol
As white as midnightes arsehole, or vir
Where be ye: come together in a cluster
In faith and these three will make a nobl
Ere ye escape my fingers, ye shall all be t
For these be they which haue al this agai
I wrought not a stroke this day but led I
Yf I wrought one stroke to day, lay me o
Hence than, get thee in, and do against me
I care as much for you now, as I did befo
What saiest thou little thefe: yf I may the
Ye shall runne apace then I wene, so god
Now to go Mido, or thou art caught in a
Nay for this sake, Abra, ye shall drinke of t
Nay for gods loue good swete maister Esa
Hurt not me for Mido: speake for me Rag
Sir spare litle Abra, she hath done none
A litle fende it is, and will be a right deuill
And she is one of them that loue not me a
Yfyr let me go, I will serue you very wele.
And neuer ... more ado against me make
Ragau shall be surety.
Sir I undertake.
Than hens out of my sight at ones & get t
Adew, I se[...]t a strawe by you nor a pin
What saiest thou thou Tib? ones ye shall h
he best ende of suretiship is to get a clapp

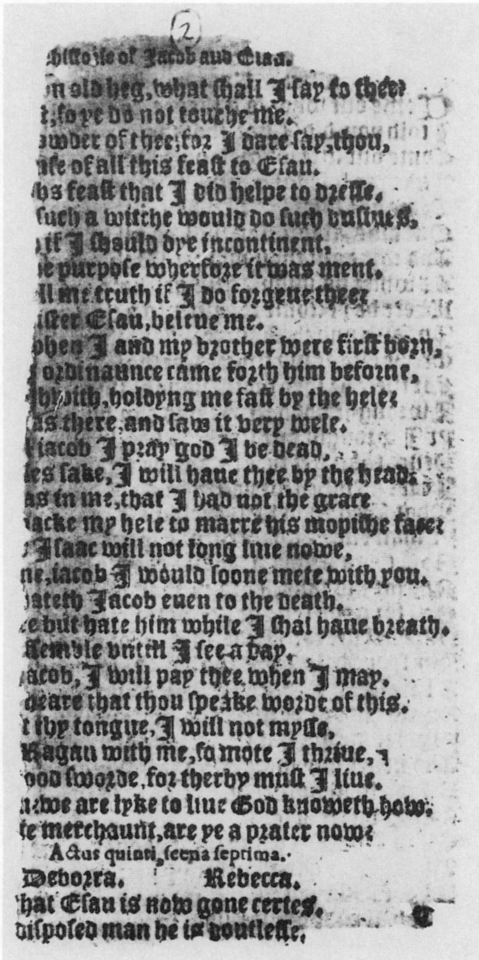
(2)
historie of Jacob and Esau.
n old heg, what shall I say to thee?
t, so ye do not touche me.
owder of thee; for I dare say, thou,
use of all this feast to Esau.
hs feast that I did helpe to dresse,
such a witche would do such busines.
if I should dye incontinent,
e purpose wherfore it was ment.
ll me truth if I do forgeue thee?
ister Esau, beleue me.
when I and my brother were first born,
ordinaunce came forth him beforne,
th, holdyng me fast by the hele?
as there, and saw it very wele.
iacob I pray god I be dead,
es sake, I will haue thee by the head:
as in me, that I had not the grace
acke my hele to marre his mopishe face?
Isaac will not long liue nowe,
ne, iacob I would soone mete with you.
ateth Jacob euen to the death,
e but hate him while I shal haue breath.
semble vntill I see a day.
acob, I will pay thee when I may.
eare that thou speake worde of this.
t thy tongue, I will not mysse,
agan with me, so mote I thriue,
ood sworde, for therby must I liue.
: we are lyke to liue God knoweth how:
e merchaunt, are ye a prater now?
Actus quinti, scena septima.
Debora. Rebecca.
hat Esau is now gone certes.
disposed man he is doutlesse,

yet am I no gladder of his departure
Then I am that Rebecca is come in
Debora, what doost thou tarying her
I came, still yt afeard, least some thyng
For Mido and Abra tolde me of Esau
In dede here he was, & departed hens
And one thyng I tell you dame, let Ja
For Esau to mischiefe Jacob dothe pre
Call Jacob hyther, that I may shew h
Sende hym hyther quickly, and tary
That he geue place awhyle, it is expe
And howe he may be sure, I wyll the

Actus quinti, scena octaua.

Jacob. Rebecc

MOther Rebecca, dyd ye sende for
yea & the cause is this, thou must
To hyde thy from thy brother Esau a sp
In dede to mens malice we must some
He lieth in awayte, to slea thee if he ca
Thou shalt therfore by my rede flee her
And lye with my brother Laban a man
Tyll Esaus wrath be somwhat asswag
When all thynges are forgotten, and hi
I shall sende for the agayn in all goodly
Yea, but howe wyll my father herewit
Thou shalt see me wynne hym thereto
And here he commeth happily, iacob he
Make a signe to Mido, that he doo no
Than gette thee in priuily tyll I doo th
As ye commaunde me mother Rebecca,

Actus quinti, scena nona.

Ysaac. Mido. Rebecc

Where be ye good wyfe
My dame Rebecca is here.

ehistorie of Jacob and Esau.

husband that I see you appere,
orde or two unto you to say.
e tell [illegible] I you pray.
at now our life dayes are but short,
er so great nede of comfort,
wiues beyng Hethites both,
se us are much unwilling and lothe.
e should take any Hethite to wife,
uld we both haue or comforte of our lyfe,
his well, and I will prouide therfore,
sly, that he appeare me before.
are for him if ye bidde me go.
ones than like a good sonne Mido.
ou my sonne from miscaryping.
acob, ye must make no tarying.
shall be shent if you be slacke,
nne iacob now, maister Isaac.
make the ready as fast as thou can.
possible get thee unto Laban.
e uncle, and a right godly man,
aughters, and not of Canan.
nia shalt thou leade thy lyfe.
per thee there, without debate or strife.
f Abraham prosper thee in peace,
y sede, and make it to encrease,
deare sonne iacob, and so go thy waye.
wete sonne, and hens without delay.
der parentes as wel with hert and word,
l to fare, and leaue you to the lord.
acob let me haue an hande also.
l my heart [illegible] well little Mido.
eparte hence into the tent agayne.
od and you, but I will here remayne.
Actus quinti, scena decima.

Esau

The historie of Jacob and Esau.

Beware by the example of Caym I thee rede,
That thou bryng not the lordes curse upon thy head.

Esau. And what should I take al this wrong at Jacobs hande?

Rebecca Forgeue, and the Lorde shall prosper thee on the lande.
My sonne Esau heare me, I am thy mother:
For my sake leat passe this grudge against thy brother.

Ragau. Syr, your mothers request is but reasonable,
Whiche for you to graunt shal be muche commendable.

Esau. Mother, though it be a great thyng that ye require:
yet must all malice passe at your desire.
And for your cause mother, this myne angre shal slake.

Rebecca I thanke thee my sonne, that thou doost it for my sake.

Esau. For your sake with Jacob I will be at accorde.

Rebecca And shall I call thy father to be as a recorde?

Esau. As pleaseth you mother, I can be well content.

Rebecca Then wyll I go call hym hyther incontinent.
And where he doothe already loue thee very well,
This wyll make hym to loue thee better a greate deale.

Ragau. Truely syr, this is of you a right gentill part:
At least yf it come from the bottome of your harte.

Esau. It must nowe be thus, but when I shall Jacob fynde,
I shall than doo, as god shall put into my mynde.

Rebecca He hath at my woorde remitted all his quarele.

Isaac. Forsoothe I loue hym the better a great deale.
And if he be here, I woulde commende his doyng.

Esau. All prest here father to tary on your commyng.

Isaac. Sonne Esau, thou haste thy selfe well acquited,
That all quarell to Jacob thou haste remitted.
It was the Lordes pleasure that it should thus be,
Agaynst whose ordinance to stande is not for thee,
But nowe to the entent it may please the Lorde,
To knitte your hartes one day in a perfect concorde,
We shall first in a song geue laude unto his name,
And than with all gladnesse, within confirme the same.

And

(7)

The historie of [illegible] and Esau.

As ye thinke best dere husbande I agree therto, *Rebec.*
Me ye may commaunde to what ye wyl haue me to do: *Esau.*
And so maye ye doo also Ragau my man.
I see none, but praise we the Lorde the beste we can. *Isaac.*
Call foorth all our household that with one accord, *Ragau calleth*
We may all with one voyce syng unto the Lorde. *al to sing*

This is the last song, & must be song after the prayer.

O Lorde the God of our father Abraham,
Howe deepe and unsearchable are thy judgementes:
Thy almightyfull hande dyd create and frame,
Bothe heauen and earthe and all the elementes.
Man of th[e ea]rthe thou haste formed and create,
Some doo the[illegible]hyp, and some straye alwaye,
Whome plea[se]th thee, thou doeste choose or reprobate,
And no flesh [c]an aske thee wherfore or why:
Of thyne owne will thou dydst Abraham electe,
Promysyng hym seede as sterres of the skye,
And them as thy chosen people to protecte,
That they myght thy mercies praise and magnifie.
Perfourme thou O Lorde, thyne eternall decree,
To me and my seede the sonnes of Abraham:
And whom thou haste chosen thyne owne people to bee,
Guyde and defende to the glorie of thy name. Finis.

Thā entreth the Poete, & the rest stād still, tyll he haue done.

When Adam for breakyng Gods commaundement *The Poetes part*
Had sentence of death, and all his posteritie:
Yet the lorde our God who is omnipotent,
Had in his owne selfe by his eternall decree,
Appointed to restore man, and to make him free,
He purposed to saue mankynde by his mercye,
Whome he ones had created unto his glorye.

Yet not all fleshe dyd he than predestinate,
But onely the adopted chyldren of promyse:
For he forknewe that many would degenerate,
And wylfully geue cause to be put from that blisse;
So on Gods behalfe no maner default there is,

But

The historie of Jacob and Esau.

But where he chooseth, he sheweth his great mercye
And where he refuseth, he doth none iniury,

But thus farre surmounteth mans intellection,
To attayne or conceiue, and much more to discusse:
All must be referred to Gods election,
And to his secrete iudgement, it is mete for us,
With Paule the Apostle to confesse and say thus:
O the depenes of the richesse of Gods wisedome,
How unsercheable are his wayes to mans reason!

Our parte therfore is first to beleue [illegible]
Not doutyng but that he wil his elect [illegible]
Than to put full trust in the goodnesse [illegible]
That we be of the number which shal [illegible]
Thirdely so to liue as we may his promise [illegible]
Thus if we do, we shall Abrahams chyldren [illegible]
And come with iacob to endlesse felicitie.

All the rest of the actours aunswer Amen.

Then foloweth the prayer.

Isaac. Now unto God let us pray for all the whole clergy,
To geue them grace to auaunce gods honor and glory.
Rebecca Than for the Quenes maiesty let us pray,
Unto god to kepe her in helth and welth night and day.
And that of his mere mercy and great benignitie,
He will defend and maintayne her estate and dignitie,
That she beeing greued with any outward hostilitie,
May against her enemies, alwaye haue victorie.
Jacob. God saue the Quenes counsailours most noble & true,
And with all godlines their noble hertes endue,
Esau. Lord saue the nobilitie and preserue them all:
And prosper the quenes subiects universall.

Amen.

[illegible] endeth this Comedie or Enterlude of
Jacob and Esau.

APPENDIX B

The Institutes of the Christian Religion

by John Calvin: Selected Passages

Calvin's *Institutes* was a major literary source for *Mary Magdalene* and probably influenced *Jacob and Esau* as well. For the relationship of Calvin's work to the plays, see Introduction pp. xxxii-xxxiv, and xliii-xliv. The location of direct borrowings in Wager's play are identified in the Notes. For purposes of convenience I use Thomas Norton's English translation of 1562, although it is probable that both playwrights were familiar with an earlier Latin version, perhaps the *Institutio* of 1539.

1. *The Law*

The first is, that while it [the Law] sheweth to euery man the righteousness of God, that is, the righteousness which only is acceptable to God, it admonish, certifie, proue gilty, yea and condemne euery man of his owne vnrighteousnesse. For so is it nedefull that man blinded and dronke with loue of himselfe, be driuen both to the knowledge and the confession of his owne weakenesse and vncleannesse: for asmuch as if his vanitie be not euidently conuinced, he swelleth with madde affiance of his owne strength, and can neuer be brought to thinke of the scle(n)dernesse therof, so long as he measureth it by the proportion of his owne will (*Inst.* II.vii.6).

So the lawe is like a certaine looking glasse wherein we beholde, first our weakenesse, and by that our wickednesse, and laste of all by them both our accursednesse, euen as a glasse representeth vnto vs the spottes of our face. For when power faileth man to follow righteousnesse then muste he needes sticke faste in the mire of sinnes. And after sinne by and by followeth curse (*Inst.* II.vii.7).

2. *Faith*

First we must be put in minde that there is a generall relation of faith to the worde, and that faith can no more be severed from the worde, than the sunnebeames from the sunne from whom they procede. . . . Wherefore if faith do swerue neuer so litle from this marke, to which it ought to be directly leuelled, it kepeth not her own nature, but becometh an vncertaine lightnesse of beliefe and wandring errour of minde. The same Worde is the foundation wherewith faith is vpholden and susteined, from which if it swarue, it falleth downe. Therefore take away the Worde, and then there shall remaine no faith. . . . But we say that the worde it selfe, howesoeuer it be conueied to vs, is like a mirrour when faith may beholde God. . . . For this is not the onely purpose in the vnderstanding of faith, that we knowe that there is a God, but this also, yea this chiefly, that we vnderstand what will he beareth towards vs. For it not so much behoueth vs to knowe what he is in himselfe but what a one he will be to vs. Nowe therefore we are come to this point, that faith is a knowledge of the will of God, perceyued by his worde. . . . But also it sufficeth not to beleue that God is a true speaker, which can neither deceiue nor lie, vnlesse thou further holde this for vndoubtedly determined, that whatsoeuer procedeth from him, is the sacred and inuiolable truth (*Inst.* III.ii.6).

Nowe we shall haue a perfect definition of faith, if we say, that it is a stedfast and assured knowledge of Gods kindnesse toward vs, which being grounded vpon the trueth of the free promise in Christ, is both reueled to our mindes, and sealed in our heartes by the holy Ghost (*Inst.* III.ii.7).

3. *Repentance*

Wherfore in my iudgement, repentance may thus not amisse be defined: that it is a true turninge of our life vnto God, proceeding from a pure & earnest feare of God, which consisteth in the mortifying of the flesh and of the olde man, and in the quickening of the spirite (*Inst.* III.iii.5).

4. *Relation of Faith to Repentance*

As for them that thinks that repentance doth rather go before faith than flow or spring foorth of it, as a frute out of a tree, they neuer knewe the force therof, and are moued with too weake an argument to thinke so. . . . Yet when we referre the beginnings of repentance to faith, . . . we meane to shewe that a man can not earnestly apply himselfe to repentance, vnlesse he know himself to be of God (*Inst.* III.iii.1-2).

5. *Relation of Faith to Love*

This womans sinnes [i.e., the woman who washed Christ's feet] are forgiuen her, because she hath loued much. In which wordes (as you see) he maketh not her loue the cause, but the proofe of the forgiuenes of her sinnes. For they are deriued vpon a similitude of that debtour, to whom fiue hundred was forgiuen, to whom he did not say that therefore it was forgiuen, because he had loued much: but therefore loued much, because it was forgiuen. . . . By what means she obtained forgiuenesse of sinnes, the Lord openly testifieth: Thy faith, saith he, hath saued thee. Therefore we obtain forgiuenesse by faith: By charitie wee giue thankes, and testifie the bountifulnesse of the Lord (*Inst*. III. iv. 37).

6. *Predestination*

[Predestination is] the eternal decree of God, wherby he had it determined with himselfe what he willed to become of euery man. For all are not created to like estate: but to some, eternal life, and to some eternal damnation is foreappointed (*Inst*. III.xxi.5).

When they [i.e., Jacob and Esau] were not yet born, and hadde not done any good or euill, that according to election the purpose of God might abide, not of works, but of him that calleth, it is sayd, The elder shall serue the younger: as it is wrytten, Iacob I have loued, but Esau I haue hated (*Inst*. III.xxii.4).

Esau and Iacob are brethren, issuing both of one the same parents, enclosed yet both in one wombe, not yet brought out into the world. In them all things are equall, yet of [the] iudgement of God is diuerse. For he taketh the one and forsaketh the other. But this also being passed ouer, that thing is giuen to the yonger which is denied to the elder (*Inst*. III.xxii.5).

Iacob therefore is chosen, and Esau is reiected: and by the predestination of God is made different from him from whom he differed not in any deseruinges (*Inst*. xxii.6).

NOTES ON *MARY MAGDALENE*

Title Page

2. *entreating*: treating.

17. *Foure may easely play this Enterlude*. "Foure" is either a misprint or a miscalculation, for the play is designed for five professional touring actors. The casting chart, along with this line, indicates that the play was "offered for acting" to other regular companies. See Introduction, pp. xxiii-xxiv, and Bevington, *From Mankind to Marlowe*, pp. 173, 268.

The Prologue

1f. In other plays of the time, the Prologue is delivered by the author or "poet" (e.g., JE). Wager may have followed the example of John Bale who delivered the prologues to his own plays (introduced as "Baleus Prolocutor" in *God's Promises*, *Johan Baptystes Preachynge*, and *Three Laws*) as a member of the acting troupe performing them.

1-2. "There is no state, however modest and happy, that is able to escape the bite of malice." The quote may be traced to Valerius Maximus, *Factorum ac dictorum memorabilium*, IV.vii.

11. *This comely and good facultie*: i.e. playing, as in ll. 24, 31, and 39.

14. *affect*: affection, passion. *geason*: rare, uncommon.

16. "You will neither praise your own tastes [or pursuits], nor find fault with those of others." Horace, *Epistles*, I.xviii.39 ("To Lollius"). As with most Latin tags in the play, this one is loosely translated in the following lines.

22. Proverbial: "Ill will never said well." See Dent, *Proverbial Lang.*, App. A, 141.

24. *detract*: depreciate.

26. *Yea, we have vsed this feate at the vnuersitie*. For troupes visiting Oxford and Cambridge, see Introduction, p. xxiv.

30. *A horse wil kick if you touche where he is galled!* proverbial; Dent, *Proverbial Lang.*, App. A, H700.

31. This constitutes the first known English Protestant defense of the stage, and judging from the preceding remarks by the Prologue, was precipitated by puritan opposition to playing, which emerged in the 1560s. For excerpts of printed criticism see Chambers, *Eliz. Stage*, IV, 192-95, 266-67.

32. *al thing: everything.*

37. *frequented*: made use of, patronized.

38. *fautes:* faults; see also l. 660.

39. *let*: hinder, damage, harm.

43. *whether you geue halfpence or pence*. Contemporary records indicate that there were two methods of payment to visiting players in provincial communities. One was in the form of a gift from the local authorities, say, five shillings from the town chamberlain's purse; the second, which occasionally was in addition to the above, was by way of collections or admission receipts. See Westfall, *Patrons and Perform.*, ch. 3; and Dawson, *Records of Kent*, pp. xv-xxii. According to Carpenter, MM, pp. 87-88, the line cited above suggests "possibly a double scale of admission to the play, perhaps according to location or accommodation."

45. See Job 28:12-19.

47. *sapience*: wisdom, doctrine.

49. *chargeable:* costly, burdensome.

53. *beleue*: belief; see also ll. 1265, 2105.

67. Caxton's *Golden Legend*: "Mary Magdalene had her surname of Magdalo, a castle. . . . She with her brother Lazarus, and her sister Martha, possessed the castle of Magdalo, which is two miles from Nazareth" (cited in Carpenter, MM, p. 88).

68, 69. See Mark 16:9 and Luke 8:2.

70. The Western church identified the Mary Magdalene of Luke 8 with the woman out of whom seven demons were expelled in Luke 7. See Introduction, p. xxvi, and Blackburn, *Biblical Drama*, p. 132.

77. *freate*: fret, trouble.

78. *erected*: raised up.

80. Compare William Wager, *The Longer*: "We desire no man here to be offended" (l. 1907).

80-83. Once again the author seems sensitive to charges of immorality levelled against the play.

The Text

87f. I am less inclined than Carpenter to read much of Infidelitie's opening speech as "a medley of nonsense" (see his comment to ll. 5-16). He is certainly right, however, in discerning the parody of Catholic worship which is more in the spirit of corresponding passages in Bale's *Three Laws* and *King Johan*, than in that of the Mahound speech of the Digby *Mary Magdalene*, ll. 1185f. For Catholic parody in Bale, see Miller, "The Roman Rite," pp. 802-22.

88. *Savaltor mundi Domine:* opening phrase of the ancient Advent hymn. *Kyrie eleison:* follows the Introit in the Mass.

89. *Ite Missa est:* chanted at solemn Mass.

90. *Sed libera nos `a malo:* this part of the Lord's Prayer is repeated at Mass.

91-102. This passage is obscure, but its allusions to the Lord's Supper and the Crucifixion may be an attack on the Catholic Mass.

95. *deace*: dais. Carpenter, MM, p. 89, glosses the word as "table, estrade."

97. *meace:* mess, *i.e.,* a helping of food.

101. *knacke*: trick.

107. Like most central Vice figures, Infidelitie assumes several identities. His duplicitous nature is reproduced in his fellow vices; see ll. 127-34.

118. *mischeue:* injure.

123. *conuey:* manage, conduct; see also l. 759.

124-6. *visour* : diguise. The term sometimes means a mask worn over the face, as in the "terrible visure" and "an ill fauoured visure" worn by God's Judgement and Confusion in *The Longer* (l. 1758; l. 1806), but here the sense is metaphorical.

127-13 Infidelitie's *impes* are the seven deadly sins commonplace in medieval theology and literature.

130. *sentence:*opinion,judgment.

144. *bungarliest:* clumsiest, most awkward; see also l. 158, *bungarly*.

147. *ouerbody*: outer garment.

150. *geare*: dress; see also ll. 160, 162, 164, 168, 488.

155. *gis*: an oath; euphemistic form of *Jesus*.

155. *holde*: bet, wager; see also l. 1846.

169. *myddes*: midst, middle.

177. *I know that you come of a worshipful stock.* According to Caxton's *Golden Legend*: "Mary Magdalene . . . was born of

right noble lineage and parents, which were descended of the lineage of kings" (qtd. in Carpenter, MM, p. 90).

185. *almose*: alms.

194. *Feate*: elegant.

200. *worshipfully*: in high regard.

207. "The words of women lighter than falling leaves, go all for naught, swept away by the whim of wind and wave." Ovid, *The Amores*, II, xvi, 45.

214. *Iurie*: Jewry, the land of the Jews.

215. *a worshipfull disposition*: honored position.

216. *Iwis*: indeed.

226. *can little skill*: have but little skill.

238. *pastance*: pastime.

251. *nourtred*: nurtured.

251. *ornature*: "manners."

258. *dearlyng*: darling, favorite.

260. *Puellae pestis, indulgentia parentum.* Criticism of parental indulgence and negligence is a popular theme in contemporary Protestant plays of youth, including *Nice Wanton*, *The Disobedient Child*, and *The Longer* where "*Indulgentia parentum*" (l. 1023) is blamed for the hero Moros' insolence and incorrigibility.

261. *suferance*: tolerance.

270. *purtenance*: appurtenances.

273. *want*: lack.

275. *plant*: i.e., Magdalene castle.

277. *decent*: proper.

285f. In seeking counsel to help handle the affairs of her newly inherited wealthy estate, Mary's circumstances mirrored those of many young members of the Tudor ruling class whose parents died while they were adolescents. The ensuing exchange among Mary, Infidelitie, and her other newly appointed "councillors" appears to be a topical comment on the abuses to which Tudor wards and other aristocratic minors were subject as a result of self-promoting guardians and ill-chosen advisors. Young King Edward's successive relationships with Somerset and Northumberland offer cases in point. For these problems and others matters concerning the upbringing and education of the aristocracy, see Simon, *Education & Society*, pp. 14-15, 333-68. *In*] *in* in 1566, 1567 eds.

305. *wanton*: lewd, reckless person; see also l. 706.

313. *by my maydenhood.* A rather unusual phrase coming from a male character, but as Carpenter notes, probably "is nothing

more than a common expletive" (MM, p. 90). This also seems to be true of Vice's *Faith of my body* on l. 215.

318. *dresse*: in the sense of "prepare" as well as "apparel" (verb); see also ll. 329, 365, 1388.

321-26. For a similar self-definition speech, see the opening remarks of Natural Inclination in *The Trial*, sig. B1ᵛ. Carpenter, MM, p. 90, compares Infidelitie's speech here to Sinne's in *All for Money*, sig. B2ʳ.

326. *habitacle*: habitation.

332. Infidelitie motions to exit. *Life*] *lyfe* in 1566, 1567 eds.

333. *Pride of Life*] *Pride* in 1566, 1567 eds.

339. *mynikin*: little.

341. *Pride of Life*] *Pride* in 1566, 1567 eds.

342. *Cupiditie*] *Cupiditi* in 1566, 1567 eds.

349. Like Bale in all his extant plays, Wager equates the legalistic Jewish priesthood of Christ's day with the Catholic clergy.

351. *knauery*] misprinted as *knanery* in 1566, 1567 eds.

353. *Infidelitie in our father's cause is occupied*: Satan. Infidelitie refers to "my father Sathan" on l. 323. The genealogy of vice motif is commonplace in the drama of the time. Two more interesting visual treatments of it are found in *King Johan* and *All for Money*.

358. *Pride of Life*] *Pride* in 1566, 1567 eds.

363. *Cupiditie*] *Cupiditi* in 1566, 1567 eds.

367. *Carnall Concupiscence*] *Carnall concu.* in 1566, 1567 eds.

373. *Pride of Life*] *Pride* in 1566, 1567 eds.

381. *Carnall Concupiscence*] *Car. con* in 1566, 1567 eds. *sort*: company.

386. *alway*: always; as in ll. 436, 462, 556, 581, 674, 799, 1075.

388. *ebrietie*: drunkenness.

393. *headinesse*: headstrongness.

401. *Cupiditie*] *Cupiditi* in 1566, 1567 eds.

404. See 1 Timothy 6:10.

419. *Cupiditie*] *Cupiditi* in 1566, 1567 eds.

423f. See Proverbs 16:18.

448. "*Faustus*. How comes it then that thou art out of hell? *Mephistophilis*. Why, this is hell, nor am I out of it." *Doctor Faustus*, Scene V, ll. 77-78.

451. *Pride of Life*] *Pryde of Lyfe* in 1566, 1567 eds. *our tragedie*. Like Bale in *Three Lawes*, Wager self-consciously conceives of the Vices' plot as a play in which they act out parts for the purpose of corrupting humanity. For the Vices' plot as "demonic play" in Bale, see Kendall, *Drama of Dissent*, ch. 3.

457. *Carnall Concupiscence*] *Concupiscence* in 1566, 1567 eds.

461. *Pride of Life*] *Pryde* in 1566, 1567 eds.
463. *Carnall Concupiscence*] *Car.concupiscence* in 1566, 1567 eds.
467. *Pride of Life*] *Pride* in 1566, 1567 eds.
477-86. See Isaiah 59:17; 61:3, 10; Ephesians 6:13.
482. *wittily*: cleverly.
487. *Pride of Life*] *Pride* in 1566, 1567 eds.
488. *geare*: see l. 150.
493. *Cupiditie*] *Cupiditi* in 1566, 1567 eds.
495. *Carnall Concupiscence*] *Car.cupiscence* in 1566, 1567 eds.
497-98. *He that looketh with one eie, and winketh with an other, / I would not trust (say they) if he were my brother*. Proverbial (see Dent, *Proverbial Lang.*, App. A, E241), but some additional comic meaning seems to derive from the fact that Prudence (Infidelitie's diguise) is emblematically depicted with a third eye in the back of her head. See Wickham, *Early Eng. Stages*, III, 105.
501. Mary's cue to enter the playing area; while the Vices comment on her appearance, she perhaps waits "at the door," (See stage direction for "the doore" after l. 1388). In *Enough*, characters in some instances stand by the door to listen to those standing before the audience (see, for example, l. 1250).
503. *Pride of Life*] *Pride* in 1566, 1567 eds.
505. *Cupiditie*] *Cupiditi* in 1566, 1567 eds.
507. *Carnall Concupiscence*] *Car.cupiscence* in 1566, 1567 eds.
510. *accumbred*: encumbered.
511. *to*: too.
513. *of*: of.
517. "All your great houses are full of saucy slaves." Juvenal, *Satires,* V, 66. Carpenter suggests that the Latin *superbis* is closer in meaning to "haughty" than to "naughty" and that therefore the latter might have been a misprint.
528. *Infidelitie*] speech prefix reads *Infideli* in 1566, 1567 eds.
532. *Pride of Life*] *Pride* in 1566, 1567 eds.
534. *Cupiditie*] *Cupiditi* in 1566, 1567 eds.
536. *Carnall Concupiscence*] *Car.cupiscence* in 1566, 1567 eds.
542. *A*: *Ah!*
546. *Quo magis tegitur, magis aestuat ignis*: from Ovid, *Metamorphoses,* IV, 64. The following lines in English were proverbial (Dent, *Proverbial Lang.*, App. A, F265).
558. *commoditie*: advantage.
567. *Pride of Life*] *Pride* in 1566, 1567 eds.
574. *backare*: back of.
580. Said with obvious sexual overtones.
581. *Carnall Concupiscence*] *Concupiscence* in 1566, 1567 eds.

589f. See John 1:18.
591. *Pride of Life*] *Pryde* in 1566, 1567 eds. "Man is God to man" is proverbial (Dent, *Proverbial Lang.*, App. A, F265), but Carpenter traces the Latin tag to Caecilius Statius: "Man to man is a god if he knows his duty" (Caecilius, #257).
598. *Carnall Concupiscence*] *Concupiscence* in 1566, 1567 eds.
608. *Pride of Life*] *Pride* in 1566, 1567 eds. *Mistress Mary*] *M. Mary* in 1566, 1567 eds. *gree*: agree; see also l. 1320.
609 *Mistress Mary*] *M. Mary* in 1566, 1567 eds.
611. *witte*: intelligence; as in l. 1336.
612. *Pride of Life*] *Pride* in 1566, 1567 eds.
612f. Here begins the topical satire on Tudor noblewomen's fashions and manners.
618. *by*: about.
619. *Pride of Life*] *Pride* in 1566, 1567 eds.
620. *Cupiditie*] *Cupiditi* in 1566, 1567 eds.
622. *Carnall Concupiscence*] *Carnall concu.* in 1566, 1567 eds.
627. *attire*: headdress.
636. *Pride of Life*] *Pride* in 1566, 1567 eds. *tusks*: tufts of hair.
640. *Cupiditie*] *Cupiditi* in 1566, 1567 eds.
644. *Carnall Concupiscence*] *Concupiscence* in 1566, 1567 eds. *geare*: appliances; see also ll. 848, 2009.
647. *courage*: spirit, wilfulness. See the Vice Courage in *The Tide Tarrieth No Man.*
651. *dispaire*: decay.
652. *Infidelitie*] *Infide.* in 1566, 1567 eds. *Mistresse Mary*] *M. Mary* in 1566, 1567 eds.
652-59. *pox*: venereal disease; thus the intentional pun.
653. *Pride of Life*] *Pryde* in 1566, 1567 eds.
654. *Master Prudence*] *M. Prudence* in 1566, 1567 eds.
655. *Pride of Life*] *Pride* in 1566, 1567 eds.
656. *Carnall Concupiscence*] *Car. con* in 1566, 1567 eds.
662. *Pride of Life*] *Pride* in 1566, 1567 eds.
664. *Carnall Concupiscence*] *Car. con* in 1566, 1567 eds.
668. *Pride of Life*] *Pride* in 1566, 1567 eds.
676. *Cupiditie*] *Cupiditi* in 1566, 1567 eds.
678. *Carnall Concupiscence*] *Concupiscence* in 1566, 1567 eds.
683. *noses wil blede*: a common bawdy expression.
684. *corage*: see l. 647.
688. *Infidelitie*] *Infidli.* in 1566, 1567 eds. *past*: paste; i.e., make-up.
690. *ouerbody*: see l. 147.
694. *Pride of Life*] *Pride* in 1566, 1567 eds.
695. *Cupiditie*] *Cupiditi* in 1566, 1567 eds.

696. *gymmes*: links.
698. *Some women*. Misprinted as *Som ewoman* in original.
702. *Carnall Concupiscence*] *Concupiscence* in 1566, 1567 eds.
704. *Infidelitie*] *Infideli.* in 1566, 1567 eds. *skilleth*: be important.
705. *Carnall Concupiscence*] *Car. con* in 1566, 1567 eds.
707. *Pride of Life*] *Pryde* in 1566, 1567 eds.
716f. *It is a stock (they say) right honorable and good, / That hath neither thefe not whore in their blood*: proverbial; see Dent, *Proverbial Lang.*, App. A, F49.
718. *Mistresse*] *M.* in 1566, 1567 eds.
720. *Infidelitie*] *Infideli.* in 1566, 1567 eds.
724f. *This is a true prouerbe, and no fained fable, / Few womens words, be honest, constant, and stable:* see Dent, *Proverbial Lang.*, App. A, T551.
726. *Carnall Concupiscence*] *Concupiscence* in 1566, 1567 eds. *Mistresse*] *M.* in 1566, 1567 eds.
728. *Voluptas autem est sola quae nos vocet ad se, et aliciat suapte natura*: Cicero, *De Finibus*, I, xvi; translated in the following lines.
731. *allecteth*: allures.
733. *abiected*: cast off.
734. *a worde or two in your eare*. Concupiscence draws Mary aside to whisper in her ear, as in JE, l. 524, and *The Longer*, ll. 814-21.
735. *geare*: matter; see also ll. 764, 767, 1653, 1668, 1758.
740. Juvenal, *Satires*, vi, 269. Slightly misquoted; the original reads (qtd. in Carpenter, MM, p. 92):

> Semper habet lites, alternaque jurgia, lectus
> In quo nupta jacet; minimum dormitur in illo.

Cupiditie] *Cupiditi* in 1566, 1567 eds.

746. *Pride of Life*] *Pride* in 1566, 1567 eds.
748. *Carnall Concupiscence*] *Car. con* in 1566, 1567 eds.
752. *hardely*: boldly.
754. *lese*: lose.
758. *Carnall Concupiscence*] *Concupiscence* in 1566, 1567 eds.
760. *Pride of Life*] *Pride* in 1566, 1567 eds.
762. *Cupiditie*] *Cupiditi* in 1566, 1567 eds.
766. *Carnall Concupiscence*] *Concupiscence* in 1566, 1567 eds.
774. *Carnall Concupiscence*] *Concupiscence* in 1566, 1567 eds.
778. *Pride of Life*] *Pride* in 1566, 1567 eds.
780. As Carpenter notes (MM, p. 92), the word *laugh* seems to be a stage direction the printer (or troupe prompter) let slip into the text, although it repeats in l. 1013.

793. *Forma bona*, etc. From Ovid, *De Arte Amandi*, II, 113; translated in the following lines.

803. *maude*: hag.

809. *Pride of Life*] *Pride* in 1566, 1567 eds.

810. *cast:* trick, device; see also l. 821: *castes.*

811. *Cupiditie*] *Cupiditi* in 1566, 1567 eds.

827. *hart rote*: term of endearment: "sweetheart."

831. *Pride of Life*] *Pride* in 1566, 1567 eds.

833. *Cupiditie*] *Cupiditi* in 1566, 1567 eds.

835. *Carnall Concupiscence*] *Concupiscence* in 1566, 1567 eds.

837. *Infidelitie*] *Infideli.* in 1566, 1567 eds. *virginals*: a small keyboard instrument popular in courtly circles, especially among young ladies. Both princesses Mary and Elizabeth were skilled on the virginals from a very young age. See Pattison, *Music & Poetry*, p. 3.

838. *regals*: a small, portable reed organ popular from the 1540s.

841-44. Infidelitie's bawdy humor with its explicit sexual punning is fairly typical of vice comedy, and here may have been accompanied by some lewd gesturing.

845. *Pride of Life*] *Pride* in 1566, 1567 eds.

848. *Carnall Concupiscence*] *Car. con* in 1566, 1567 eds.

851. *Cupiditie*] *Cupiditi* in 1566, 1567 eds.

853. *Infidelitie*] *Infideli.* in 1566, 1567 eds.

855. *Pride of Life*] *Pride* in 1566, 1567 eds.

859. *Mistresse Mary*] *M. Mary* in 1566, 1567 eds. *a song of .iiii. partes*. Four-part harmony was not uncommon for popular singing of the time, including in the drama. In *King Johan*, e.g., it is required for two songs (at ll. 913 and 1141). Since music figures so prominently in contemporary troupe interludes (as in those of amateur auspices), it is likely that most professional actors had some musical training. Some no doubt were recruited from the choir schools and of course every monk who had to participate in divine office would have had some experience with plainsong and perhaps even with the polyphony fashionable in Tudor anthems, antiphons, and popular songs. With the dissolution of the monasteries, many of the religious, now out of work, were able to offer their talents for secular purposes.

861. *Cupiditie*] *Cupiditi* in 1566, 1567 eds.

865. *Infidelitie*] *Infide.* in 1566, 1567 eds.

867. *Infidelitie*] *Infideli.* in 1566, 1567 eds. *of*: about, concerning.

869f. *The song*. Carpenter, MM, p. 92, observes that the comparisons of Mary with Lais, Thais, and Helen, recall similar comparisons in the Balade in Chaucer's *Legend of Good Women*, The Prologue, ll. 249f.

882. *Huffa*. Carpenter compares this to the *Hoff* of evil spirits in the mystery plays (MM, p. 92).

891. *Pride of Life*] *Pride* in 1566, 1567 eds. *conglutinate*: attached.

893. *Cupiditie*] *Cupiditi* in 1566, 1567 eds.

895. *Carnall Concupiscence*] *Car. concupiscence* in 1566, 1567 eds.

899. *Infidelitie*] *Infide.* in 1566, 1567 eds.

900. *Mary*] *Marie* in 1566, 1567 eds.

901. *Iugge*: term of affection.

906. *inquired*: sought.

931. *Malicious Iudgement*] *Malicious iugement* in 1566, 1567 eds. *the Citie of Naim* [Nain]. See Luke 7:11. Given as *Naim* in the sixteenth-century versions of the Bible.

936. *rayse*: i.e., resurrect; see Luke 7:12-15.

937. *Malicious Iudgement*] *Malicious iudge.* in 1566, 1567 eds. See Luke 11:14f.

939. See Matthew 9:10-11.

941. See Matthew 11:9.

946. See Matthew 23.

948. See Matthew 12:1-14.

950. See John 8:58.

959. See Matthew 12:14.

967. *on*: of.

969. *Malicious Iudgement*] *Malicious iudge.* in 1566, 1567 eds.

973. *pretence*: intention.

981. *Malicious Iudgement*] *Malicious iudge.* in 1566, 1567 eds. *Ne credas tempori*. No known source for this tag. *Trust not the tyme he doth say*: Carpenter glosses this as "do not trust the date he names" (Carpenter, MM, p. 93).

991. *Malicious Iudgement*] *Malicious iudge.* in 1566, 1567 eds.

996. *marchant*: fellow.

997f. See Luke 9:58.

1021. *Malicious Iudgement*] *Malicious iudge.* in 1566, 1567 eds.

1023. *Infidelitie*] *Infide.* in 1566, 1567 eds.

1037. *Malicious Iudgement*] *Malicious iudge.* in 1566, 1567 eds.

1050. *fashion*: behavior, actions; see also l. 1065.

1055. *Malicious Iudgement*] *Malicious iudge.* in 1566, 1567 eds.

1069. *Infidelitie*] *Infide.* in 1566, 1567 eds.

1071. *Malicious Iudgement*] *Malicious iudge.* in 1566, 1567 eds.

1086. *for you*: so far as concerns you.

1093. *false eye*: see ll. 497-98n.

1099. *afrayde*: Carpenter suggests that this is a printer's correction of *afeard*, which is required by the rhyme. See l. 1963.

1113. *The Lawe*. The Lawe enters carrying stone tablets. The Lawe logically doubles with Cupiditi who sings the bass part in the song (see l. 863), he may have spoken in a deep voice appropriate for this Moses-like figure. For the doubling, see Bevington, *From Mankind to Marlowe*, p. 173.

1125-26. See Calvin's *Inst.*, III.vii.6. Here is the first among many passages in the play that are directly indebted to *The Inst.*. Calvin's work as a source to the play is discussed in the Introduction, p. xxxii, and Appendix B.

1127. *proude enterprise*: pride and boldness.

1131. See 1 Peter 2:9.

1137-39. See Calvin, *Inst.*, III.vii.7.

1148. *iust*: righteous. *mans fragilitie*: i.e., the weak human race.

1166-67. See Ecclesiastes 7:20; Psalm 14:3.

1183. *Women haue no soules, this saying is not newe*: proverbial (Dent, *Proverbial Lang.*, App. A, W709).

1186. *vndertake*: ppl. for undertaken, i.e., understood, included (Carpenter, MM, p. 93).

1189. See Romans 3:20.

1201. *Knowledge of Sinne*] *Knowledge of synne* in 1566, 1567 eds.

1202. *vilitie:* vileness; as in *The Longer*, l. 202.

1205. *Now wo be to the time that euer I was borne*. The familiar lament of the guilt-ridden sinner; see Judas's outcry in *All for Money*, sig. E2^{v}.

1221. *Knowledge of Sinne*] *Knowledge of synne* in 1566, 1567 eds.

1249. *Knowledge of Sinne*] *Knowledge of sinne* in 1566, 1567 eds.

1261-64. See Psalm 118:22; Matthew 21:42; Mark 12:10; 1 Peter 2:6.

1286. *I haue the sicke*: *haue* seems to be a misprint for *leaue* (Carpenter, MM, p. 93).

1292. *taking*: condition.

1293. *Knowledge of Sinne*] *Knowledge of synne* in 1566, 1567 eds.

1298. *Was thy conscience sicked*: sickness-stricken.

1301. *You bottell-nosed knaue*. This is one indication of the ugly appearance of Knowledge of Sin, who is earlier described as "a pocky knaue, and an yll fauoured" (l. 1198). In *All for Money*, "bottel nosed knaue" is applied to Satan, traditionally depicted with a large, ugly snout. Similar phrases appear in *Like Will to Like* ("bottel nosed godfather") and *Susanna* ("crookte nose knaue"). The matter is discussed in Craik, *Tudor Interlude*, p. 51.

1305. *Knowledge of Sinne*] *Knowledge of synne* in 1566, 1567 eds.

1308. *Knowledge of Sinne*] *Knowledge of synne* in 1566, 1567 eds.

1310. *away the mare*: proverbial; see Dent, *Proverbial Lang.*, App. A, M646. The meaning is "Away with care!"

1317. *Here entereth Christ Iesus.* According to Roston, *Biblical Drama*, p. 69, this is one of the last appearances of Christ on the English stage for some 350 years. The one other contemporary Protestant play depicting Christ (but only after the Resurrection) is John Foxe's *Christus Triumphans*, performed at Trinity College, Cambridge, in 1562/63. There, he appears in one brief scene (Act 1, Scene 4), carrying a Bible.

1321-32. See John 3:17; Luke 19:10; Matthew 4:17.

1335f. The action here, with Mary perhaps positioned between Christ, on the one hand, and Infidelitie, on the other, seems to re-enact the traditional stage psychomachia of Vice and Virtue figures competing for the soul of mankind, a configuration repeated by Marlowe in the Good and Bad Angel sequences in *Doctor Faustus*. For this, see Dessen, *Elizabethan Drama*, ch. 6.

1339. *harlot*: knave.

1357. *Christ Iesus*] *Christ* in 1566, 1567 ed.

1357-61. See John 5:21-24.

1373. *Christe Iusus*] *Christ*e in 1566, 1567 ed. *preuent, preuented* (l. 1394): to hinder from sin. See Bale's *Temptation*, l. 47.

1382. *the father*. Plural, as it is shown by the *they* of the following line, and possibly a misprint for *fathers*.

1388. *Cry all thus without the doore, and roare terribly*. Based on Luke 8:2f., the spectacular casting out of seven devils from Mary is depicted in the Digby *Mary Magdalene* (see Part I, ll. 678f.) and earlier in the mysteries. The devils roaring terribly is also a traditional piece of stagecraft. In the Digby *Mary* Satan beats them for their failure. The stage direction is additionally significant in that the reference to the door indicates clearly an indoor performance, most of which occurred in halls.

1390. See Matthew 8:29.

1395. *reiected*: expelled, specifically exorcised.

1400. *repend*: repay, requite.

1412. *strength*: strengthen; as in l. 1468.

1413. See John 6:44.

1414s.d. *Repentaunce*] *repentance* in 1566, 1567 eds.

1417. *Fayth*] *Faith* in 1566, 1567 eds.

1421. *Repentaunce*] *Repentance* in 1566, 1567 eds.

1425f. The speeches of Faith and Repentaunce are based on Calvin, *Inst.*, III.iii.5; III.ii.7; III.ii.6. See Introduction, pp. xxxii-xxxv, and Appendix B.

1438. *returnyng*: turning away.

1451. *miseration*: commiseration

1472. *forthinke*: repent, review.

1476. *ascertain*: assure.

1485. *promission*: promise.

1488. See Ephesians 1:13; 2 Corinthians 1:22.

1489. *Repentaunce*] *Repentance* in 1566, 1567 eds.

1497. *Fayth*] *Faith* in 1566, 1567 eds. See James 1:23f.

1505. *Repentaunce*] *Repentance* in 1566, 1567 eds.

1509. *Fayth*] *Faith* in 1566, 1567 eds.

1517. *Repentaunce*] *Repentance* in 1566, 1567 eds.

1520. See Ephesians 2:8-9.

1529. *Christ Iesus*] *Christ* in 1566, 1567 eds.

1533. *Fayth*] *Faith* in 1566, 1567 eds.

1535. *Repentaunce*] *Repentance* in 1566, 1567 eds.

1541. *Christ Iesus*] *Christ* in 1566, 1567 eds.

1542-56. See Matthew 11:25f.

1543-44. See Matthew 9:12-13.

1555. *slake*: decrease, cease.

1561-64. See Luke 15:7.

1565s.d. *Simon biddeth Christ to dynner*. This statement is more of a description of the action that follows than an actual stage direction.

1573. *Christ Iesus*] *Christ* in 1566, 1567 eds.

1575f. See John 5:19.

1581. *Malicious Iudgement*] *Malicious iudge.* in 1566, 1567 eds.

1588. *semble*: seem.

1590. *To take some repast*] This might be a printer's error for "some repast to take," which would restore the rhyme with l. 1592 (Carpenter, MM, pp. 93-94); compare to l. 1664.

1592. *puruiance*: provision.

1593. *Christ Iesus*] *Christ* in 1566, 1567 eds.

1601. *Christ Iesus*] *Christ* in 1566, 1567 eds.

1605. *Malicious Iudgement*] *Malicious iudge.* in 1566, 1567 eds.

1612. *Malicious Iudgement*] *Malicious iudge.* in 1566, 1567 eds.

1623. *rablement*: disorderly crowd, rabble.

1629. *As for a gowne*. This presumably is the "Pharisies gown" Infidelitie mentions earlier (l. 1025) "About the which the preceptes of the testament / Must be written in order one by one" (ll. 1077-80)

1638. *aldermen*: politicians.

1643. With the re-entry of Simon and Christ the stage area is transformed into the dining room in Simon's house, with the table, stools, and cushions, along with a wash basin, "trenchers, spoones, salt and bread," brought in with the players (l. 1649; ll. 1665-70). Infidelitie fetches and brings in the food and drink (l. 1663).

1649. *Malicious Iudgement*] *Malicious iudge.* in 1566, 1567 eds.

1655. *byr*: contraction for *by our*.

1671. *Infidelitie*] *Infideli.* in 1566, 1567 eds.

1673. *hither to*: misprinted *hitherto* in the original.

1675. *Christ Iesus*] *Christ* in 1566, 1567 eds.

1680. *ghostly*: spiritual.

1697. *Malicious Iudgement*] *Malicious iudge.* in 1566, 1567 eds.

1703. *Malicious Iudgement*] *Malicious iugement* in 1566, 1567 eds. *grutch*: trouble.

1715. *Christ Iesus*] *Christ* in 1566, 1567 eds.

1716-40. See John 5:31f.

1737. *the*: the original has y^t, a misprint for y^e.

1749. *Christ Iesus*] *Christ* in 1566, 1567 eds. *xi. houres*] a misprint for *.xii.* See John 11:9.

1757. *Malicious Iudgement*] *Malicious iudge.* in 1566, 1567 ed

1763. *Christ Iesus*] *Christ* in 1566, 1567 eds.

1764s.d. *sadly apparelled*: Mary's costume change signifies her change of heart. She carries a jar of ointment with her (l. 1813).

1767. *greuance*: trouble, grief.

1795. *obsequie*: service; see Bale's *Temptation*, l. 306.

1808. *detrimentes*: losses, damage.

1828s.d. *Let Marie . . . doe as it is specified in the gospell.* Mary applies the ointment to Christ's feet. This stage direction is perhaps the clearest evidence that the playscript was originally intended for actors, rather than for readers.

1837. *Malicious Iudgement*] *Malicious iudge.* in 1566, 1567 eds.

1839. *intromit*: to enter among, to have to do with.

1841-46. In the the original, these lines are given mistakenly to *Malicious iudgement*.

1847. *Malicious Iudgement*] *Malicious iudge.* in 1566, 1567 ed.

1849. The rhyme might be restored here (albeit imperfectly) by reading l. 1851 as *whereabout looke you* (cited in Carpenter, MM, p. 94).

1853. *Christ Iesus*] *Iesus Christ* in 1566, 1567 eds.

1857. *Christ Iesus*] *Christ* in 1566, 1567 eds.

1857f. See Luke 7:40f.

1860. *ought*: owned.

1867. *Christ Iesus*] *Christ* in 1566, 1567 eds.

1873. See Luke 7:39.
1874. *a:* used as a preposition: *of.*
1889. *Christ Iesus*] *Christ* in 1566, 1567 eds.
1901f. See Luke 7:44.
1921. *grutch*: complain.
1922. *iust,*] *iust* in 1566, 1567 eds.
1929-41. See Luke 7:40-49.
1937. *Malicious Iudgement*] *Malicious iudge.* in 1566, 1567 eds.
1941. *Christ Iesus*] *Christ* in 1566, 1567 eds.
1953-58. A thinly veiled reference to the Reformation.
1957. *Malicious Iudgement*] *Malicious iudge.* in 1566, 1567 eds.
1966. *blasphemer and*] Misprinted as *blasphemerand* in original.
1981. *Christ Iesus*] *Christ* in 1566, 1567 eds.
1993. *Christ Iesus*] *Christ* in 1566, 1567 eds.
2004. *obseruation*: observance.
2011. *Christ Iesus*] *Christ* in 1566, 1567 eds. *thee,*] *thee* in 1566, 1567 eds.
2019. *Infidelitie*] *Infide.* in 1566, 1567 eds.
2021. *Malicious Iudgement*] *Malicious iudge.* in 1566, 1567 eds.
2041. *Malicious Iudgement*] *Malicious iugement* in 1566, 1567 eds.
2047. *Infideltie*] *Infideli.* in 1566, 1567 eds.
2049f. The rhyme-scheme changes here from alternate quatrains to couplets. To restore the rhyme in the opening couplet, line 2050 may be altered to read *of his mercy great* .
2058. *reproued*: refuted, disproved.
2066f. See Matthew 22:37-39.
2096. *simulate*: simulated.
2101. *perfite*: perfect.
2109-12. Carpenter notes that the same sentiment about wearying the audience and excuse given for ending the action is found toward the end of *The Longer* (ll. 1973-76). See also *Enough*, ll. 1621-22.
2130. *munificence*: magnificence.

NOTES ON *IACOB AND ESAU*

Title Page

7-9. *the Players / who are to be consydered to be Hebrews / and so should be apparailed with attire.* This is the earliest known stated intention in English drama of dressing the characters in "period costume." Historical realism is also attempted with the use of biblical coins, the shekel and talent (although "ten thousand pounds" slips in), by avoiding anachronistic oaths, "by Jesu," "by our Lady," etc., and by addressing prayers to the God of Abraham (see Blackburn, *Biblical Drama,* pp. 152-53).

10. *The Prologue, a Poete.* It is probable that "the Poete," who delivers the epilogue as well, was the schoolmaster in charge of the original production, since it was a common practice in Tudor England for such masters as Richard Hunnis, Nicholas Udall, Thomas Ashton to write plays for their own students. In Kilkenny, Ireland, John Bale directed his "boys" in the staging of *God's Promises, The Temptation of Our Lord,* and *Three Laws.* In these, he functions as Prologue.

10-19. *Hanan, Zether, Ragau, Deborra.* As Blackburn observes (p. 153), these four names do not derive from the Genesis narrative of Jacob and Esau, but they are all Hebrew. Zethar, one of Isaac's neighbors, is the name of Ahazuerus' chamberlain in Esther 1:10. His companion, Hanan (meaning "gracious"), is called after the Benjamite of 1 Chronicles 8:23. Ragau, Esau's servant, is derived from Luke 3: 35. Rebekah's nurse, Deborah, is taken from her more famous counterpart in Judges 4 and 5.

The Prologue

1-7. God's promise to Abraham first appears in Genesis 12:1-3, and is repeated several times throughout the Abrahamic narrative as well as in the New Testament (see Galations 3:15; Hebrews 6:13-18).

5. See Genesis 25:21-26.

8-14. For the possible debt to Calvin's *Institutes* here, see Introduction, pp. xliii-xliv, and Appendix B.

10. *Malachie and Paule*: Malachi 1:1-3; Romans 9:13.

13. *renuing*] Crow and Wilson, JE, suggests that this should read *renning*.

17. See Romans 8:15; 9:4; and Galatians 4:5.

The Text

22s.d. *greyhounds*. For use of dogs and other animals in Tudor dramatic productions, see Introduction, p. xxxvii.

28. *.vif.*] this (from 1568 ed.) appears to be a misprint of *five.*

31. *hogges head*: sleepy head.

38. *yallyng*: howling, yelling.

39. *for from he call:* i.e., from the time he calls.

40. *stounde*: moment, time.

47. *Fette*: fetch.

54. *freshe*: afresh, anew.

61. *sute:* pursuit(?)

67. *fashions*: manner, behavior.

69-70. *passeth*: careth, regardeth.

71s.d. *appereth in sight . . . ere he enter*: Southern (p. 364) cites this stage direction as evidence that the play was performed in a hall, since only in such a setting would the actor be able to appear in sight *before he entered*, standing in the entrance framed by one of the doors at the screen end of the hall.

77. *disease*: trouble, discomfort.

79. *draffesack*: a term of abuse. *draff* means dregs, refuse, specifically brewer's grains (Farmer, JE, p. 357).

93. *haue at it*: try it, begin it.

94. *haile peale*: greeting, salutation.

106. *meales meate*: food eaten at a meal.

107. *Teg*: a young deer.

108. *hoe*: stop, enough.

117. *mome*: fool, buffoon.

124. *wene*: think.

125. *brother myne*: No family relationship is implied here nor in l. 108 (*childe*).

127. *take the law of the game*: *take* in the sense of receive. The sense seems to be "receive what the law requires"; Esau now begins to beat Ragau.

130. *scapes*: misdemeanors. As Farmer notes, "Ragau has presumed to sneer at Jacob and Esau, who, while reviling Jacob himself, resented a servant taking a liberty" (p. 445).

131. *iertes*: jerks, strokes, with the whip; *for the nonce*: for the particular purpose. *must haue*] *musthaue* in 1568 ed.
135. *cheuerell*: garment made from young goat skin.
137. *mopyng*: grimacing; scowling.
142s.d. *Exeant ambo*: let both exit.
150. *addresseth*: gets ready, prepares for.
158. *boote*: avail.
161. *stay*: state.
164f. *See* Psalm 22:6; Proverbs 13:24; 22:15; 23:13-14; 29:15.
165. *ensue*: follow after, practice.
175. *here in the Tentes*: This might suggest that several tents make up the play's scenery, but for this aspect of staging, see Introduction, p. xxxviii, note 42, and Southern, *Staging of Plays before Shakespeare*, pp: 361-74:
176. *any whan*: any time.
179. *Yong it pricketh (folk do say) that wyll be a thorne*: proverbial (Dent, *Proverbial Lang*. Appen. A., T232). The title page of *Nice Wanton* similarly states, "Early sharp, that will be thorn; / Soon ill, that will be naught."
191. *documents*: precepts, teaching, example.
193. *retchelesse*: reckless.
195. *speciall grace*: It is only through "special grace," we are told, that the "godlye" child Barnabus is saved from damnation in *Nice Wanton* .
213. *sad*: serious, sober-minded.
216. *mell*: interfere, meddle.
222. *lende*: give, afford.
223. *purse*: Farmer, JE, glosses: "offer, as an insult or jibe, to pay Jacob for his interference" (p. 433).
236. See Romans 11:33.
237. *pointed*: appointed.
238. See 1 Timothy 2:21.
242f. See Genesis 25:23.
244. *fashions*: kind, sort.
252. *not)*] 1568 ed. read *not* (the parenthesis is missing).
253. *assay*: try, attempt.
258. *withouten*: without.
268. *sprite:* spirit
269. *assay*: See l. 253.
283. *leade me forth of doores*: i.e., lead me forth out-of-doors.
290. *my wife*] *myfe* (printer's error?) in 1568 ed.
297. *Rebecca*] 1568 ed. read *Rebecc.*
298. *Isaac*] 1568 ed. read *Isaac.a.*
303. *Rebecca*] erroneously faced l. 304 in 1568 ed.

305f. See James 1:2-3; 1 Peter 4:12-13.
318f. See Job 2:10.
336. *knack*: trick, joke.
344. *perfight*: perfect.
355. *wourne*] Hazlitt substitutes *scorn*. Crow and Wilson, JE, notes that the original makes perfect sense: 'warn,' to refuse to grant.
368. *retchelesly*: recklessly.
379. *In deede*] 1568 ed. read *I deede*.
385. *oneth:* variation of *uneath*, scarcely, hardly.
398. *fordonne*: undone. The ensuing dialogue in alternate lines is one of several passages in the text employing stichomythia, perhaps in imitation of the classics.
403. See Deuteronomy 21:17; see also l. 419.
431. *I vse not for to lye*: I am not accustomed to lying.
445. *knowlage*: recognize, acknowledge.
457. *Yea, womens answers are but fewe times to seeke*: proverbial (Dent, *Proverbial Lang.* App. A., W670).
481. *siely*: trivial, silly.
496. *Esau*] faces l. 497 in 1568 ed.
499. *force*: care.
509. *braune:* muscle.
521. *If had thee*] Farmer follows Hazlitt in reading *If* [I] *had thee*.
524. *let me tell thee a worde in thine eare*. See *Mary Magdalene*, l. 734 and note.
525. *nere*: nearer.
529. *whelpe*: puppy. *King Johan*, l. 663: "He regardyth no more the Pope than he dothe a whelpe."
530. *lust*: wish, desire.
531. *And plucke a good crowe ere ye brake your fast with me*: proverbial (Dent, *Proverbial Lang.* App. A., C855). "Pluck at the crow" was a game or sport in which one person was pulled ("plucked") around by others. *Misogonus*: "Throw the knave down and with him pluck at a crow" (I.i. 427 and note).
532. *mankene*: furious, mad.
538. *grannt*] the first *n* seems to be an inverted *u*; thus, *graunt*.
543. *thee,*] Crow and Wilson, JE, says the comma is doubtful.
546. *throst*: thirst.
548. *fremman*: Stranger, one not related.
559. *hodypeake:* a fool, simpleton, blockhead
563. *tratling*: prattling, talking idly. *boying*: boylike.

567. *wrabbed.* rabid (?). Farmer notes that the word is used in this sense in Heywood's *Four P.P.*, where it also rhymes with "crabbed."

571. *lulleth a sow*: pulls by the ears.

589. *peake*: mope, act dejectedly.

598. *sticke*: scruple, hesitate.

607. *indent*: execute, make compact.

610. *stounde*: see l. 40.

611. *cicle*: shekel.

628s.d. *Esau entring into Iacobs tent*: This is the first s.d. in which the word *tent* is used, and it suggests that Jacob, along with Isaac, Esau, and the neighbors Hanan and Zethar, has his own tent represented in the acting space. This I believe to be plausible for a court performance, but as Southern (p. 366) observes, elsewhere in the play it is implied that Jacob lives with his parents in Isaac's tent. He would interpret the s.d. to mean Jacob's part of Isaac's tent. The discrepancies might be explained by a playscript only partially revised for simpler, sparser staging after performance at court.

647. *stabbe*: Farmer: "a variant of *stub* = to root up--to wallow in food as doth a hog in a swill."

655. *As ere was eate Iacob*: *ere* used as a contraction for *ever*; *eate* used as noun, i.e., food; hence, phrase may be glossed "as ever was food, Jacob."

657. *Esau a dawe*: i.e., "Esau is a daw." A *daw* is a small crow; the term was applied contemptuously to a foolish, silly person; as in *The Disobedient Child*: "I never saw One . . . in so easy a matter . . . thus play the daw."

670. *cogeld.* Farmer suggests "'tucked in' at his meal," which sounds more plausible to me than the OED gloss: "To foist in, esp[ecially] in a wheedling way"; *cries ka kob*. The "caw" (sound) of the jackdaw, perhaps when it is most hungry (see l. 657n). *Mido*] in 1568 ed., the *M* is upside down.

673. *wotte*: know, think.

682. *auant*: boastfully (from the French).

684. *stomachere*: stomach cheer; i.e., food.

685. *shent*: blamed, reproached, put to shame.

686. *licence*: leave, permission.

688. *thanke*: thanks.

692. *Clawe a churle by the tayle, and he will file your hand*: proverbial. A variation on this proverb is "Grease a fat sow in the tail and he (or she) will beray (defile) your hand." See Dent's *Proverbial Lang.* App. A., C386.

694. *meated*: fed, supplied with food.

703. *hound*] *honud* in 1568 ed.
726. *no*] *uo* in 1568 ed.
738. *or a*] *ora* in 1568 ed.
742. *Esau*] faces l. 743 in 1568 ed.
745. *bidden*: gone without; abstained from.
746. *mawe*: stomach.
755. *clattering*: chattering; talking idly; as in l. 910.
761. *twelfe*: twelve.
765. *lyther*: bad, worthless (usually physically).
771. *with a mischiefe*: popular expression interchangeable with *with a vengeance*. See also l. 825.
788. *Nay soft brother mine*: see l. 125.
790. *delicates*: delicacies, tidbits.
794. *euer ye*] *euerye* in 1568 ed.
800. *maship*: mastership; in abbreviated form, as used here, it often implied disrespect.
804. *mease*: *meale;* see also l. 854. *pardy*: verily (a form of oath).
806. *toye*: trifle, whim, fancy.
808. *lob*: lout, bumpkin.
812. *syr reuerence*: English proverb. This is a proverbial expression of apology for saying something possibly offensive, a clipped version of "Saving your reverence."
820. *falchion*: a small broad sword, slightly curved at the point, popular in Medieval England.
825. *drawlatch*: thief, rogue (general word of contempt).
831. *my parte of the tent*: this seems to suggest that Esau does not live in his own separate tent but in a section of a larger tent, perhaps Isaac's as Southern maintains.
832. *I go incontinent*: immediately, at once.
834. *[quinta]*] mistakenly labelled *quarta* in 1568 ed.
836. *as streight as a threde*: a proverbial expression borrowed from spinning.
838. *scudde*: run nimbly, briskly.
841. *all to*] *allto* in 1568 ed.
847. *sonne*: in the sense of "boy."
859. *shrewe:* rebuke or scold.
872. *The firste song* (s.d.). The song is a simple anthem, perhaps in four parts, similar to those written by the Chapel Royal composers in the mid-sixteenth century (see Le Huray, *Music & Reform. in England,* pp. 57-89, and 185-226). It is impossible to know from the text itself whether this piece was accompanied by instruments, but if performed at the Chapel Royal, it probably involved at least the organ and possibly viols or regals. The organ is specified for sacred

music in Bale's *God's Promises* (see l. 178 s.d.) performed by boys. All the above-mentioned instruments were used in boys' plays at court from the latter part of Henry VIII's reign onwards. See Stevens, *Music & Poetry*, pp. 252-59; Craik, *Tudor Interlude*, pp. 45-48,Wickham, *Early Eng. Stages*, pp. 150-55.

912s.d. *exeant omnes*: let everyone exit.

914. *slack*: lax, remiss, neglectful; see also l. 937 and l. 1061.

934. *poule*: variation of poll. the crown of the head or nape of the neck.

942s.d. *Enter Rebecca unseen*: I follow Farmer in inserting this stage direction. As Rebecca reveals a few minutes later she has eavesdropped on the exchange between Isaac and Esau. At this point, the entrance would provide dramatic irony (*Isaac:* "Is none here but we? / *Esau*: "None to herken our talke father, that I doo see").

950. *ruth*: sorrow, pity, compassion.

959f. See Genesis 27:1-4.

966. *koosse*] kiss.

968. *With*] *Wits* in 1568 ed.

971. *withouten*: without, as on l. 258.

987. *(thinke this to be true)*] the first of the two parentheses is missing in 1568 ed.

1021. *is*] *his* in 1568 ed.

1023-24. *I shall with a trice make such meate certain, / As shall say come eat me*: proverbial. "Here is a pigion so finely roasted it cries, Come eat me" (Dent, App. A., P315). *with a trice*: in an instant.

1038. *deuoire*: duty, service (from the French *devoir*).

1049. *I am at all assayes*: "I am ready for anything." See *Ralph Roister Doister*, p. 40.

1051. *quarter sacke*: a sack capable of holding a quarter of grain.

1061. *slacking*: see l. 914.

1071. *vessell*] Farmer, JE, emends to *vessells*.

1095. *smell*: detect, perceive.

1098. *As trimme as a trencher*: proverbial; see *King Johan*: "For he hath crosse keyes with a tryple crowne and a cope, / Trymme as a trencher, havynge hys shoes of golde" (ll. 2560-61). *tricke*: neat.

1104. *Yong doth it pricke that wyll be a thorne*: proverbial; see l. 179n.

1135. *And here again I trow, ere an horse licke his eare*: proverbial; see William Wager's *Enough*: "We will be here again or a horse can lick his ear" (l. 1218).

1144. *Cat after kinde (saith the prouerbe) swete milke wil lap*: proverbial. "That cat is out of kind that sweet milk will not lap" (Dent, *Proverbial Lang*. App. A., C167). Similarly, in Bale's *Three Lawes*: "I shall kepe ye as well from that / As my grandame kept her cat / From lyckynge of her creame" (l. 340-43).

1153. *farcing*: stuffing.

1156. *percelie*: parsley.

1157. *Endiue*: the name of two species of chicory. *suckorie*: chicory. *lacteux*: lettuce (?). *Violette*: violet petals were used in salads.

1158. *Liuerworte*: Soaked in wine, this was believed to have been good for liver and lung disease. *marigolde:* Marigold flowers were often made into jam.

1159. *Peniryal*: a species of mint, often used for medicinal purposes. *buglosse*: a plant used to treat snake and other venomous bites.

1183-88. *see thou bee a stone*: i.e., as silent as a stone, as Rebecca makes clear five lines later.

1187. *preatie*: i.e., pretty.

1188. *saye.] saye* in 1568 ed.

1211. *is so possible*] Hazlitt, *Dodsley's Plays*, and Farmer, JE, emend to *is so impossible.*

1212. *beck*: nod, bow (as salutation).

1213. See Matthew 6:10; Acts 21:14.

1243 *stall:* applied to a sheath or receptacle of various kinds.

1248s.d. The stage direction instructing Rebecca to put the goat-skin sleeves on Jacob refers to Genesis 27:15-16.

1256. *triksie*: see l. 1098.

1270. *assaile*: approach.

1272. *bewray:* betray, expose.

1290f. Isaac's deception is found in Genesis 27:18f.

1294. *benison:* the pronouncing or invocation of a blessing, benediction.

1302. *sowneth*: soundeth. Hazlitt, *Dodsley's Plays,* revises as *soconeth,* but as Farmer, JE, maintains, the original derives from *soune* (meaning noise/sound in Anglo-Saxon).

1305. *pittance*: a portion or allowance of food or drink.

1306. *suffisance*: sufficiency, plenty.

1309. *slightly*: cunningly, craftily.

1310. *the blinde eate many a flye.* The phrase, which needs explanation here, is proverbial, as in *Magnificence*: "By God, we have made Magnyfycence to ete a flye" (l. 503). See also Dent, *Proverbial Lang.* App. A., B451.

1322. *Abra*] *Mido* is the speech-prefix in 1568 ed., an apparent mistake.
1332f. The blessing of Jacob is found in Genesis 27:26f.
1349. *missay*: slander, say ill of.
1382. *take no greefe*: take no offence, find no fault.
1392. *cock on houpe*: an obscure proverbial expression, the original meaning of which seems to have been to "turn on the tap and let the liquor flow" (OED). However, it came to be an exclamatory expression of merriment and celebration; same application in *The Longer*, l. 322.
1400. *swayne*: servant, herdsman.
1411. *wonne my spurres*: i.e., achieved honor, proven myself. "To win one's spurrs" was a proverbial expression for gaining knighthood, the spur being the distinctive mark of a knight.
1425. *ruffle*: swagger, flaunt.
1426. *port*: way of living, in Esau's instance, a better and preferred way of living.
1428. *quinti*] *quarti* in 1568 ed.
1434f. See Romans 11:33.
1441f. Esau's discovery that he has been impersonated and the following events are found in Genesis 27:30 f.
1446. *ioyly*: splendid, excellent.
1457. *scath*: harm, hurt.
1459. *preuented*: forestalled, go before (from the French, *prevenir*). Bale's *Johan Baptystes Preaching*: Whose wholsom commynge Johan Baptyst wyll prevent" (l. 5).
1477. *Wo be the day and houre that euer I was borne*. See Mary's similar outcry of despair in MM, l. 1119 (and note).
1484. *remorse*: pity, compassion.
1498. *hedgecreeper*: a general term of reproach.
1499. *fetche*: trick, stratagem.
1506. *fortune*: chance, happen.
1508. *misers*: wretches, miserable persons.
1510. *I shal coyle them till they stinke for pain*. *Ralph Roister Doister*: "I shall cloute thee tyll thou stinke." *Coyle* here means to beat, thrash, or punish as with the lash of a whip winding round the culprit's body.
1512. *I will take no daies*: lose no time.
1513. *potte*: punishment, or place of punishment; apparently originating from *melting pot* (as place of execution).
1514. *araye*: mess.
1517. *to come lagge*: late, last.
1520. *ieopard a grote*: jeopardize or wager a groat, a silver coin worth about four pence.

1521. *If he may reache them, will haue on the peticote*: The petticoat was a man's undergarment worn beneath the doublet. The expression is proverbial (see, e.g., "pay him o'th' petticoat" in *Misogonus*, II.i.12), and seems to imply a beating of the genitals.

1522. Abra, Mido, and Deborra are presumably inside "the tent" at this point, appearing one after the other before Esau. Ragau is perhaps at the entrance.

1523. *fray?*] *fray*. in 1568 ed.

1525. *renne*: run.

1526. *Gill*: wanton, girl.

1528. *Mab*: old witch, a term of abuse.

1529. *white as midnightes arsehole*: A most curious expression, which Farmer glosses as "a meridan of foulness."

1530. *cluster.*] *cluster* in 1557/58 ed.

1533. *all*] *al* in 1557/58 ed.

1535. *If*] *Yf* in 1557/58 ed. *lay me on the iacke*: a jack is a loose-fitting outergarment worn by men and women; hence, attack, lay blows upon.

1536. *then,*] *than* in 1557/58 ed.

1537. *muche*] *much* in 1557/58 ed.

1538. *sayest . . . litle theefe? if . . . thee*] *saist . . . little thefe. yf . . . thee* in 1557/58 ed.

1539. *God*] *god* in 1557/58 ed.

1541. *drinkeof the whippe*: i.e., "feel the whip." *drinkeof*] *drinke of* in 1557/58 ed.

1542. *Gods*] *gods* in 1557/58 ed.

1545. *fiende*] *fende* in 1557/58 ed.

1547. *If*] *Yf* in 1557/58 ed.

1549. *shalbe*] *shall be* in 1557/58 ed.

1551. *Then hence . . . once, and*] *Than hens . . . ones . . . &* in 1557/58 ed.

1553. *once . . . shal*] *ones . . . shall* in 1557/58 ed. *Tib*. Farmer thinks the word is allied to *fib*; hence, feign, pretend.

1554. *suretiship*: obligation undertaken by one person on behalf of another in payment of debt. *clappe*: blow, slap (with the hand).

1555. *olde . . . shal*] *old . . . shall* in 1557/58 ed.

1559. *Debora*] speech-prefix reads *Rebecca* in 1568 ed.

1560. *businesse.*] *busiues,* in 1557/58 ed.

1565. *borne*] *born* in 1557/58 ed.

1566. *beforne*: before, openly to view.

1567. *holding*] *holdyng* in 1557/58 ed.

1569. *God*] *god* in 1557/58 ed.

1570. *will*] *wtll* in 1568 ed. *God*] *god* in 1557/58 ed.
1574. *Iacob . . . meete*] *iacob . . . mete* in 1557/58 ed.
1576. *shall*] *shal* in 1557/58 ed.
1577. *day:*] *day,* in 1557/58 ed.
1579. *this,*] *this.* in 1557/58 ed.
1582. *sword*] *sworde* in 1557/58 ed.
1583. *like*] *lyke* in 1557/58 ed.
1584. *saucie merchaunt*: insolent fellow.
1588. *Than*] *Then* in 1557/58 ed.
1590. *ill . . . thing*] *yl . . . thyng* in 1557/58 ed.
1592. *and . . . hence*] *& . . . hens* in 1557/58 ed.
1593. *thing*] *thyng* in 1557/58 ed.
1596. *him*] *hym* in 1557/58 ed.
1599.. *did*] *dyd* in 1557/58 ed.
1600. *and*] & in 1557/58 ed. *somwhither*: somewhere.
1601. *thee*] *thy* in 1557/58 ed.
1603-49. See Genesis 27:42f; Genesis 28:1f
1605. *Laban,*] *Laban* in 1557/58 and 1568 eds.
1607. *thinges*] *thynges* in 1557/58 ed.
1608. *thee again*] *the agayn* in 1557/58 ed.
1611. *Iacob*] *iacob* in 1557/58 ed.
1612. *do*] *doo* in 1557/58 ed.
1613. *priuely tyl . . . do*] *priuily tyl . . . doo* in 1557/58 ed.
1619. *[Isaac]*] this speech-prefix faced l. 1618 in 1568 ed.
1620. *short*] *short,* in 1557/58 ed.
1621. *neede*] *nede* in 1557/58 ed.
1622. *being*] *beyng* in 1557/58 ed.
1623. *loth*] *lothe* in 1557/58 ed.
1624. *would*] *should* in 1557/58 ed.
1625. *life.*] *lyfe,* in 1557/58 ed.
1629. *then*] *than* in 1557/58 ed.
1633. *Iacob*] *iacob* in 1557/58 ed.
1634. *Isaac*] *Isaa* in 1568 ed. *thee*] *the* in 1557/58 ed. *fast thou*] *fast as thou* in 1557/58 ed.
1638. *life*] *lyfe* in 1557/58 ed.
1640. *peace.*] *peace* in 1557/58 ed.
1641. *seede*] *sede* in 1557/58 ed.
1642. *Iacob . . . way*] *iacob . . . waye* in 1557/58 ed.
1643. *sweete . . . hence*] *swete . . . hens* in 1557/58 ed.
1644. *parents, . . . heart*] *parentes . . . hert* in 1557/58 ed.
1645. *Lord*] *lord* in 1557/58 ed.
1647. *litle*] *little* in 1557/58 ed.
1648. *againe*] *agayne* in 1557/58 ed.
1649. *remaine*] *remayne* in 1557/58 ed.

1650. *And . . . deede*] *Ad . . . dede* in 1557/58 ed.
1652. *Iacob*] *iacob* in 1557/58 ed.
1653. *him*] *hym* in 1557/58 ed. *whirlewynd*. The sense of this line is obscure; for Farmer it anticipates the Sedgely curse, "May the great fiend, booted and spurred, with a scythe at his girdle, ride headlong down thy throat."
1654. *daye*] *day* in 1557/58 ed.
1656. *al*] *all* in 1557/58 ed.
1662. *Iacob*] *iacob* in 1557/58 ed.
1664. *shal . . . Lord*] *shall . . . lord* in 1557/58 ed.
1667. *than*] *then* in 1557/58 ed.
1670. *thine owne*] *thyne own* in 1557/58 ed.
1672. *dearlyng*] *derlyng* in 1557/58 ed. *princkore*: a saucy youth. *golpoll*: an expression of endearment.
1678. *him*] *hym* in 1557/58 ed.
1680. *Iacob . . . aduaunce . . . wyse:*] *iacob . . . aduaunced . . . wyse.* in 1557/58 ed.
1681. *of the new guise*: usually means of the latest fashion or deportment (as in the vice New Guise in *Mankind*). Here the term could have topical significance in referring to Jacob's Protestant piety.
1682. *mine*] *myne* in 1557/58 ed.
1685. *bring . . . Lordes . . . upon*] *bryng . . . lordes . . . vpon* in 1557/58 ed.
1686. *all . . . Iacobs*] *al . . . iacobs* in 1557/58 ed.
1689. *let*] *leat* in 1557/58 ed.
1691. *Which*] *Whiche* in 1557/58 ed.
1692. *thing*] *thynge* in 1557/58 ed.
1694. *mine . . . shall*] *myne . . . shal* in 1557/58 ed.
1697. *as recorde?*] *as a recorde?* in 1557/58 ed.
1700. *dooth*] *doothe* in 1557/58 ed.
1705. *then do . . . God . . . minde*] *than doo . . . god . . . mynde* in 1557/58 ed.
1708. *would . . . doing*] *woulde . . . doyng* in 1557/58 ed.
1709. *comming*] *commyng* in 1557/58 ed. *[Esau]*] this speech-prefix is misplaced facing l. 1711 in 1568 ed.
1713. *Against*] *Agaynst* in 1557/58 ed.
1719. *Mee . . . will*] *Me . . . wyl* in 1557/58 ed.
1720. *do*] *doo* in 1557/58 ed.
1721. *best*] *hest* in 1568 ed. *can.*] *can,* in 1557/58 ed.
1722. *Cal*] *Call* in 1557/58 ed.
1723s.d. *This song must be song after the prayer*: In 1557/58 ed., the stage direction here reads: *This is the last song, & must be song after the prayer*.

1725. See Romans 11:33.
1725. *unsearcheable*] *vnsearchable* in 1557/58 ed.
1726. *almightifull . . . did*] *almightyfull . . . dyd* in 1557/58 ed.
1727. *Both heaun . . . earth*] *Bothe heauen . . . earthe* in 1557/58 ed.
1729. *do . . . worship*] *doo . . . worshyp* in 1557/58 ed.
1732. *thine . . . didst*] *thynge . . . dydst* in 1557/58 ed.
1733. *Promising him . . . skie*] *Promysyng hym . . . skye* in 1557/58 ed.
1735. *might*] *myght* in 1557/58 ed.
1736. *Performe . . . thine*] *Perfourme . . . thyne* in 1557/58 ed.
1737. *Abraham,*] *Abraham:* in 1557/58 ed.
1738. *thine*] *thyne* in 1557/58 ed.
1739. *Guide*] *Guyde* in 1557/58 ed.
1739s.d. *Then . . . and . . . stand . . . til*] *Than. . . & . . . stand . . . tyll* in 1557/58 ed. *The Poet entreth*. This redundant stage direction, which appears in the right-hand margin, is slightly different from the one in 1557/58 ed., which reads: *The Poetes part.*
1745. *mercie*] *mercye* in 1557/58 ed.
1746. *once . . . glorie*] *ones . . . glorye* in 1557/58 ed.
1747. *did . . . then*] *dyd . . . than* in 1557/58 ed.
1748. *children . . . promise*] *chyldren . . . promyse* in 1557/58 ed.
1750. *giue*] *geue* in 1557/58 ed.
1751-55. For the theological and topical significance of these lines, see Introduction, pp. xliii-xliv.
1752. *mercy:*] *mercye* in 1557/58 ed.
1754. *intellection*: understanding, intellect.
1755. *attaine*] *attayne* in 1557/58 ed.
1757. *secret . . . meete*] *secrete . . . mete* in 1557/58 ed.
1759. *deepnesse . . . riches*] *depenes . . . richesse* in 1557/58 ed.
1760. *unsearcheable*] *vnsercheable* in 1557/58 ed.
1761. *parte*] *part* in 1557/58 ed.
1762. *doubtyng*] *doutyng* in 1557/58 ed.
1763. *Then*] *Than* in 1557/58 ed.
1765. *Thirdly*] *Thirdely* in 1557/58 ed.
1767. *Iacob*] *iacob* in 1557/58 ed.
1767s.d. *prayer*] *praier* in 1557/58 ed.
1769. *auance*: advance.
1770. *Then*] *Than* in 1557/58 ed.
1771. *God*] *god* in 1557/58 ed.
1773. *maintaine hir*] *maintayne her* in 1557/58 ed.
1774. *greeued*] *greued* in 1557/58 ed.
1775. *enimies*] *enemies* in 1557/58 ed.

1776. *and*] *&* in 1557/58 ed.
1777. *godlinesse . . . heartes endue.*] *godlines . . . hertes endue,* in 1557/58 ed.
1779. *Quenes*] *quenes* in 1557/58 ed.
1780s.d. *Thus endeth this Comedie*:] *endeth this Comedie* in 1557/58 ed.

GLOSSARY

A: *Ah!* MM 542
a: used as a preposition *of*. MM 1874
abiected: cast off. MM 733
accumbred: encumbered. MM 510
addresseth: gets ready, prepares for. JE 150
affect: affection, passion. MM 14
aldermen: politicians. MM 1638
allecteth: allures. MM 731
almose: alms. MM 185
al thing: *everything*. MM 32
alway: always. MM 386; as in MM 436, 462, 556, 581, 674, 799, 1075
any whan: any time. JE 176
araye: mess. JE 1514
ascertain: assure. MM 1476
assaile: approach. JE 1270
assay: try, attempt.JE 253; see also JE 269 and 272.
attire: head-dress. MM 627
auance. advance. JE 1769.
auant: boastfully. JE 682
backare: back off. MM 574
beforne: before, openly to view. JE 1566
beleue: belief. MM 53; see also MM 1265, 2105.
benison: the pronouncing or invocation of a blessing, benediction. JE 1017, 1294
bewray: betray, expose. JE 1272
bidden: gone without; abstained from. JE 745
bon grace: bonnet, or shade for the face. MM 670
boote: avail. JE 158
boying: boylike. JE 563
braune: muscle. JE 509
bungarliest: clumsiest, most awkward MM 144; see also MM 158, *bungarly*
by: about. MM 618
byr: contraction for *by our*. MM 1655
can little skill: have but little skill. MM 226
cast: trick, device. MM 810; see also MM 821: *castes*.
chargeable: costly, burdensome. MM 49
cheuerell: garment made from young goat skin. JE 135
cicle: shekel. JE 611
clappe: blow, slap (with the hand). JE 1554
clattering: chattering; talking idly. JE 755; as in JE 910
commoditie: advantage. MM 558
conglutinate: attached. MM 891
conuey: manage, conduct. MM 123; see also MM 759
corage: spirit, wilfulness. MM 684; see MM 647

daw a: foolish, silly person. JE 657
dearlyng: darling, favorite. MM 258
decent: proper. MM 277
delicates: delicacies, tid-bits. JE 790
detract: depreciate. MM 24
detrimentes: losses, damage. MM 1808
deuoire: duty, service. JE 1038, 1204
disease: trouble, discomfort. JE 77
dispaire: decay. MM 651
documentes. precepts, teaching, example. JE 191
draff: dregs, refuse, specifically brewer's grains. JE 79
draffesack: a term of abuse. JE 79
drawlatch: thief, rogue (general word of contempt). JE 825
drinkeof the whippe: i.e. "feel the whip." JE 1541
ebrietie: drunkenness. MM 388
endiue: two species of chicory. JE 1157
ensue: follow after, practice. JE 165
entreating: treating. MM title pg.
erected: raised up. MM 78
falchion: a small broad sword, slightly curved at the point, popular in Medieval England. JE 820
false eye: MM 1093; see MM 497-98n
farcing: stuffing. JE 1153
fashion: behavior, actions. MM 1050; see also MM 1065; JE 67
fashions. kind, sort. JE 244
fautes: faults. MM 38; see also MM 660
Feate: elegant. MM 194
fetche: trick, stratagem. JE 1499
fette: fetch. JE 47
force: care. JE 499
fordonne: undone. JE 398
for from the call: i.e., from the time he calls. JE 39
for the nonce: for the particular purpose. JE 131
forthinke: repent, review. MM 1472
fortune: chance, happen. JE 1506
for you: so far as concerns you. MM 1086
freate: fret, trouble. MM 77
fremman: stranger, one not related. JE 548
frequented: made use of, patronized. MM 37
freshe: afresh, anew. JE 54
gaudes or mockes: jests, tricks. MM 659
geare: dress. MM 150; see also MM 160, 162, 164, 168, 488
geare: appliances, MM 644; see also MM 848 and 2009
geare: matter, MM 735; see also MM 764, 767, 1653, 1668, 1758
geason: rare, uncommon. MM 14
ghostly: spiritual. MM 1680
Gill: wanton, girl. JE 1526
gis: an oath; euphemistic form of *Jesus*. MM 155
golpoll: an expression of endearment. JE 1672
gree: agree. MM 608; see also MM 1320
greefe: offence, fault. JE 1382
greuance: trouble, grief. MM 1767
grutche: trouble. MM 1702
grutche: complain. MM 1921
gymmes: links. MM 696
habitacle: habitation. MM 326
haile peale: greeting, salutation. JE 94

hardely: boldly. MM 752
harlot: knave. MM 1339
hart rote: term of endearment, "sweetheart." MM 827
have at it: try it, begin it. JE 93
headinesse: headstrongness. MM 393
hedgecreeper: a general term of reproach. JE 1498
hodypeake: a fool, simpleton, blockhead. JE 559
hoe: stop, enough. JE 108
hogges head: sleepy head. JE 31
holde: bet, wager; see also 1846. MM 155
I am at all assays: "I am ready for anything." JE 1049
ieopard a grote: jeopardize or wager a groat, a silver coin worth about four pence. JE 1520
iertes: jerks, strokes, with the whip. JE 131
I go incontinent: immediately, at once. JE 832
indent: execute, make compact. JE 607
intellection: understanding, intellect. JE 1754
intromit: to enter among, to have to do with. MM 1839
inquired: sought. MM 906
ioyly: splendid, excellent. JE 1446
Iugge: term of affection. MM 901
Iurie: Jewry, the land of the Jews. MM 214
iust: righteous. MM 1148
I vse not for to lye: I am not accustomed to lying. JE 431
I will take no daies: lose no time. JE 1512
Iwis: indeed. MM 216
knack: *knacke* trick, joke. JE 336; MM 101
knowlage: recognize, acknowledge. JE 445
koosse. kiss. JE 966
lay me on the iacke: attack, lay blows upon. JE 1535
lende: give, afford. JE 222
lese: lose. MM 754
let:: hinder, damage, harm. MM 39
licence: leave, permission. JE 686
lob: lout, bumpkin. JE 808
lulleth a sow: pulls by the ears. JE 571
lust: wish, desire. JE 530
lyther: bad, worthless (usually physically). JE 765
Mab, old witch, a term of abuse. JE 1528
munificence: magnificence. MM 2130
mankene: furious, mad. JE 532
marchant: fellow. MM 996
maship: mastership; in abbreviated form, as used here, it often implied disrespect. JE 800
maude: hag. MM 803
mawe: stomach. JE 746
meace: mess, *i.e.,* a helping of food. MM.97
meales meate: food eaten at a meal. JE 106
meated: fed, supplied with food. JE 694
mell: interfere, meddle. JE 216
mischeue: injure. MM 118
miseration: commiseration MM 1451
misers: Wretches, miserable persons. JE 1508
missay: slander, say ill of, JE 1349
mome: fool, buffoon. JE 117
mopyng: grimacing; scowling. JE 137
myddes: midst, middle. MM 169

mynikin: little. MM 339
nere: nearer. JE 525
nourtred: nurtured: MM 251
obsequie: service; MM 1795
obseruation: observance. MM 2004
of: about, concerning. MM 867
of the new guise: usually means of the latest fashion or deportment. JE 1681
on: of: MM 967
oneth: variation of uneath; scarcely, hardly. JE 385
ouerbody: outer garment. MM 147, 690, 147
ought: owned. MM 1860
ornature: "manners." MM 251
pardy: verily (a form of oath). JE 804
passeth: careth, regardeth. JE 69-70
pastance: pastime. MM 238
past: paste; i.e., make-up. MM 688
peake: mope, act dejectedly. JE 589
percelie: parsley. JE 1156
perfight, perfite; perfect. JE 344; MM 2101
pittance: a portion or allowance of food or drink. JE 1305
pointed: appointed. JE 237
port: way of living; deportment. JE 1426
potte: punishment, or place of punishment. JE 1513
poule: crown of the head or nape of the neck. JE 934
pox: colloquial for venereal disease. MM 652-59
pretence: intention. MM 973
preuent, preuented (MM 1394); to hinder, forestall from sin. MM 1373, JE 1459
preatie: i.e., pretty. JE 1187
prety young Iones: i.e., Joans, girls. MM 667
princkore: a saucy youth. JE 1672
promission: promise. MM 1485
proude enterprise: pride and boldness. MM 1127
purtenance: appurtenances. MM 270
puruiance: provision. MM 1592
quarter sacke: a sack capable of holding a quarter of grain. JE 1051
rablement: disorderly crowd, rabble. MM 1623
regals: a small portable reed-organ popular from the 1540s. MM 838
reiected: expelled, specifically exorcised. MM 1395
releuauit: relief. JE. 104.
remorse: pity, compassion. JE 1484
renne: run. JE 1525
repend: repay, requite. MM 1400
reproued: refuted, disproved. MM 2058
retchelesse: reckless. JE 193; see also JE 368
returnyng: turning away. MM. 1438
ruffle: swagger, flaunt. JE 1425
sad: serious, sober-minded. JE 213
sapience: wisdom, doctrine. MM 47
saucie merchaunt: insolent fellow. JE 1584
scapes: misdemeanors. JE 130
scath: harm, hurt. JE 1457
semble: seem. MM 1588
sentence: opinion, judgment. MM 130
shent: blamed, reproached, put to shame. JE. 685
shrewe: rebuke or scold. JE 859

siely: trivial, silly. JE 481
simulate: simulated. MM 2096
skilleth: be important. MM 704
slack: lax, remiss, neglectful JE 914; also JE 937 and 1061
slacking: JE 1061; JE 914
slake: decrease, cease. MM 1555
slightly: cunningly, craftily. JE 1309
smell: detect, perceive. JE 1095
somwhither: somewhere. JE 1600
sort: company. MM 381
sprite: spirit. JE 268
stall: applied to a sheath or receptacle of various kinds. JE 1243
stay: state. JE 161
sticke: scruple, hesitate. JE 598
stomachere: stomach cheer; i.e., food. JE 684
stounde: moment, time. JE 40; see also JE 610
strength: strengthen, MM 1412; as in MM 1468
suckorie chichory. JE 1157
sufferance: tolerance. MM 261
suffisance: sufficiency, plenty. JE 1306
suretiship: obligation undertaken by one person on behalf of another in payment of debt. JE 1554
sute: pursuit (?), JE 61
swayne: servant, herdsman. JE 1400
take the law of the game: "receive what the law requires." JE 127
taking condition. MM 1292
teg: a young deer. JE 107
to come lagge: late, last. JE 1517
thanke: thanks. JE 688
throst: thirst. JE 546
toye: trifle, whim, fancy. JE 1806
tratling: prattling, talking idly. JE563
tricke: neat. JE 1098
tusks: tufts of hair. MM 636
twelfe: twelve. JE 761
vndertake: ppl. for undertaken, i.e., understood, included. MM 1186
.vif.: five JE 28
vilitie: vileness. MM 1202
virginals: a small keyboard instrument popular in courtly circles, especially among young ladies. MM 837
visour: diguise. MM 124-26
wrabbed: rabid (?). JE 567
want: lack. MM 273
wanton: lewd, reckless person. MM 305; see also MM 706
wene: think. JE 124
whelpe: puppy. JE 529
withouten: without. JE 258; see also JE 971; as on JE 258.
witte: intelligence. MM 611; as in MM 1336
wittily: cleverly: MM 482
wonne my spurres: i.e., achieved honor, proven myself. JE 1411
a worshipfull disposition: honored position. MM 215
worshipfully: in high regard. MM 200
wotte: know, think. JE 673
yallyng: howling, yelling. JE 38